THE
ORIGINS
of THE
MODERN
JEW

THE
ORIGINS
of THE
MODERN
JEW

JEWISH

IDENTITY

AND EUROPEAN

CULTURE IN GERMANY,

1749–1824

Michael A. Meyer

WAYNE STATE UNIVERSITY PRESS

DETROIT

1979

Second printing, April 1972
Third printing, March 1979

Library of Congress Cataloging in Publication Data

Meyer, Michael A
   The origins of the modern Jew.

   Bibliography: p.
   Includes index.
   1. Judaism—Germany.   2.   Jews in Germany—
Intellectual life.   3.   Jews in Germany—Identity.
I.   Title.
BM316.M4 1979   943'.004'924   78-26528
ISBN 0-8143-1470-8

Grateful acknowledgment
is made to the
Hebrew Union College-
Jewish Institute of Religion
for financial assistance
in publishing this book.

for my parents

CONTENTS

PREFACE

For the Jew in the modern world Jewishness forms only a portion of his total identity. By calling himself a Jew he expresses only one of multiple loyalties. And yet external pressures and internal attachments combine to make him often more aware of this identification than of any other. Conscious of an influence which Jewishness has upon his character and mode of life, he tries to define its sphere and harmonize it with the other components of self. Such Jewish self-consciousness—while not entirely without precedent in Jewish history—has been especially characteristic of the last two centuries. In the considerable isolation of the ghetto, Jewish existence possessed an all-encompassing and unquestioned character which it lost to a significant extent only after the middle of the eighteenth century. It is with the age of Enlightenment that Jewish identity becomes segmental and hence problematic.

This historical study presents an analysis of the question of Jewish identity as it manifested itself initially within German Jewry. Although the process of Jewish entry into German life has been dealt with extensively in other works, no attempt has yet been made to analyze the process from this specific point of view. My central concern has been to probe the reactions of individual Jews, expressed in both word and deed, to the circumstance of their Jewishness. Thus I continually applied a single question to a wide variety of source material: What does being a

Jew mean to this individual? The intent was not any personal evaluation of the answer, but an understanding of what produced a particular
response and an exploration of its consequences.

The seventy-five years from 1749 to 1824 upon which this book con-
centrates witness a wide spectrum of reactions. Its termini are symbolically
marked by Lessing's play *The Jews,* which presented the Jew with a new,
favorable image of himself, and by the failure of the *Verein für Cultur
und Wissenschaft der Juden* (Society for Culture and Science among the
Jews), which had been the first attempt to interpret Jewish existence in
terms of the nineteenth century. Modern Jewish history in its intellectual
aspect begins with these years. When Moses Mendelssohn, the Jew who
became a ranking philosopher of the Enlightenment, was constrained
at one point in his life to justify his persistence in Judaism, an experienced
consciousness of the self as Jew first finds articulate expression in the language of a larger intellectual milieu. By 1824 a number of possible paths
have been taken: philosophical justifications, intense efforts to transform
both Jews and Judaism, practical struggles for political and social acceptance, and outright rejections of Jewish identity. With the *Verein,* the
circle of the young Jewish scholar Leopold Zunz, very different reasons
for remaining Jewish appear from those presented in the Enlightenment.
The members of this small society, living with full awareness in the age
of Romanticism, advanced new arguments, which—while they proved no
more enduring than those formulated earlier—by their very contrast to
what preceded point to the variety of possible solutions. Taken as a whole,
the period testifies to the modern Jew's persistent desire to explain continued Jewish identification to himself and the world in terms of the
cultural values dominant in his generation.

Since my interest centers on a problem rather than an individual or
movement, I have preferred a flexible pattern of organization. The scheme
is neither strictly chronological nor strictly topical. Where the purposes
of a chapter seemed best served by the biography of a single individual,
that form was chosen. But where a group of individuals or a periodical
or a movement proved indicative of a certain response to Jewishness, then
it was made the subject of a chapter or section. The book as a whole is
to be seen as a mosaic in which each chapter contributes a few fragments
to the total portrait of Jewish self-expression in these seventy-five years.

As this is a study in the intellectual dimension of Jewish history, it does not claim to be a comprehensive treatment of the period. Economic and social developments are discussed only as they are relevant to the primary focus of interest. Moreover, there is little attempt to seek out covert economic or psychological motivations which may underlie conscious affirmations or rejections of Jewishness. The effort is rather to discover how the impact of challenging values was consciously met by those German Jews who first became aware of European culture and refused to ignore it. These men and women were doubly a minority, both in their articulateness and in their rejection of a still prevalent, intellectually exclusive orthodoxy. But they are significant beyond their numbers, for they produced the first attempts to resolve a problem that remains central for the Jew in Western society.

I wish to thank my mentors at the Hebrew Union College–Jewish Institute of Religion, Professors Ellis Rivkin and Fritz Bamberger, for their intellectual stimulation, wise counsel, and helpful suggestions. Dr. Rivkin first led me into this phase of Jewish history, while Dr. Bamberger shared with me the rich insights of a veteran specialist in the field. I should also like to express my gratitude to the library staffs of the College-Institute in Cincinnati, New York, and Los Angeles, as well as to the staffs of the Leo Baeck Institute, Columbia University, and the Jewish Theological Seminary for their invaluable aid in providing me with rare volumes. Rabbi Richard N. Levy and Miss Roslyn Rivkin read the entire manuscript and made numerous valuable suggestions. Finally, I owe an immeasurable debt of gratitude to my wife, Margie, whose patience, forbearance, and encouragement in moments of despair made the completion of this book possible.

MICHAEL A. MEYER
Los Angeles, California, September 1966

1

Moses Mendelssohn The Virtuous Jew

*Unter allen selten
Unter den Seinigen
der Einzige* [1]

Ever since the conversion of Rome to Christianity in the fourth century, a maledictory ideology hung, like an ominous storm cloud, over the Jews of Christian Europe. Although there were long periods when the Church chose to ignore its own doctrines, the position of the Jew was never secure. A German-Jewish merchant of the tenth century who performed important economic functions for the feudal hierarchy, might enjoy privileges almost equivalent to those of a Christian noble. But the medieval Jew was always dependent upon the good graces of secular and clerical protectors who subscribed, at least in principle, to a doctrine that condemned all Jews as blasphemers and Christ-killers.

In periods of religious and social turbulence the established ideology could be used as an excuse for plunder and rapine; the Crusaders of 1096 who massacred entire Jewish communities were able to justify their actions by the latent Church doctrine. Yet, after the passing of the First Crusade, the Jews of Western Europe were allowed about half a century more of relative peace and prosperity; only thereafter did a decisive and continuing process of degradation begin. From the middle of the twelfth century, the Jews of England, France, and Germany were increasingly persecuted, impoverished, and isolated from their environment. Ritual murder accusations were raised against them, first in England, later in

France and Germany; the Second Crusade of 1147 brought further calamities. In 1215, at the Fourth Lateran Council in Rome, Pope Innocent III revived the old Christian attitude toward the Jews: they were henceforth to be reduced to the status the Church had long ago prescribed for them. By the middle of the thirteenth century the Jews of Germany had become no more than chattel, chamber serfs of the Holy Roman Emperor; by the end of that century a series of expulsions from areas in Western Europe had begun. Even in Christian Spain, where certain Jews achieved a high degree of social acceptance, mounting political and religious pressures soon brought on voluntary and forced conversions, then an Inquisition directed against these New Christians, and, in 1492, expulsion of the remaining Jews.

The intellectual life of the High Middle Ages subserved the Christian theology. By its very nature that life excluded the Jew, who was left to cultivate his own tradition within the confines of his own community. Few Jews studied Latin, which they regarded as the language of the Temple destroyers and of anti-Jewish Christian dogma, while at the same time the study of Hebrew was extremely rare among medieval Christian scholars.[2] So wide a gulf existed between Jew and gentile that there could be no question of a divided identity. The Jew identified fully with his own group and its religious aspirations. He felt himself a part of the worldwide community of Israel which God had blessed with a special revelation and which He would finally redeem by the hand of His Messiah. The world outside the Jewish community was alien. He ventured there to make his living, but as a Jew he could not identify with the Christian environment, nor make its ideals his own.

This mutual exclusion was interrupted for a time in Renaissance Italy. There a general laxity in religious observance prevailing among the upper classes and intellectual leaders made possible a much closer contact between Jew and gentile. Yet the Italian Humanists did not supplant the old ideology of the Church with a new universalism: they tried neither to overthrow nor even to reform the Church. Acceptance of the Jew was simply in keeping with the untrammeled individualism that temporarily prevailed even within the Church itself. As for the Renaissance Jew, he too was often not overly pious, and like his Christian counterpart seldom subjected his religion to serious criticism.

While the Italian Renaissance for a time permitted the Jew a role in intellectual life, in Northern Europe the Lutheran Reformation cleared away none of the barriers between Christian and Jew; on the contrary, it strove to buttress them. Luther himself, at first kindly disposed to the Jews, turned on them with bitter vituperation when after twenty years they still refused conversion to reformed Christianity. He then proposed extreme isolation of the Jews so that their beliefs might not contaminate Christians.

Nor did the seventeenth century bring a measurable change in the general attitude to the Northern-European Jew. With few exceptions he was still regarded as physically disgusting and morally contemptible. The only novelty was the utilization by various rulers of certain rich and capable Jews for mercantile ventures. Their liquid assets, connections, and willingness to take risks suited these Jews for large-scale capitalistic undertakings. Yet the "Court Jews," some of whom became exceedingly powerful and wealthy, were often victims of a downfall as rapid as their ascent. They were accepted because they served the interests of monarch or noble, not because there had been any change in thinking about the Jew. The Court Jews were acquainted with great political figures, spoke a number of languages, and were often assimilated in their manners and dress. But in the realm of Christian intellectual life even the exceptional Court Jews were not participants. Though business connections between Jews and non-Jews were common, cultural and social relationships were virtually non-existent.[3]

As late as the eighteenth century, in literature and on the stage, writers and dramatists continued to picture Jews as greedy moneylenders or errant fools,[4] while ritual murder fables were still believed by large segments of the population.[5] However by the close of the seventeenth century there was rising, first in Holland and England, then in France and Germany, a new ideology which tore down the medieval structure and substituted reason for belief and human nature for sacred texts. Because it strove to be universal, it perforce had to include even the Jew.

The Enlightenment of the eighteenth century had its roots in the two centuries that preceded it. In the midst of religious wars between Catholics and Protestants a few courageous souls dared to argue for toleration based on a law of nature that transcended both religious and national boundaries. At the height of the Reformation the Dutch scholar Desiderius Erasmus proposed a humanized Christianity based on mutual toleration among Christians. In marked contrast to Luther, he could find no objection to entering into friendship even with a Jew, though he added the condition "that in my presence he did not blaspheme Jesus Christ." [6]

The pioneer labors of Erasmus were carried forward in the seventeenth century by another Dutchman, Hugo Grotius,[7] and by his disciple, the German baron Samuel Pufendorf. The universalism of Erasmus, limited by the higher esteem in which he held Christians, was gradually broadened into an all-encompassing conception of humanity.[8] Pufendorf, in his great work *Of the Law of Nature and Nations,* first published in 1672, approached this idea when he entitled a section "That all Men are to be accounted by Nature equal" and concluded that "it follows as a command of the law of nature, that every man should esteem and trust another as one who is naturally his equal; or who is a man as well as he." [9] The new universal spirit even reached into Holland's Jewish community where a few men like Uriel Acosta and Baruch Spinoza, at odds with their co-religionists, sought a larger community of rational men, beyond the pale of Judaism.

However, it was in England in the last years of the seventeenth century that the characteristic philosophy of the Enlightenment first reached maturity.[10] Its progenitor was the pioneer empiricist and political philosopher John Locke. Though no foe of religion, Locke brought about an epistemological revolution that tore away much of the foundation upon which Christianity had been built. By arguing that all knowledge depended upon simple ideas taken in by the senses, he discredited divine mysteries that could only be grasped by faith or intuition. Locke's theory of knowledge begins with sensation rather than revelation, and his Christianity is entirely reasonable; thus the intellectual and spiritual worlds are both made to rest upon healthy human reason, common to all mankind.[11]

Like his epistemology, Locke's theory of the state is based on the rational human being. As ideologist of the Revolution of 1688, Locke opposed religious intolerance as interfering with the peace and well-being of society.[12] On the grounds that they politically or morally endangered society, Locke rejected Catholics and atheists but held that "neither Pagan nor Mahometan, nor Jew, ought to be excluded from the civil rights of the commonwealth because of his religion." [13]

The religious and political philosophy of John Locke was carried into the eighteenth century by such disciples as John Toland who argued that "true religion must necessarily be reasonable and intelligible." [14] More explicitly than Locke, Toland drew inferences from the universal nature of reason to an attitude toward the Jews. In 1714 he published a pamphlet entitled *Reasons for Naturalizing the Jews in Great Britain and Ireland on the Same Foot with all other Nations.* Though motivated by the practical interest of the state, he makes clear both the inhumanity of hating the Jews and its inconsistency. As in all other groups there are undesirable elements among them, but there are as well "men of probity and worth, persons of courage and conduct, of liberal and generous spirits." He refuses to apply a special standard to the Jews. In matters of the state they can be judged only as human beings. They are, Toland concludes, "not otherwise to be regarded, than under the common circumstances of human nature." [15]

As the eighteenth century wore on, it became more and more apparent that the concepts of a universal human nature, universal natural law, and universal rationality made the exclusion of the Jew a gross anomaly. But it was one thing to draw the conclusion abstractly and another to apply it. For most of the writers of the eighteenth century, particularly on the Continent, the flesh-and-blood Jew with his beard, strange garments, and wholly irrational ceremonial law seemed somewhat less than a human being. Was it possible that among this most wretched people there might be found a philosophically minded Jew? Even Voltaire, who accepted Jews in general much more readily than Jews in particular, hoped that at least some of them might develop the traits of a philosopher.[16] As yet there were no outstanding examples. However, the more imaginative writers of the Enlightenment saw no need to wait for empirical proof; they began to create idealized Jews in fiction and drama.

The first important work to present a new image of the Jew was the *Lettres juives,* supposedly a correspondence between three Jews but in reality the creation of a remarkably imaginative Frenchman, the Marquis d'Argens.[17] The *Letters,* which appeared from 1735 to 1738, aroused widespread protest. For the Marquis had put into the mouths of intelligent, enlightened Jews all his criticisms of French ecclesiastics, theology, manners, and morals. He achieves a sublime irony when he lets one of his Jews argue that, after all, Christians too have a place in heaven:

Lay aside for one moment, dear Isaac, the prejudices imbibed in thy childhood, and look with a philosophical eye upon an honest Nazarene who lives in the midst of Paris. He believes and serves the same God as we do.... Why should'st thou think, dear Isaac, that God would bind this Nazarene by such strong bands, and hinder him from entering into the faith of Israel, only to have the pleasure of destroying him? [18]

It is not surprising that a portrayal of enlightened Jews should flow from the pen of an ardent exponent of critical deism and the philosophy of common sense.[19] The Marquis considered the existence of God self-evident from the order in the universe, and ethics derivable from the laws of nature. Since he made all truth dependent upon empirical reason and denied any super-rational revelation, it was perfectly possible for him to put all his own ideas into the mouths of Jews, though his Jews were understandably as critical of Jewish orthodoxy as they were of Christianity. But these enlightened Jews whom the Marquis invents are only a device for him to express his own religious and social criticism. His principal concern was not to point out philosophical or virtuous Jews, although the very creation of such Jews indicates that he thought their existence not unlikely. It was left to the German writer, Christian Gellert, to portray a virtuous Jew with the explicit intent of impressing upon his readers that such an individual might really exist.

Gellert was a popular moralistic writer whose works were intended to appeal to large segments of the population. In 1746 he published a novel of exotic adventure, *Leben der Schwedischen Gräfinn von G*** (*Life of the Swedish Countess of G***), in which a fictitious Swedish countess relates the colorful story of her life. At the outset we learn that here is an enlightened family. She explains that she received a proper training in religion: her cousin taught her "religion in a rational way." [20] Through one of her husband's letters we are introduced to a Polish Jew whose life the count has saved and who then becomes her husband's friend and benefactor. Gellert wanted to show that a Jew could be "grateful in the noblest manner" and that "there are good hearts even among this people, which seems to have them less than any other." [21] Not surprisingly, Gellert's Jew remains nameless; he is an example, not a flesh-and-blood individual.

The Countess was well received in Germany; its portrayal of a noble Jew may have had an effect on English literature,[22] and probably was also an influence upon the young Lessing who three years later proposed his own noble Jew in his stage play *Die Juden* (*The Jews*).[23]

Gotthold Ephraim Lessing, among the outstanding representatives of the German Enlightenment, from his youth manifested an independent and unconventional spirit. The son of a small-town Lutheran preacher, he refused to accept uncritically his father's orthodoxy; to the marked displeasure of his parents he associated with actors and wrote comedies.[24] In 1749 he wrote to his father, "As long as I do not see one of the foremost commands of Christianity, to love one's enemy, better observed, so long do I doubt whether those are Christians who pass themselves off as such." [25] In that same year, when still a very young man, he wrote his one-act comedy *The Jews*. It was intended to demonstrate that even among the people which Christianity had so long reviled as the enemies of Christ a virtuous individual could be found.[26] The play concerns a nameless traveler who saves the life of a baron set upon by highway robbers whom the baron erroneously believes to be Jews.[27] In the course of the play, the noble, magnanimous character of the traveler becomes ever more apparent. Finally, when the baron is about to give the stranger his daughter's hand in marriage, the high-minded traveler reveals that he is himself a Jew. The marriage now of course cannot take place, but the baron's gratitude is undiminished. Fervently he exclaims, "O how worthy of esteem the Jews would be if they were all like you!" To which the Jew can only answer, "And how worthy of love the Christians if they possessed all your qualities!" (Scene 22).

It is most significant that when Lessing wrote *The Jews* he had not yet met Moses Mendelssohn, and it is doubtful if he had had any extensive contact with Jews.[28] The noble Jew of his comedy was a product of Lessing's desire to show that such a phenomenon was possible, before he had a concrete instance. However, by the time that his play appeared in print in 1754, and drew the criticism of the Göttingen theologian Johann David Michaelis, he had found his living example.[29]

In his review of the play Michaelis stressed how unlikely it was that such a noble individual could be found among the Jews. The improbability bothered him all the more, he wrote, since he wished that "the noble and lovely picture" were true.[30] Lessing replied in the first issue of his *Theatralische Bibliothek* with a letter written by Mendelssohn to his friend and mentor Dr. Aaron Gumperz criticizing Michaelis' review. Lessing sent the issue to Michaelis with a personal letter. "He is really a Jew," he wrote of Mendelssohn, "a man of twenty and some years who without any guidance has achieved a great strength in languages, in mathematics, in philosophy, in poetry. I regard him as a future honor to his nation...." [31]

Lessing began to cultivate the friendship of this noble-minded Jew in whom not he alone but the Enlightenment as a whole was to find concrete proof that the universal ideals of the age were valid. Mendelssohn was granted the unique opportunity of being accepted by the gentile world as no Jew had been before him. His circle of friends and acquaintances grew as the fame of the Jewish savant spread outward from Berlin. Visitors in the Prussian capital sought him out to inscribe a few words of wisdom in their autograph books.[32] How eager they all were to meet him and speak with him, to observe this remarkable phenomenon at first hand. But the *Aufklärer* were no more anxious to make Mendelssohn an example than he was to become one. Though he grew up and remained his entire life a traditional observant Jew, in the early years of manhood it was the great world outside that claimed his interest. He was to show that a Jew could be philosopher, aesthete, even Prussian patriot. But what Mendelssohn wanted to prove most of all was that, despite Michaelis, a Jew could be virtuous.

German thought in the mid-eighteenth century witnessed an upsurge of interest in natural theology. Spurred by the influx of deistic ideas from England, a widespread movement arose which intended to displace the old Christian orthodoxy along with the fervent pietism which had been prominent a few decades earlier. In 1748, without revelation, without so much as mentioning the Bible, and without abstruse philosophical speculation, the enlightened Berlin theologian Johann Joachim Spalding presented to his fellow Christians a common sense religious philosophy. Simple logic led him from the sensual to the spiritual, to God, and finally to immortality. God had created man, Spalding insisted, to be upright, and in being upright to be happy.[33] Seven years later Hermann Samuel Reimarus, professor in Hamburg, published a book on the "most eminent truths of natural religion." [34] It was the result of reflection upon the first truths common to all religions. These fruits of reason must be presupposed by individual revealed religions, for "how," asked Reimarus, "can one have reason to believe that revelation came from God, unless he was first convinced that there was a God?" [35]

This tradition of *theologia naturalis* in Germany went back to the great Leibniz and his popularizer Christian Wolff; it had an overpowering appeal for the young Mendelssohn who soon became and remained a Wolffian. His ready acceptance of rational religion finds its explanation both in what Mendelssohn brought to natural theology and in what it offered him.

Mendelssohn was early drawn to philosophy. While still living in Dessau, the young Moses at twelve became acquainted with Maimonides' *Guide of the Perplexed* and developed a love for the medieval Jewish philosopher which he retained for the rest of his life.[36] Maimonides' philosophy, though medieval in character, served Mendelssohn as a bridge from Talmudic Judaism to the religion of reason that he encountered a few years later in Berlin.[37] The Rambam affirmed the divine revelation at Sinai—and gave it a much wider significance than Mendelssohn was to do in his *Jerusalem*—but like Locke, Toland, and the enlightened German theologians of a later age he minimized the conflict between reason and revelation and strove to render a rational account of his faith. In Berlin Mendelssohn found the same adherence to the ideal of rationality. But he found it principally in the intellectual world outside the confines of a Jewish community which was not, in general, intellectually inclined.[38] Rational discourse became his greatest pleasure, for which he thirsted when business or private matters deprived him temporarily of learned conversation or writing.[39]

The natural theology which Mendelssohn so quickly adopted was interested from the very first in discovering the basic religious truths that might unify mankind.[40] Christian Wolff, through his deduction of religious from logical truths, undermined the traditional claim of theologians that Christianity possessed unique truths of its own. His disciples, recognizing revelation as a divisive factor, limited it to the Bible and then compromised it to fit the demands of reason. Enlightenment theology in Germany, however, remained much more conservative than the radical religious criticism that prevailed in France and, to a lesser extent, in England. Only a few extremists rejected revelation entirely. Most of the *Aufklärung* theologians (Spalding, Reimarus, Jerusalem) preferred not to deny revelation—at least in their published works—while, however, concentrating their attention on the "humane, cheerful, this-worldly, practical, simply understood and modern religion of healthy common sense." [41] This religion set forth the principles of God, Providence, and immortality as the common foundation of all faiths, excluding only the atheist from its "religion of humanity." And so not only was Mendelssohn unable to find in natural religion anything that seemed to him to contradict Judaism, but also enlightened Christians included the upright Jew among those who, because they believed in the three tenets of the common faith, were worthy of salvation. A letter of Thomas Abbt to Mendelssohn expresses the genuine kinship that a Christian could feel with a Jew. He writes, "May our common God, who is not the God of Jews or Christians, but the God of all human beings and all spirits, keep you as well as my heart wishes it for you...." [42]

Mendelssohn was thus able to feel that the deepest stratum of religion produced no differences between himself and his Christian friends. The ideal of the moral life, derivable by unaided reason and the surest way to bliss on earth and hereafter, was the common aspiration of all good men. As early as 1763, twenty years before he wrote *Jerusalem,* Mendelssohn insisted that morality needs no revelation. In a sermon which he wrote for the occasion of the Peace of Hubertusburg he urged: "Let us, my dear brethren, serve our God and love our neighbor as ourselves. This is all that the Lord requires of us; and this we should do even if God had not required it of us: for these are the true means to our happiness." [43]

Although Mendelssohn was honored by the Berlin Jewish community, which even freed him from all community taxes in 1763, he did not care much personally for the "protected" Jews of the Prussian capital. He told his fiancée Fromet Guggenheim that she had little in common with the rich Jews of Berlin whose characters he considered beneath hers; Jews of the middle class, closer to his own station, appealed to him more. [44] But apparently he managed to maintain excellent relations with all segments of the Jewish community. A Christian visitor to Mendelssohn's home in 1763 remarked in a letter to a friend: He is "a brother to his brothers, obliging and respectful toward them, also loved and honored by them." [45]

Mendelssohn was in correspondence with the great rabbis of his day: Jonathan Eybeschütz and Jacob Emden. The former wrote to him in the most flattering terms; the latter shared with him a considerable interest in secular studies, though Mendelssohn could not agree with Emden's slavish acceptance of tradition. [46] As Mendelssohn's reputation grew, Jewish communities all over Germany wrote to him for advice or to ask his intercession with local government officials.

Even in the early period of his life, when German philosophy and letters claimed his time and interest, Mendelssohn devoted some of his energy to Jewish matters. Specifically, he sought to instill morality and rationality in the Jewish community through the medium of the traditional literature. In 1758,[47] together with a friend, he issued a Hebrew weekly, *Kohelet Musar,* which contained homiletic commentaries to passages from the Talmud and urged use of the holy tongue. Surprisingly, these rather innocuous pamphlets aroused the opposition of the Berlin rabbis who suppressed their publication after two issues.[48] A decade later he wrote a Hebrew commentary to Maimonides' logic, *Milot ha-Higayon,* which gained a somewhat more favorable reception. It went through three editions in Mendelssohn's lifetime and a number more thereafter.[49] To the Jewish community as well as to the outside world Mendelssohn was trying to show the worthwhileness and good sense of the Jewish tradition. He reassured his cousin, Elkan Herz, that he was far from considering the rabbinical literature worthless; he considered himself a Rabbinite, not a Karaite.[50] When the first part of a German translation of the Mishnah done by a Christian, Johann Jacob Rabe, was announced in 1759, Mendelssohn used the occasion to defend study of Talmud. He wrote anonymously in the *Litteraturbriefe:*

> I cannot possibly convince myself that the best minds of a people (and certainly the Jewish people has no lack of very good minds) should have been for so many centuries occupied exclusively with a work composed only of insipid foolery. The uncommon diligence with which they apply themselves to this study and the oriental fervor with which I have so often seen them dispute over certain matters indicates to me that a man of genius could find full sustenance in this kind of learning.[51]

Some years later Mendelssohn himself translated selections from the Talmud and Midrash which then appeared in an anthology of popular philosophy as "Specimens of Rabbinical Wisdom." [52]

Not even the mystical tradition of the Kabbalah received an unqualified rejection. In conversation with enlightened non-Jews, Mendelssohn defended kabbalistic philosophy in its pristine essence as really quite reasonable. Only when it was adulterated by taking the allegory literally and heaping on imaginative commentaries did it grow into nonsense and fanaticism.[53] His attitude to the Talmud was similar: when studied in the proper manner it was beneficial. It produced that "certain subtleness of mind" which, as Mendelssohn wrote to Kant, "seems to be characteristic of the nation." [54] But the overly clever pilpulistic mode of Talmud study was as revolting to him as the excesses of the Kabbalah. Both were a degeneration; both revealed a gulf between Judaism and the healthy human understanding, a gulf Mendelssohn wished to deny. To Jacob Emden he wrote that he loathed the pilpulism of most of the rabbis, who thereby thought themselves wise; since his youth he had disdained this method of study.[55]

Though Mendelssohn had received a thorough education in rabbinic literature, and unlike the following generation never deprecated it in favor of the Bible, Talmud did not possess sufficient interest for a young student with an insatiable desire for achievement in all areas of human knowledge and creativity. He accepted without regret the constraints of being an observant and loyal Jew, but he was determined to be a German as well—and this at a time when the concept of a German national culture was still but a vision in the minds of a few intellectuals.

It seems a strange paradox that nascent German culture should have been championed by a Jew. What could be more ironic than the young bearded Moses, at the time only "tolerated" in Berlin, audaciously criticizing Frederick the Great for writing poetry in French instead of German? [56] And yet it was not so strange. Mendelssohn's friends, particularly Lessing, were seeking to break away from the idolization of French letters that reigned supreme in Germany. It was a new and open cause which had not yet received official sanction. A master of German prose, as Mendelssohn was soon universally acknowledged to be,[57] was a welcome ally whether or not he was a Jew. Thus the son of a poor Torah scroll writer could teach the Germans to write their own language.[58]

Mendelssohn's proficiency in German, his desire to maintain the friendship of Lessing and his circle, and his youthful aspiration to identify himself with a cause—all these contributed to his cultural nationalism. These factors were abetted by Mendelssohn's special regard for German philosophy. He was the lifelong foe of French atheism and of the skepticism which he found in the Scottish philosopher David Hume. Though he considered Locke, Clarke, and Shaftesbury "truly philosophers," he preferred the German philosophy with its serious, thoroughgoing rationalism.[59]

But while Mendelssohn could fully share the aspirations of incipient German culture, it was far more difficult for him as a Jew to participate in the rising wave of Prussian patriotism which welled up in all segments of the population during the Seven Years' War. This awakening of a Prussian national spirit was largely the result of personal enthusiasm for Frederick the Great, whose courage and sense of duty to the state in time of war produced a hitherto nonexistent attachment to the Prussian *Vaterland*. In honor of Frederick's battles the poet F. W. Gleim wrote ecstatic war poems which breathed the life of a great experience shared by the people with its "hero-king." [60] Even the cosmopolitan Goethe later admitted that the first heightened consciousness of life was brought into German poetry through Frederick the Great and the Seven Years' War.[61]

But could the Jewish community share in this tremendous enthusiasm? Judging from their legal and political status it would seem not. Eighteenth-century German thought applied the term "nation" to any "natural linguistic and cultural community," [62] and the Jews were recognized as such by both Christians and themselves.[63] There was special legislation relating to them as a group; they differed in manners and customs; few spoke a pure German. In 1671 Jews had been readmitted to Brandenburg for purely economic reasons: "the promotion of trade and commerce." They were excluded from the rights and duties of citizenship and made subject to personal letters of privilege and general regulations affecting the entire community. They were limited to those crafts, industries, and trades in which they would not be competing with Christians. Finally, their numbers in Prussia were strictly controlled by the government, which made every effort to expel those who illegally crossed the borders.

Frederick the Great had no more love for the Jews than did his predecessors. His Jewry regulation of 1750 was in many respects even stricter than previous decrees. But he fully recognized the importance of religious toleration for the political and economic interests of the state,[64] and was aware that Prussia could gain considerable wealth by encouraging enterprising Jews to enter neglected branches of commerce and to found new industries. Despite increased tax burdens the Jewish community prospered under Frederick the Great and produced a number of extremely wealthy individuals.

It is wholly understandable that whenever the occasion presented itself Prussian Jewry should try to ingratiate itself with the king,[65] and that therefore it should mark the occasion of Frederick's victories in the Seven Years' War with special sermons and poems of praise. It is, however, difficult to determine whether the Jewish community, participating so little in the national life of the state, was genuinely caught up in the wave of Prussian national sentiment or was simply discharging a perfunctory obligation. On the one hand there are the epigrams of the Jewish poet Ephraim Kuh that manifest an enthusiasm for Frederick which is parallel to that of Gleim and is shared by the Polish-Jewish poet Issachar Falkensohn Behr.[66] On the other hand there is the withdrawing, reflective attitude of Mendelssohn as expressed in a letter to Lessing of June, 1757. Here he asks his friend to rejoin the circle in Berlin:

> Come to us! In our solitary arbor we may forget that the passions of men devastate the globe. How easy it will be for us to forget the unworthy squabbles of greed when we continue orally our dispute regarding the most important matters that we began in writing! [67]

In this passage Mendelssohn, though perhaps merely assuming a philosophical stance, seems at best indifferent to the war. There is nothing of Prussian patriotism here and it may well be that his attitude at the time was representative of the bulk of Berlin Jewry.[68]

Yet by the end of the year Mendelssohn had written two German sermons in commemoration of the victories wrought by Prussian arms at Rossbach and Leuthen, and had translated Hebrew poems of thanksgiving for both of these occasions. Since Mendelssohn was asked to do this work by the leaders of the Jewish community, we cannot know for certain whether he undertook the tasks with reluctance or enthusiasm. After the Rossbach sermon he wrote sheepishly to Lessing, "You needn't even write what you think of this sermon. I can already more or less imagine." [69] However Lessing, who was not a Prussian but a Saxon, held a dim view of patriotism, which he considered "an heroic infirmity" he was "most happy in not sharing." [70] It is therefore possible that Mendelssohn was not ashamed of his sermon but knew very well that Lessing would treat it with an indulgent smile.

But even if Mendelssohn was not enthralled with the task of writing patriotic sermons and esteemed his creations—though perhaps out of modesty—rather lightly,[71] it is apparent from another source, his literary reviews, that in the course of the Seven Years' War he began to take patriotic sentiments very seriously. Writing anonymously in the *Bibliothek der schönen Wissenschaften* and later in the *Litteraturbriefe,* Mendelssohn could forget that he was a Jew and regard the patriotic ideal as might the fully privileged member of a nation-state. When J. G. Zimmermann's *Vom Nationalstolze* first appeared in 1758, Mendelssohn reviewed it quite favorably but objected to the author's placing the patriot above the philosopher.[72] Three years later Mendelssohn bestowed greater praise upon a new edition of the same work. In this new edition the Swiss Zimmermann had added a section on national pride in a monarchy with obvious reference to Prussia. Mendelssohn's review leaves no doubt that he now had the greatest sympathy for the nation and its monarch. The pariah Jew, feeling for the moment fully a Prussian, could write of Zimmermann's work:

> Hereupon follows a description of the prince of whom the nation has cause to be proud. This description affects us so immediately that I take pleasure in copying it entirely. It flatters our egos in the most pleasant way in that it justifies our basking in the greatness of a monarch which others must be satisfied with admiring from afar.[73]

Later the same year, reviewing Thomas Abbt's *Vom Tode für das Vaterland*,[74] Mendelssohn reproached the modern nations for lacking the great love of country that was the spiritual possession of the ancient Greeks and Romans. The exhortations, so understandable in an Abbt, become bitterly ironic when they are expanded upon by a politically outcast Jew. In discussing Abbt's work the anonymous reviewer, who signed his articles with a cipher, could term Prussia "our fatherland." But Mendelssohn the Jew, whose very residence in Berlin depended entirely upon his position as bookkeeper in the silk business of the wealthy Isaac Bernhard, could only vicariously share the sentiments of his friend Abbt. "My countrymen ... ?" he once mused in a letter to Abbt, "which countrymen, the people of Dessau or the citizens of Jerusalem?" In a later letter he completely denied that he had a fatherland.[75] It is apparent, then, that Mendelssohn was poignantly aware of how little material cause he had to be a patriot, though he paid genuine tribute to the ideal.

Fortunately, political privilege was not of the utmost importance to the young Mendelssohn who had to be coaxed into submitting a personal petition to the government for the status of "protected Jew." Of far greater significance to him was his acceptance by the German intellectual elite.

He looked upon his acquaintance with the finest minds of Germany as the great good fortune of his life.[76] They in turn were eager to accept Mendelssohn as the exception Jew par excellence, without generally altering their opinions of the Jewish people as a whole.[77] They asked him to join a private coffee house for intellectuals then being formed in Berlin; they came to visit him, read his publications, and entered into correspondence with him. One of them, the aforementioned young philosopher Thomas Abbt, yearned to be his close friend and poured out to the sympathetic Mendelssohn the deepest meditations of a troubled soul.[78]

The impression that Mendelssohn made on the intellectual world in those years of young manhood is astounding. Through Lessing he met the dedicated *Aufklärer* Friedrich Nicolai who remained his lifelong friend and admirer. A few months after becoming acquainted with the Jewish prodigy, Nicolai wrote to Lessing of Mendelssohn: "I am indebted to him for the most cheerful hours of the past winter and summer: I never left him, regardless of how often we were together, without becoming either better or more learned." [79] And Nicolai was by no means the only one who felt that way.[80]

Those who knew Mendelssohn personally were even more impressed by his *Tugend,* his personal virtue, than by his philosophy or literary criticism.[81] The ideal of virtue, so prominent a value of the Enlightenment,[82] became the nub of Mendelssohn's religious philosophy. Like Leibniz [83] and like Lessing [84] he considered the moral life—not dogma—the essence of religion. In his popular dialogues on immortality, the *Phaedon,* Mendelssohn argued quite traditionally that all the virtuous will receive their just reward in the world to come. Even the search for metaphysical truth he regarded as only a means to the final goal of the moral life. "The highest level of wisdom is indisputably *doing good*," he wrote later in life. "Speculation is a lower level that leads to it." [85]

Although there is no reason to doubt the sincerity of Mendelssohn's own virtue, it remains true that he was quite aware of its inestimable value in gaining admission to the intellectual world outside of Judaism. Michaelis' critique of *The Jews* dealt Mendelssohn such a crushing blow precisely because it denied the possibility that a Jew could be virtuous. Any other kind of affront would not have hurt as much. "Let them further expose us to the scorn and derision of all the world," Mendelssohn wrote to Gumperz, "only virtue, the one solace of distressed souls, the one refuge of the forsaken, let them not seek wholly to deny us." [86]

Mendelssohn realized as well as Lessing that the gentile community had formed its image of the Jews largely on the basis of what it saw of them at the trade fairs. There the poorer Jews hawked their wares, drove hard bargains, and repelled the Christians by their strange manners and language. Mendelssohn was prepared to admit that insatiable avarice existed among "the common rabble" (though he suggested the Christians were probably responsible), but he objected to the conclusion that all Jews were like these.[87] He considered Gumperz a living example of Lessing's traveler whose virtue, we may be sure, was Mendelssohn's own ideal.[88] The cultivation of *Tugend* seemed to him the most effective assault upon the stereotype of the greedy moneylender that was still prominent even in intellectual circles. He was particularly disturbed that the denial of Jewish virtue should come from a distinguished professor. "The common people of the Christians have ever regarded us as the dregs of nature, as ulcers of human society. But from learned people," he wrote, "I always expected a fairer judgment." [89]

During the fifteen years that followed Mendelssohn's 1754 letter to Gumperz, his reputation as a German intellectual grew rapidly. After he published the *Phaedon* in 1767 he was widely recognized as a principal spokesman for the German Enlightenment.[90] No longer was it possible to view him as a mere curiosity, the living proof that even a Jew could master a modicum of philosophy and literature. As long as he was not a figure of the first rank on the intellectual scene, the enlightened Jew was welcomed even by those of less universalistic outlook. But could a Jew be one of the dominating spirits of Western European culture and still remain a Jew? For those whose surface devotion to *Aufklärung* thinly overlay deep commitment to orthodox Christianity, it was inconceivable that the noble Mendelssohn should not accept their faith.

Johann Caspar Lavater, a Swiss theologian, expressed these sentiments when in 1769 he issued an open challenge to Mendelssohn either to refute Christianity publicly or to join its ranks. His challenge forced the Enlightenment Jew, living in two worlds, to reconcile one with the other, to define for himself and his Christian contemporaries the basis for his continuing identification with Judaism. Lessing's traveler had merely stated that he was a Jew, and Mendelssohn too had tried to leave it at that. "The contemptuous opinion one holds of a Jew," he wrote to Lavater, "I wished to be able to refute through virtue and not through polemics." [91] Now Lavater's open challenge made that impossible, and thereby opened a new phase in Mendelssohn's life: he was constrained to explain his persistent adherence to the faith of his fathers. While the intellectual world looked on, Mendelssohn the philosopher confronted Mendelssohn the Jew.

2

An Ephemeral Solution

It had long been Mendelssohn's judicious policy to avoid discussing revealed religion with gentiles. In his philosophical writings he dealt with natural not "positive" religion, restricting himself to only those truths "which must be of equal importance to all religions." [1] When he wrote on immortality he put his largely Leibnizian thoughts into the frame of a Socratic dialogue, choosing a pagan protagonist to escape the controversial question of revelation.[2] He was well aware that he had much to lose and little to gain by publicly expressing his thoughts on Judaism or Christianity. If he were overly partial to his own faith he would alienate those Christians who preferred to think of Moses Mendelssohn as being unlike the rest of Jewry. If, on the other hand, he proved himself at variance with traditional Judaism, he would arouse the ire of much of the Jewish community.

Behind the wishes of Christians to discuss religion with Mendelssohn usually lurked the desire to convert him. Once the subject was broached with any but the most emancipated, the inevitable question—How can you, a learned man, a philosopher, remain a Jew?—was bound to arise. It was better to steer the conversation to a more comfortable topic. Thomas Abbt once wrote to Mendelssohn that Christian Ebert, professor at the Carolinum in Brunswick, had recently expressed to him his high esteem for "Herrn Moses." But for Ebert, as undoubtedly for many others, admiration led to an irrepressible query—and Abbt had to quickly change the subject: "When he put to me the question, whether there was no hope you would become a Christian," reports Abbt, "I asked him to show me his English books, of which he has an excellent collection." [3] Had the question been posed directly to Mendelssohn, he would doubtless have resorted to a similar evasion.[4]

When Lavater visited Mendelssohn in Berlin in 1763 and tried to engage him in conversation on Christianity, he succeeded only after the utmost urging and the extraction of a strict promise of secrecy.[5] Yet, in the course of their talk, he mistakenly gained the impression from Mendelssohn's favorable comments concerning Jesus that the Jewish philosopher was ripe for conversion. The conversation was still on his mind when, six years later, he translated into German the specifically Christian portion of a religious-philosophical work by the Genevan naturalist and philosopher Charles Bonnet. He rushed off an unbound copy fresh from the press to Mendelssohn who was most astonished to find it dedicated to himself. The dedication called upon him either to refute publicly Bonnet's arguments for Christianity or, if he could not, to do "what good sense, love of truth, honesty would enjoin upon you—what Socrates would have done if he had read this book and found it irrefutable." [6] Mendelssohn had no choice but to answer the public challenge. To have remained silent would have meant that he had indeed found Bonnet irrefutable but was unwilling to accept the consequences. And yet he was not prepared to criticize Christianity publicly, for he realized, as did Nicolai, that it would certainly stir up a hornet's nest and he would bear away many painful stings.[7]

In his *Open Letter* replying to Lavater, Mendelssohn sought refuge in a cherished ideal of the Enlightenment: the salvation of the righteous of all faiths. He noted that Judaism stressed this same doctrine and therefore did not proselytize. Mendelssohn was urging Lavater that the difference between Jew and Christian was not really crucial, since it did not affect man's final destiny, the most consequential aspect of religion. Why could not whatever else a Jew or Christian believed or did on account of his religion remain a private matter as long as salvation depended upon a shared morality? In an argument reminiscent of John Locke, Mendelssohn held that only a religion whose doctrines were detrimental to the peace of society demanded refutation. To destroy the religious base of a genuine morality could serve no good purpose. He concluded:

> I can therefore quite well believe that I recognize national prejudices and erroneous religious views among my fellow citizens and yet be *bound* to remain silent if these errors do not *directly* condemn either *natural* religion or *natural* law, but are, on the contrary, linked *coincidentally* to the furtherance of the good.[8]

This is the way Mendelssohn proposed to look upon Christianity; it was the way he hoped Christians would look upon Judaism.

His argument fitted the thinking of a Lessing, but not of a Lavater.[9] For Lavater, beneath the veneer of enlightenment, was a Christian of the utmost fervor and zeal. Rawidowicz has aptly designated him a representative of "storm and stress" in the realm of religion.[10] For this impassioned Christian even the most virtuous Jew, as long as he denied Christ, would have great difficulty in attaining salvation. To a Jew of Mendelssohn's noble character Lavater could only have the attitude which, according to Mendelssohn, Judaism disavowed: What a pity for the beautiful soul! [11]

In his *Reply* to Mendelssohn [12] Lavater apologized for his audacity, but reaffirmed an earnest desire to know how Mendelssohn as a philosopher could defend the divinity of Judaism and yet deny Bonnet's contentions for Christianity. Lavater was not to be easily satisfied. He tried to entice Mendelssohn by suggesting that the philosophical seriousness already shown in the *Open Letter* made it quite apparent that further writings on religion from his pen could not possibly arouse ill feeling against himself or his fellow Jews. He even proposed that a book on Judaism would lead to a better understanding by Christianity of its mother religion. But in the end, zeal for his faith overwhelms him: "That it were but God's will that you were a Christian!" he exclaims.[13] If Mendelssohn does not want to pursue the matter, Lavater promises he will trouble him no further, but he has not lost hope: someday he will see him among the blissful worshippers of his Lord Jesus Christ.

Lavater's *Reply* was published by Nicolai in Berlin together with a *Postscript* by Mendelssohn. Despite his previous protestations of reluctance, Mendelssohn here briefly criticizes Bonnet, and for the first time publicly unveils a small part of his philosophy of Judaism. For him it is a revealed religion [14] based not on miracles witnessed by a few, as were those of Jesus, but, as Judah Halevi had argued, on the testimony of the entire nation. Mendelssohn goes no further. He wants to accept Lavater's offer to let the curtain drop, and he falls back, as at first, upon the "holy truths" which "the best Christians and the best Jews have in common." [15]

For the next twelve years Mendelssohn published nothing else of an apologetic or polemic character. But during the course of the Lavater dispute he wrote a number of private letters and fragments, unpublished until after his death, which give us a much more complete picture than the published material. They illustrate his struggle to retain his ties with the gentile world without sacrificing his adherence to Judaism. A careful study of these documents reveals the impact of the dispute upon Mendelssohn. His conviction that close ties of mutual respect might exist between the cultured and virtuous of both religions is badly shaken by his utter disillusion with the majority of learned Christians. Inwardly he is torn between identification with the universal community of humanity, which now seems only a dream, and the more limited Jewish community, which has not for many years occupied the center of his interest and which has always harbored bitter resentment against Christianity.

Mendelssohn mistakenly assumed from Lavater's dedication that Bonnet had directed his work to the Jews and authorized the translator's public challenge. In his *Open Letter* he therefore attacked Bonnet by suggesting that his arguments could not be expected to convince a Jew; they could only confirm Christians in their faith. On January 12, 1770 Bonnet wrote to Mendelssohn that Lavater had not informed him of his intention to dedicate the translation to Mendelssohn, that he disapproved of Lavater's action, and that his book "was not at all addressed to the venerable house of Jacob." [16] Mendelssohn was deeply touched by Bonnet's letter. It now seemed that Lavater had been the villain and that there need not be ill feeling between him and Bonnet. He was grateful for the proffered friendship of the highly respected Swiss scholar and expressed the conviction that they were in accord on all essentials. Moreover, it was the area of agreement which needed to be stressed:

> The truths which we hold in common are still too little disseminated that we could expect much good to come of the discussion of these disputed points. Are the designations Christianity and Judaism tied up with ... particular doctrines?

What difference does it make? In our ears these names will be no more inimical than Cartesians and Leibnizians. What a happy world we would live in if all men *accepted* and *practiced* the truths that the *best* Christians and the *best* Jews have in common.[17]

Mendelssohn stated the same thought publicly, as we have seen, a short time later in his *Postscript*. He was in fact expressing the radical sentiment that he felt closer ties to an enlightened Christian—as he then thought Bonnet to be—than to the average uneducated Jew of Berlin. Mendelssohn still thought that there was a realm of mutual understanding for exceptional individuals from both sides of the religious division.

In the beginning he had harbored no such hopes of rapprochement with Lavater, the actual instigator of the dispute. In a page of brief reflections on Lavater's challenge, which must be dated before Mendelssohn's *Open Letter*,[18] he is certain that Lavater was not motivated by friendship. But in his *Open Letter*, to bring the matter to a rapid conclusion, he restrained his bitterness. Later, Lavater's *Reply* gave Mendelssohn some faith in the integrity of his opponent. In a letter written in early March,[19] Mendelssohn offers his friendship to Lavater in the same Enlightenment spirit which had animated his letter to Bonnet a few weeks earlier: "Come, let us embrace each other in our thoughts! You are a Christian preacher, I a Jewish bookkeeper. What difference does it make? If we return to the sheep and the silk-worm what they have given us, then we are both *human beings*." [20]

Thus, in the first days of March 1770, Mendelssohn possessed a sense of spiritual kinship with both Lavater and Bonnet; and he had every reason to feel as he did. Both Christians had shown him the utmost respect: it seemed as if Bonnet was not concerned with converting Jews, and Lavater had openly expressed his regrets. Then, after Lavater's *Reply* and Mendelssohn's *Postscript* had already gone to the printer, a set of "additions" to the *Reply* arrived from Lavater. These additions (which unfortunately are not extant) upset Mendelssohn considerably for he saw in them the impetus to further dispute.[21] His disillusion with the Christian world was exacerbated at the same time by the rash of tracts that appeared after his *Open Letter*, some of them moderate in tone, others less so, and one by a certain Johann Balthasar Kölbele positively vicious in its insinuations.

Mendelssohn slowly came to realize what he must have suspected before the Lavater dispute but was not able to believe for a time even after it had begun: the vast majority of Christians, including even the best educated, could not admire and respect a virtuous Jew—particularly one who had gained fame in the intellectual world—without endeavoring to convert him. Mendelssohn felt rebuffed; he was no longer so concerned about arousing further controversy since he now began to feel that a bridge was not really possible. His change in attitude is best shown by a letter he wrote in Hebrew to his friend Avigdor Levi on March 30, 1770. He had hoped to avoid dispute, but since it had come, he would not falter:

All my life I restrained myself from religious disputes and polemics, for they are of no avail.... After I began to speak out and answer the words of that impetuous one [Lavater], all the adherents of that faith and those who support it set themselves against me. Some were vehement, others flattering; some got angry, others mocked—because that is their manner—and, whichever way, they trouble me with their words and fancies. But I trust in the Lord, my Fortress; He will gird me with strength for His battle and will put in my heart what I shall speak, and I know I shall not be ashamed.[22]

Mendelssohn was confirmed in his suspicions when, in July 1770, he received a new French edition of the proofs for Christianity which had been contained in the second part of Bonnet's work.[23] It was prepared by the author himself, who sent a copy to Mendelssohn. This new edition included a set of notes which so irritated Mendelssohn that he permanently broke off all contact with Bonnet. The notes incensed him for two reasons: some of them directly addressed the Jews in such a way that Bonnet, despite his previous protestations to the contrary, now seemed to Mendelssohn as much a proselytizer as Lavater; secondly, a single note endeavored to refute objections that Mendelssohn had made against Christianity in his *Postscript*, without however mentioning his name. Mendelssohn erroneously[24] thought that Bonnet had pre-dated his new preface to the edition to make it appear as if Mendelssohn had taken his objections, as contained in the *Postscript*, from those already refuted by Bonnet. This hurt Mendelssohn's pride, and it is likely that he now would have preferred the objections stated properly in his name with due reference to the *Postscript*.[25]

Earlier in the dispute Mendelssohn had begun to formulate detailed counter-remarks against Bonnet, but he did not publish them. The question arises whether he would have liked to make them public and thus accept Lavater's challenge, or whether he prepared them only for the eventuality that he might have no choice. Taken together the evidence suggests that, in the course of the dispute, growing disappointment and disgust turned Mendelssohn's unquestionable desire to preserve the peace into a belated regret that he had failed to fight the battle. On November 16, 1770 Mendelssohn wrote a letter to his relative and business associate Elkan Herz which contains a paragraph completely out of keeping with his previous attitude toward non-Jews. It has been a puzzle to scholars for it seems to reveal a very different Mendelssohn. But the writer of the Elkan Herz letter is neither a false Mendelssohn placating overly zealous fellow Jews,[26] nor an "inveterate anti-Christian"[27] whose earlier expressions of spiritual kinship with Lavater and Bonnet were not indicative of his genuine sentiments. He is rather a Mendelssohn transformed, a Mendelssohn who, at least for the moment, has lost faith in the greater community of Christians and Jews and who now both as Jew and as radical enlightener is sorry he has not made a more forceful effort to crush the "abominable structure of nonsense," as Lessing called orthodox Christianity.[28] Although at first Mendelssohn himself had favored reticence, after his disillusion he doubted the wisdom of his attitude. He now claimed that his restraint was from the beginning wholly due to the wishes of others; his timorous fellow Jews, afraid of the consequences, had held him back. So he wrote to Elkan Herz:

> You ask me why I got involved in a dispute? I only wish I had gotten involved a bit more. As yet, thank God, I have no regrets about it. I don't bother about any of the trash that is published against me. Whoever has a brain in his head realizes that it is in bad taste. If I might only have another such opportunity, I would do again what I did this time. Though some think it necessary always to keep silent, I don't believe it. If I consider what one is obligated to do for the sanctification of the name of God, I don't at all comprehend how considerable numbers of our people always cry out that for God's sake I should not write anything more on the subject. Also, God knows, I was not happy to disengage myself from the dispute. I bent my will to the will of others. If it would have gone my way, I would have liked to give a completely different answer.[29]

This "completely different answer" that Mendelssohn now insists he would have liked to give publicly may best be derived from a letter to the Crown Prince of Brunswick-Wolfenbüttel of January 25, 1770, and from his aforementioned counter-remarks to Bonnet. Taken together, they constitute the first complete expression of Mendelssohn's religious philosophy.

They anticipate his *Jerusalem,* which they precede by thirteen years, on almost every major point.

The Crown Prince of Brunswick-Wolfenbüttel, an enlightened young noble with an interest in philosophy, had, like many others, been impressed by Mendelssohn's *Phaedon.* When he came to Berlin in October of 1769, he sought the company of the Jewish philosopher and treated him with great respect. A short time thereafter the prince received a copy of Mendelssohn's *Open Letter* to Lavater and became curious how Mendelssohn could accept the divinity of Judaism while rejecting that of Christianity. He therefore wrote to Mendelssohn asking to see his counter-remarks to Bonnet. Mendelssohn replied, on January 25, 1770, that the counter-remarks were more in his mind than on paper. Nonetheless, he proceeded to give the prince a rather extensive answer to his question.

Mendelssohn's letter is masterfully composed in a calm, friendly, and totally unpolemic tone.[30] It does not give the impression of being a severe attack on Christianity, and yet it is just that. He lays down a criterion for all religious truth which the prince, a student of the enlightened theologian J. F. W. Jerusalem, is unable to reject: rationality. "I cannot repeat it often enough," writes Mendelssohn, "it all depends upon the logical truth of the doctrine, not upon the historical truth of the mission." Whatever is patently irrational cannot come from God. Given his criterion Christianity fares rather badly. Mendelssohn audaciously itemizes the dogmas of the Christian faith which he, qua rational individual not qua Jew, cannot accept. But it is the brilliance of Mendelssohn that he does not limit himself to a critique of Christianity—that would make it seem as if he were setting an unbridgeable gulf between himself and the Christian prince. He not only makes clear the differences between Christianity and Judaism as he sees them, but he proposes how they might be resolved. There could be a religion that would embrace both faiths. If Christianity would divest itself of its irrational dogmas and would agree that its founder had never freed the Jews from the Mosaic law, then Judaism in turn would recognize Jesus as a "prophet and messenger of God," sent "to preach the holy doctrine of virtue and its rewards in another life to a depraved human race."

There is no reason to believe that Mendelssohn seriously expected such a total rapprochement. But the proposal made it seem as if the gulf were not really unbridgeable without in any way mitigating the rational critique of Christianity. Mendelssohn succeeded in expressing his true point of view without antagonizing the prince. Thereafter the friendship between them continued and even grew stronger.

Like the letter to the crown prince, the counter-remarks to Bonnet put Christianity to the test of reason and found it wanting.[31] However, the greater significance of this latter document lies in the philosophy of Judaism which Mendelssohn formulated here fully for the first time.

Mendelssohn's concept of God seems at first not to differ from that of the exponents of natural religion. God is not mysterious; his attributes are not qualitatively different from those of men: the goodness of God is but the goodness of men in the highest degree. Human reason provides a perfectly adequate bridge to the Deity, enabling man to explain God's relationship to him by a single motive: his intention that the entire human race should be happy (glückselig). Since God desires only the best for man it is inconceivable that he should, as Christianity claims, make salvation dependent upon a revelation bestowed upon only a small fraction of the human race. Judaism draws the much more logical conclusion that all mankind may achieve happiness and salvation simply by leading a virtuous life. Mendelssohn realized that as long as Christianity insisted upon exclusive salvation it would always regard the Jew as an outsider; it would see in him only a prospective convert. If, however, Christians would accept the doctrine of the universal salvation of the righteous, this attitude toward the Jew would presumably cease.

A difficulty arises when Mendelssohn tries to explain the revelation at Sinai. Why should a rational God have bestowed a special revelation upon a small Asiatic people if all men already possessed the moral sense which is the sole prerequisite for salvation? How can such a special revelation be harmonized with the conception of a universally benevolent God? It is a problem that Mendelssohn is unable to solve satisfactorily. If he were to carry his reasoning to its logical conclusion he would be a deist. But he does not. God did once reveal himself to Israel, not to single it out exclusively for salvation, but to bestow certain laws as a "special favor" for "very special reasons." In return for obeying these laws the Jews can expect a "particular reward" since God would not have laid this extra burden upon them without some special compensation. What God's "special reasons" were for giving the revelation, or in what the "particular reward" consists, Mendelssohn does not say.

Embracing the revelation at Sinai freed Mendelssohn from the charge of deism, but at the same time exposed him to the Christian contention that if God had spoken to Israel through Moses He could once again have spoken through Jesus. Mendelssohn was therefore compelled to make a sharp distinction between the authority of Moses and that of Jesus. The authority of the former, he claimed, did not rest upon the miracles which he performed but upon the revelation itself, witnessed by the entire people. Nothing comparable to it ever happened before or after; its authority was indisputable and unique. Christianity could be subjected to the double-edged argument that few had witnessed the miracles performed by its founder and far greater numbers had attested to miracles performed by false prophets; but Judaism rested on no such tenuous basis.

Since the divine character of the Sinaitic revelation was beyond doubt and wholly unique, no Jew, bound by this revelation, could free himself from the laws which it imposed even though he no longer knew the purpose of some of them. God alone, as the source of the law, could rescind it, but had not done so. "In a great public manifestation, He spoke distinct words; in a similarly great public manifestation He would have abrogated His law." Until such an event occurs, the Jew, though not the Christian, must continue to obey the divine commandments.

The Mosaic law, the content of this special revelation, plus two truths of natural religion, God and Providence, constitute for Mendelssohn, as they did for the medieval Jewish philosopher Joseph Albo, the three cardinal tenets of Judaism. In the Mosaic legislation Mendelssohn finds the means for the preservation of the other two:

> The ceremonial laws of the Jews, aside from other causes we cannot discover, seem to have as a secondary purpose to set this nation visibly apart from all the rest and remind it constantly, through the performance of many religious acts, of those holy truths which should be unforgettable for all of us.[32]

In sum, Mendelssohn's Judaism, as he formulated it in 1770, consists of natural religion combined with a singular revelation of law intended only for the Jews and binding upon them alone. Unlike Christianity Judaism demands no belief in a dogma contrary to human reason. Although he could not admit it even to the crown prince, Mendelssohn was convinced that Judaism because of its greater rationality was vastly superior to orthodox Christianity. What was implicit in the letter to the crown prince and in the counter-remarks, Mendelssohn made explicit when writing to a fellow Jew. On July 22, 1771 he wrote the following to Elkan Herz:

> We have no principles which are contrary to or beyond reason. We add nothing to natural religion but commandments, statutes and just ordinances—thank God. But the principles and fundamentals of our religion are based upon pillars of reason and agree in every respect with true analysis and speculation, without any contradiction or controversy whatever. And that is the superiority of our true and divine religion over all the other lying [33] religions. The Christians will all charge that our principles are those of deism or naturalism. . . . Our people should verily recognize all of this by themselves, because it is our pride and glory, and all the books of our sages are full of it.[34]

When Mendelssohn wrote these words the dispute was over. Stricken by a lengthy and debilitating nerve disease, he was for many years unable to devote himself to philosophy. But he had taken a position; his adherence to Judaism could no longer be in doubt. In the *Postscript* he had publicly affirmed his acceptance of the Sinaitic revelation, while privately he had so interpreted Judaism that it harmonized perfectly with the religion of reason. Judaism was simply natural religion together with a special revelation of law—and that was its glory.

But the real significance of the Lavater dispute for Mendelssohn personally was that it forced him to realize the insufficiency of merely setting an example. He had gained fame as a philosopher and as a man of great personal virtue. Yet, fifteen years after Michaelis' review of *The Jews,* the bulk of the Christian community was still unwilling to believe that a man like himself could sincerely be a Jew.[35] Now he had made it perfectly clear that he was indeed a Jew and he was prepared to justify his Judaism by the tenets of the Enlightenment. Although he wrote to Lavater that he had not just begun to examine his religious beliefs, being a Jew had never loomed so large as it did when he was forced to render account for it. Hereafter, Mendelssohn's Jewishness remained in the forefront of his consciousness. In the succeeding years he was to devote his attention to two questions which he had neglected as litterateur and philosopher: what was the type of society whose political and religious institutions would enable the Jew to live fully within it and yet remain a

Jew? and secondly, what was there within Jewish life itself that prevented full freedom for the individual Jew and his integration—as a Jew—into the larger society?

After the dispute, as before, Mendelssohn continued to cherish both his ideals: a community of Jews and Christians characterized by full tolerance and respect flowing from a common natural religion; and an enlightened, moral, unfanatic Jewry. But now he also concerned himself with the real situation before him, and the rest of his life was largely devoted to bringing the real closer to the ideal.

The character of the German-Jewish community of the seventies and eighties must have gravely troubled Mendelssohn. Although Berlin Jewry honored and esteemed its famed philosopher, a narrow-minded suspicion still prevailed among the more fanatic orthodox. There were some who could believe the accusations of a Kölbele that Mendelssohn was at heart a deist; [36] and in the midst of the Lavater dispute, the Berlin rabbinate saw fit to summon Mendelssohn to render it account.[37] Yet, at the same time, the number of Jews breaking away from traditional Judaism was increasing rapidly. In 1783 the artist Chodowiecki described the situation of Berlin Jewry in a letter to the Countess of Solms-Laubach: "It seems that where you live the Jews are still orthodox; here, with the exception of the lower classes, they are so by no means. They buy and sell on Saturdays, eat all forbidden foods, keep no fast days, etc." [38] Even if Chodowiecki's description is exaggerated, it is nonetheless evident that the rift within Jewry was becoming more and more apparent.

Mendelssohn, ever the conciliator, strove to curb the excesses of both factions. He had admitted in his *Open Letter* that he could not consider all that passed for Judaism as its genuine essence. "I will not deny it," he wrote, "that I have detected human additions and abuses in my religion which, sadly, all too much dim its lustre." He had even admitted that some of the more recondite rabbinic writings were of little value (*Scharteken*).[39] But he remained an observant Jew, retained his respect for Talmud as for Bible, and opposed sharp attacks on the orthodox.[40]

Mendelssohn was a revolutionary in neither his thinking nor his actions. Just as in his philosophy he followed the lead of the German rationalists and the British empiricists without striving toward a system of his own, so in affairs of the Jewish community he was reluctant to embark upon radical reforms. Even before his illness weakened him, he recognized that he lacked the courage and perseverence to set out upon untrodden paths:

> He who dares to make innovations must carry them through with stoutness of heart, patiently bear the consequences, double his courage and rather go out of his mind than let himself be silenced.... My temperament is not for innovations.[41]

And yet, despite his immense respect for tradition and the conservative bent of his character, in some ways Mendelssohn was unquestionably a reformer of Jewish life—a temperate one to be sure, but a reformer nonetheless.

It was a long-standing and widespread custom among Jews to bury their dead as soon as possible after death. In 1772 the continuance of this established practice was imperiled when the Duke of Mecklenburg-Schwerin issued an edict requiring his Jewish subjects to delay burials for at least three days since certainty of death could not be immediately established. On May 18th of that year, the Jewish community of Schwerin wrote to Mendelssohn urgently requesting him as a man of some influence to intercede on its behalf through the submission of a petition to the duke.

Although Mendelssohn acceded to the request and prepared the desired schema,[42] he sent it to the Jewish community together with a letter that supported the position of the duke. He argued on the basis of both Jewish law and medical opinion that late burial was distinctly preferable. He realized, however, that his arguments would probably not meet with the approval of the Schwerin community, since opposition to any change of the status quo was to be expected. His reply concluded thus: "I know, however, that you will not agree with me for the hand of custom is mighty and strong and it is possible that in your eyes I shall seem a heretic—but I have a clear conscience." Mendelssohn's viewpoint did arouse the opposition not only of Mordechai Jaffe, rabbi of the Schwerin community, but also of Jacob Emden, who could see in the duke's order only an occasion for compelling the Jews to adopt Christian customs and thus break down the divinely ordained separation of the Jew from the Christian community and its laws.[43]

Mendelssohn, too, favored the continued existence of a separate Jewish community and saw the ceremonial law as its chief preserving force.[44] But he was unhappy with the practical reality: not many of his coreligionists had followed his own example. Among the orthodox the pilpulistic method of Talmud study and the Judeo-German jargon persisted, while in wealthy homes German and French culture began to appear but were seldom combined with serious intellectual endeavor. Excessive concern with economic well-being prevailed in an ever more affluent Jewish community.[45] There were few of his fellow Jews with whom Mendelssohn could discuss an intricate philosophical problem. To Herz Homberg, one-time tutor in his home, he complained, "I have no friend among our nation around me who will really get involved with me in speculative matters."[46]

Out of a sense of his own isolation grew an interest in promoting a more modern, yet nonetheless Jewish, education for the new generation. The small circle of avid young admirers which would gather weekly in Mendelssohn's home to discuss and dispute must have been a great source of pleasure for the Jewish philosopher. One of them, David Friedländer, reports that in Mendelssohn's home "educational and cultural institutions were the outstanding topic of conversation. Improvement of instruction and recommendation of the German mother tongue were Mendelssohn's favorite themes."[47]

Although Mendelssohn was not overly impressed by Director Campe's invitation to Jewish students and teachers to participate in his Dessau Philanthropin, his interest in practical efforts to improve Jewish education was clearly apparent in his active support of the Berlin *Freischule,* founded in 1778.[48] This "free school," intended primarily for Jewish children whose parents could not afford a private tutor, offered a curriculum including "Hebrew, German, French—all grammatically taught; arithmetic and mechanics; geography, history and science."[49] For the use of this school David Friedländer composed a reader [50] to which Mendelssohn contributed a translation of Maimonides' Thirteen Articles of Faith and a prayer entitled "Devotional Exercise of a Philosopher." The latter invokes God as the "Author of Wisdom" and in the Enlightenment spirit entreats: "Let us be wise that we may be happy."

It was precisely this "wisdom," which consists of knowledge combined with piety, that Mendelssohn found lacking in the Jewish community. There had always been study of the traditional literature, and now secular learning was becoming widespread. But to the minds of his fellow Jews there was no connection between the two. It was with no less an aim in mind than the bridging of this gulf that Mendelssohn carried through his most controversial project: the translation of the Pentateuch into pure German. For the orthodox it would open the door to culture; for the assimilated it would make possible a return to Torah.

Despite his protestations to the contrary, it is likely that from the first Mendelssohn had at least some remote intention of making his translation a vehicle for the propagation of culture among his fellow Jews. However, in this, as in every other matter that was not purely intellectual, Mendelssohn was reluctant to become involved in controversy. He knew very well that the translation would arouse bitter opposition, and it was therefore only upon the urging of Solomon Dubno that he decided on publication.[51] But having once made the decision Mendelssohn refused to retreat, although he immediately encountered angry objections. In fact, it was the opposition of certain of the rabbis that made him see more clearly how necessary his translation was. The truest expression of Mendelssohn's motivation is unquestionably his letter of June 29, 1779 to his Christian friend, the Danish state-councilor August von Hennings. Here he writes that his illness had largely incapacitated him for philosophy, but:

> After some examination I found that the remainder of my powers could still suffice to render a good service to my children and perhaps to a considerable part of my nation if I were to put in their hands a better translation and explanation of the Holy Books than they had heretofore. This is the first step to culture, something from which my nation, sadly, is kept at such remove that one might almost despair of the possibility of an improvement. However, I felt myself obligated to do the little that is in my power and leave the rest to Providence, which, for the most part, takes longer to carry out its plan than we can see in advance. Now the more opposition this weak attempt meets the more necessary it seems to me and the more zealously I shall seek to carry it through.[52]

In his introduction to the translation Mendelssohn of course could not mention this intention to disseminate "culture." For, although by culture (*Cultur*) he meant nothing more than an improvement of morals, manners, and taste—certainly not an attack upon orthodoxy—such a forthright statement of purpose could only hinder the success of the project.

Cultural improvement, the growth in the next generation of a Jewry traditional yet able to move with dignity and understanding in the educated gentile society, was, however, not the only purpose of the translation and its accompanying commentary. An increasing percentage of Jewish youth was unable to read the Hebrew text without a translation.[53] They were thus forced to avail themselves either of a Judeo-German translation or a Christian one.

The Judeo-German jargon symbolized for Mendelssohn, as for the generation of Maskilim who followed him, that foreignness and illegitimacy which is the sad mark of the pariah. It evoked the image of the "wretched rabble which roams about at the fairs," as Lessing had called these strange, unmannered hawkers. Or perhaps it was the image of his brilliant but rather intemperate friend Solomon Maimon which came to Mendelssohn's mind when he considered the jargon. Maimon, a far more creative thinker than Mendelssohn, lacked his friend's equanimity of spirit. He was known to get terribly excited in discussing even trivial matters and at such times to revert unwittingly to the Yiddish of his Polish youth. The usually logical Mendelssohn was so set against the jargon that he saw it as part of a cause-and-effect relationship which could hardly be proven: "I fear that this jargon," he wrote in 1782, "has contributed not a little to the immorality of the common man; and I expect a very good effect from the increasing use of the pure German idiom." [54] Psychologically there seems to be a trace of self-hate or simple shame in Mendelssohn's strange reasonings; ideologically the old speech represented for him the past which must be overcome and the very counterpole of the "culture" which must be achieved.

The Christian translations, the most notable of which was the epochal masterpiece of Luther, were as objectionable as those in Judeo-German since they were slanted to read the New Testament into the Old. In the Hebrew preface to his Pentateuch, Mendelssohn called attention to the distortions perpetuated by Christian scholars who, unfamiliar with the tradition of Jewish interpretation, often misconstrued the text.[55] While Mendelssohn's own translation was by no means literal, it strictly adhered to the traditional Jewish interpretations.[56] In contrast to some of the Christian scholars of his day he was not a devotee of Biblical criticism. He disapproved of textual emendations and hoped they were only a passing fad. Mendelssohn thought the work of the great English Bible scholar Benjamin Kennicott and his circle dealt "rather too arbitrarily" with the text,[57] and a Jewish commentary by Avigdor Levi, abusive of orthodox interpretation, aroused his thorough displeasure.[58] In view of this conservative approach to the Bible, his surprisingly traditional opinions in his Pentateuch introduction are not likely to be dissimulations. Here he asserts that Moses wrote the entire Torah, including the last eight verses dealing with his own death. It was handed down so faithfully through the generations that the Pentateuch has remained exactly as it was when God dictated it to Moses, even to the vowels and accents.[59]

It was therefore not possible for the Jewish opponents of Mendelssohn's Pentateuch to argue convincingly that the translation did violence to traditional interpretation, nor that it was critical of the received text. Neither did the Hebrew commentary accompanying the translation, done by Mendelssohn in association with others, give any evidence of radicalism. In fact it was the translation, not the commentary, that stirred up all the furor.[60]

The hostility with which the translation was greeted from the very beginning in certain quarters can only be understood as a deep-seated anxiety on the part of the more traditional Jewish elements who, not without some measure of justification, could equate study of pure German with casting off the yoke of the commandments. Berlin Jewry (which officially approved the translation) had gained a reputation for laxity paralleling that of the so-called *religion de Berlin* among the Christians.[61] And indeed, Mendelssohn, though his own conduct was unimpeachable, associated with non-observant Jews, one of whom, Herz Homberg, participated in writing the commentary.

As the opposition continued and grew, the normally equanimous Mendelssohn became more forceful in striking back at his opponents. In the Lavater dispute he had learned the bitter lesson of how far removed he was from the leadership of orthodox Christianity; now he experienced gradual disaffection with the leadership of orthodox Jewry. Hennings had offered to use his influence to silence Raphael Cohen, rabbi of Hamburg-Altona and the most vociferous early opponent of the translation. At first Mendelssohn objected: "I wish that he be left undisturbed," he wrote to Hennings from Strelitz on June 29, 1779, "and that nothing be brought to bear upon him from the outside, in order to see what truth alone, free of all other considerations, is able to accomplish in my nation.... Perhaps a little ferment will best serve the cause with which I am really concerned, and I would only harm it if I sought to intervene." Yet only two weeks later, back in Berlin, Mendelssohn had changed his mind. He now wrote to Hennings that if the Danish king or several high officials were to subscribe to the translation perhaps the rabbi of Altona would take it as "a hint to proceed more correctly in the future." [62] Hennings obtained the subscriptions and Raphael Cohen was eventually silenced.[63] But the heated opposition convinced Mendelssohn that the translation, originally intended for the common man, was yet "much more necessary for rabbis." [64]

These rabbis were the ones whom Mendelssohn had in mind when early in 1782 he wrote the preface to a German translation of *Vindiciae Judaeorum,* an apologetic work by the noted seventeenth-century Amsterdam rabbi, Menasseh ben Israel. Mendelssohn concluded his prefatory remarks with an appeal to the leaders of Jewry. The Jew could not expect to be tolerated by the gentile community as long as he himself was intolerant. Freedom of conscience had to be established within the Jewish community first, before the Jew could plead for tolerance on the part of the gentiles.

> Oh, my brothers! You have until now all too severely felt the oppressive yoke of intolerance and perhaps thought to find a kind of compensation in the power granted you to impose an equally severe yoke upon your people. . . . If you want to be cherished, tolerated and spared by others, then cherish, tolerate and spare one another! [65]

It was Mendelssohn's old philosophy of the virtuous Jew, which had been so badly shaken in the Lavater dispute, that he asserted here in a new guise. Not only within the individual Jew, but within the Jewish group as a community, inner reform would have to precede and make possible social acceptance and political equality.

The battle for Jewish rights, Mendelssohn thought, might be waged more effectively by Christians than Jews since their pleas could not so easily be discounted as mere self-interest. When the Alsatian Jewish community asked Mendelssohn to write a tract in favor of Jewish emancipation, he preferred to pass the task on to the enlightened Prussian war-councilor Christian Wilhelm Dohm. Mendelssohn realized that the average man is swayed more by the stature of the writer than the cogency of the arguments. And, unquestionably, Dohm's *On the Amelioration of the Civil Status of the Jews* would not have had the same profound and lasting influence had it been written by a Jew. A few years after Dohm's book appeared Mendelssohn wrote to Baron Hirschen:

> Among people of the common sort, reasoning works only a bit and most has to be done by the recognized authority of the writer and his lack of self-interest. For this reason I have always regarded it with great pleasure whenever the prejudice of Christians against the Jews is opposed by a Christian writer.

The Jews themselves, rather than struggling against civic inequality, should show their own worth. Then, eventually, the Christians would realize their error. "The greater the difficulties, the more we must exert ourselves. There must arise more and more individuals among us who distinguish themselves without making a clamor and show merit without making any loud demands." [66]

Thus for Mendelssohn political emancipation of the Jews was a slow process in which Christians must be the chief spokesmen, while Jews furthered the cause best by making their own lives show the truth of the contentions made for them by their Christian defenders. Only when a Jewish community was faced with utter disaster, as the Dresden community was in 1777, did Mendelssohn use his considerable influence among Christians for a political purpose.[67] Grandiose plans proposed to him by certain Christians for a Jewish state in Palestine, or a wholly new society where Jews and Christians would live in full equality, were unable to arouse Mendelssohn's enthusiasm.[68] Nor did the Austrian edict of toleration of Joseph II produce the same hopes in Mendelssohn that it did in most of the other Maskilim.[69] He tried to protect his friend Wessely from the ire of the rabbis who condemned his *Words of Peace and Truth,* written in favor of Joseph's reforms, but Mendelssohn himself harbored increasingly grave doubts about Joseph's motives. He feared that behind the mask of toleration lay a different intention on the part of the Austrian government: assimilation and eventual conversion.[70]

Mendelssohn's preface to Menasseh ben Israel's work was welcomed by most Jews and enlightened Christians.[71] The gentile intellectual world was pleased that Mendelssohn was again writing for the German public,[72] while the greater part of the preface, an apology for the Jews' occupational status, could not but meet the approval of his own people. It was the uncompromising stand taken against all ecclesiastical authority in the latter portion of the preface that disturbed the vested interests of both parties.[73]

The most significant response came in an anonymously published pamphlet titled *The Search for Light and Justice*.[74] The author, who was probably the Austrian convert Joseph von Sonnenfels,[75] branded Lavater an "importunate fanatic," but then proceeded to issue his own challenge. In the preface Mendelssohn had publicly and of his own accord opposed the authority of the rabbis. How was it possible to do so without denying Judaism itself? The pamphlet confronted Mendelssohn with a clear dilemma: either ecclesiastical authority is not essential to Judaism and can be eliminated or, if it is essential (as the author thought it was), "then you my most worthy Mr. Mendelssohn have left the faith of your fathers—but yet another step and you have become one of ours." [76]

Like the Lavater dedication thirteen years earlier, this open challenge demanded a reply.[77] This time, however, Mendelssohn answered not with a protestation of his right to silence, but with what was to be his most remembered work. He called it *Jerusalem* for it embodied his vision of the ideal,[78] and he incorporated into it most of what he had already privately noted down years before as counter-remarks to Charles Bonnet.

In the first part of his *Jerusalem* Mendelssohn developed the outlines of an ideal society in which religion and toleration would be closely linked. Its central theme is best epitomized not in *Jerusalem* itself but in what Mendelssohn once wrote in an autograph book:

> Statecraft speaks:
>   Who recognizes a God must be tolerated;
> Religion teaches:
>   Who will not tolerate him recognizes no God.[79]

It was an appeal for a pluralistic society that offered full freedom of conscience to all those who accepted the postulates of natural religion: God, Providence, and a future life. Neither state nor church should have authority to encroach upon freedom of thought and expression. It was the very essence of religion, Mendelssohn thought, to teach rather than coerce. Religious sentiment could not be induced forcibly; it must be spontaneous. Excommunications have served no good purpose for they have rebuffed the sincere and been scorned by the despisers of religion. Again and again the greatest men were denounced as heretics:

Peruse the names of all the unfortunate who ever were supposed to be improved through ban and condemnation; reader! to whatever church, synagogue or mosque you outwardly adhere! examine whether in the mass of the banned you do not meet with more true religion than in the disproportionately greater mass of the banners? [80]

In the first part of his *Jerusalem* Mendelssohn disputed the authority of the rabbis no less than that of all other ecclesiastical officials. Excommunications, prohibition of heretical works, any measures of coercion were all out of keeping with the true spirit of religion. In Judaism these were the "abuses" to which Mendelssohn had alluded in his *Open Letter* to Lavater. Now, in the second part of his work, he developed a Judaism free of ecclesiastical authority, but one which did not correspond to empirical reality. Many Jews, he admitted, regarded their religion in much the same light as the anonymous pamphleteer—yet he himself could not.[81]

In the second part of his *Jerusalem* Mendelssohn projected an ideal Judaism to match the ideal society of the first part. It contains Mendelssohn's own religious philosophy, the product of his lifelong endeavor to sustain within himself a twofold spiritual bond. As a rational human being, he felt tied to the universal world of the intellect that transcends all barriers of time, place, and religious denomination; as a Jew he was bound by the revelation at Sinai to a particular law, divinely given to a people into whose midst he was born. *Jerusalem* was above all a personal defense of Mendelssohn's own existence and the goals of his life. He sought to strengthen the universal bond of reason against the pernicious influence of narrowing dogma and its coercive implementation, while upholding the bond of Sinai against its detractors among both Christians and Jews.

For Mendelssohn there could be no conflict between the universal realm of reason and the particular realm of Jewish law. Unlike orthodox Christianity, which retained impenetrable mysteries, Judaism could be fully rationalized. It was for him, in Rawidowicz's excellent image,[82] the second story of a spiritual home in which the lower floor, the "common religion of humanity," was shared by all, while a small portion of mankind was singled out to dwell in the upper story as well. Mendelssohn could live comfortably on both floors since Judaism, as he conceived it, embraced the natural religion of mankind, even while complementing it with "revealed legislation," the continual practical reminder of universal religious truth. "All [Jewish] laws refer to or are based upon eternal truths of reason or remind and awaken one to the contemplation of them, so that our rabbis correctly say: the laws and teachings are related to one another as body is to soul." [83] And in Mendelssohn himself, though sometimes strained, there was indeed such an organic relationship.

His Christian and Jewish contemporaries, however, found difficulty in reconciling the two parts of *Jerusalem*.[84] In the first part Mendelssohn spoke as a philosopher of the Enlightenment, very much in the spirit of John Locke. In the second he spoke as a Jew, justifying the continued separate existence of his people exclusively by the unconvincing argument that divine law may be abrogated only by the spoken retraction of the Lawgiver. His conception of Judaism as uniquely law bore a significant resemblance to that of Spinoza in the *Theologico-Political Treatise*. But, unlike Spinoza,[85] Mendelssohn did not regard the ceremonial law as inseparably linked to the ancient theocracy. Only those laws dependent upon the land of Palestine were no longer binding.

Athough respect for the Mosaic legislation was shared by Christian Bible scholars, its perpetuation after the destruction of the Judean state seemed to them a gross anomaly,[86] and, gradually, the Christian view of the temporary character of the Mosaic law crept into Jewish circles as well. Herz Homberg, after he had read *Jerusalem,* insisted on engaging Mendelssohn upon the subject. In reply to Homberg's questions Mendelssohn forsook his theoretical justification of the law (non-abrogation) for a pragmatic one: its importance lies in preserving the Jews as a separate nation. For only Judaism is a pure theism and must therefore be saved from adulteration:

> The ritual laws ... have not ceased to be necessary as a bond of unity; and in the scheme of Providence this unity itself will have to be preserved, in my opinion, as long as polytheism, anthropomorphism and religious usurpation still rule the globe. As long as these troubling spirits are united against reason, the genuine theists must also provide for a kind of union among themselves if the former are not to trample everything under foot. And wherein shall this union consist? In principles and beliefs? then you have dogmas, symbols, formulas, reason in fetters. Therefore in acts, meaningful acts—i.e. ceremonies.[87]

This was an argument Mendelssohn had included in his counter-remarks to Bonnet.[88] But, to avoid unnecessary controversy, he had chosen to omit it from *Jerusalem*.

However, even when the pragmatic argument is added to the theoretical, Mendelssohn's own adherence to the law still warrants further exploration. We know that, although he was not excessively severe in his observance, he wore a beard, kept the dietary laws, and would not ride or write on the Sabbath.[89] Unquestionably, there is more to be said in explanation of his orthodoxy in religious practice than what he wrote either in *Jerusalem* or to Homberg. Although his objective arguments for keeping the law were not mere rationalizations,[90] certain personal factors must have supplied motives for his justification. Mendelssohn's ancestor was the great talmudist and codifier Moses Isserles; as a boy he had received a thorough traditional education in Dessau and Berlin and had grown to manhood before there was any movement within Judaism to eliminate ritual observance. Moreover, he was by nature inclined to be respectful of tradition: "As long as we have not yet achieved complete certainty, we must, in regard to matters of practice, adhere to the principles according to which we were brought up and which we have received from other men worthy of our respect." [91]

Personal inclination was abetted by a practical consideration. It must have been clear to Mendelssohn that he would have lost all effectiveness as an educator and cultural reformer of his people had he freed himself from the law. The opposition aroused by the Pentateuch translation, sufficiently disturbing as it was, would unquestionably have been far more clamorous and effective had its author not been meticulous in keeping the commandments. If Mendelssohn's orthodoxy in practice had been subject to the slightest doubt, the logic of his opponents that culture leads away from Torah would have been irresistible.

Yet despite his own devotion to Jewish tradition, Mendelssohn's attitude toward the Jewish education of his children was more indulgent than energetic. To Homberg he wrote, "My son Joseph has as good as given up his Hebrew studies." And, about a year later, "He ... has forgotten nearly all of the Hebrew you taught him. I let him go his own way; as you know, I am no friend of coercion." [92]

There was a new attitude toward Judaism in the younger generation of educated Jews. They gathered around Mendelssohn, admired, honored, and respected him. But they tolerated rather than emulated his attitude toward the tradition. Out of regard for his feelings they made it a rule not to talk about talmudic controversies or ritual laws in his home. Friedländer recalls: "The sophistries of the former, the insignificance and pettiness of the latter, had already become objects of scorn in everyday life, yet, nonetheless, in Mendelssohn's presence one refrained from mentioning them either seriously or in jest." [93]

The ceremonial law, which Mendelssohn had made the unique feature of Judaism, was falling into disrepute. Although his admirers tried to hide their new attitude from him, it must still have been painfully obvious.[94] Nonetheless, Mendelssohn might have ended his days in peace had not the lower story of his spiritual home been threatened along with the upper. For in the last years of his life the philosophy of the Enlightenment was being shaken by the first wave of romanticism, the Leibnizian metaphysics assailed by Kant, and, most disturbing of all, the concept of eternal reason was being displaced by Lessing's idea of development.

Mendelssohn was not an *Aufklärer* in that narrow, derogatory sense of "arch-rationalist" which nineteenth-century critics gave to the term. He was no enemy of emotion or of religious enthusiasm.[95] His philosophy inclined away from the prevailing subordination of aesthetics to metaphysics and toward an autonomous aesthetic faculty.[96] Only when emotion freed itself completely from the restraints of reason or was proposed as a more profound key to reality than was healthy common sense did Mendelssohn reject it.[97]

For most of the eighteenth century, the strict, conservative rationalism of the Leibniz-Wolff school dominated German thought and creativity. Not until the seventies was there a powerful reaction against the unlimited control of reason. In literature the revolt appeared in the form of the "storm and stress" movement, which produced Goethe's early novel *Sorrows of Young Werther,* published in 1774. Mendelssohn, who was still very much interested in literature, read this highly personal effusion of emotion and was moved by it, but he was hardly carried away with enthusiasm for Goethe's work. On the contrary, he was somewhat taken aback and exclaimed: "What do those people want who arouse nothing but fiery passion and provide their heated imagination with no guide to get them safely through it?" [98]

The rise of emotionalism in literature was accompanied by the rebirth of fanaticism (*Schwärmerei*) [99] in religion. Men such as Johann Georg Hamann and Friedrich Heinrich Jacobi, precursors of the Romantic movement, forsook the banner of reason and retreated to the flag of faith. It seemed to the defenders of *Aufklärung* as if the flame of enlightenment were about to sputter out and a new age of darkness engulf the spirit. Mendelssohn greeted this development with the utmost apprehension. To his long-time Swiss friend Johann Zimmermann he wrote:

> We dreamed of nothing but enlightenment and by the light of reason hoped to find the environs so lit up that fanaticism certainly would no more show itself. But we see that already from the other side of the horizon night with all of its ghosts is again ascending. The most dreadful part of it is that the evil is so active, so effective. Fanaticism *acts* while reason is satisfied to *speak*.[100]

In his last two published works, the *Morgenstunden* (*Morning Hours*) and *An die Freunde Lessings* (*To the Friends of Lessing*), Mendelssohn attempted to repair the breaches in the besieged fortress of reason. He assured Jacobi that, as for himself, he would recognize as valid no conviction which was not the result of rational demonstration.[101] But all the philosopher's efforts were in vain; except for a few near-sighted diehards, the day of natural religion was clearly over.

The religion of reason was being subjected to a two-pronged attack. Pressing hard upon it from the one side were the religious fanatics; from the other, the materialists—*Aberglauben* and *Unglauben*.[102] The atheism of a Hume was no more palatable to Mendelssohn than the mystifications of a Jacobi. When he read Hume's *Dialogues Concerning Natural Religion* he became quite irritated,[103] and later, with obvious contempt, pronounced them not worthy of serious refutation.[104] But fanatics and atheists could be brushed off as extremists. Far more disconcerting, because both rational and moral, was the work of the "all-crushing" Kant.

Unlike the pre-romantics Kant was not a foe of the Enlightenment; rather, he overshadowed it while at the same time representing its final glorification.[105] Mendelssohn could accuse him neither of lack of seriousness nor of excessive emotionalism. Indeed, he wished that he had known Kant more intimately when he was still a young man and receptive to new ideas.[106] But when the *Critique of Pure Reason* appeared in 1781 Mendelssohn found himself unable to understand it, a fact he was not ashamed to admit.[107] It was almost pathetic how hard he tried to explain away the *Critique,* how he was totally unable to recognize the epochal character of the work. At first he was apparently convinced that Kant did not really mean to strike down pure reason. When he conceived a medallion in honor of the Königsberg philosopher, he seriously proposed it should depict on the reverse side the leaning tower of Pisa, representing the structure of reason, and be inscribed, "Critique of Pure Reason," with the motto: "Threatens to fall but does not." Even shortly before his death he thought Kant was perhaps only trying to ban uncritical acceptance of authority from philosophical studies.[108] Mendelssohn did sense, however, that his own philosophy was out of date and that he was too old and weak to begin anew. He was gratified to hear of anyone who like himself was still a Wolffian.[109] In regard to Kant he hoped only that he "would build up again in the same spirit in which he had torn down." [110]

At the same time that critical philosophy was destroying metaphysical rationalism the static view of the world based upon the eternal immutability of reason was subjected to the first attacks of historicism. Critics of Mendelssohn have frequently pointed out that he had little knowledge of history and even less historical sense. On the testimony of Nicolai we know that early in life Mendelssohn was interested only in philosophical speculation; [111] he could not understand how a man of Lessing's caliber might be interested in historical details.[112] Well known are his disdainful words to Abbt in a letter of February 16, 1765:

> What do I know of history? Whatever so much as bears the name history: natural history, geological history, political history, intellectual history, never wanted to enter my head; and I always yawn whenever I have to read something historical —only the style of writing can arouse me.[113]

It is less often noted that Mendelssohn became ashamed of his ignorance and proceeded to acquire considerable historical knowledge.[114] But there is no question that he lacked a sense of the philosophical significance of history. To Herder, the great pioneer of historical thought, Mendelssohn wrote that he could not follow him upon the course where he was making such great strides.[115] Nor was he able to follow the path that his friend Lessing discovered only shortly before his death—and therein lies the final tragedy of Mendelssohn's life.

In April 1779, thirty years after he wrote *The Jews,* Lessing published his justly famous *Nathan the Wise,* an apotheosis of Enlightenment toleration and the religion of humanity. Having been forbidden to publish further religious polemics he once again made the stage his pulpit. The figure of Nathan, it is commonly supposed, was patterned after Mendelssohn, although more, it seems, after the public image of the "Jewish Plato" than the flesh-and-blood individual.[116] Mendelssohn himself considered Lessing's play the crowning achievement of his friend's life. It was impossible that he could have risen to greater heights. To Lessing's brother, Karl, he wrote in February of 1781, "Fontenelle says of Copernicus: he made known his new system, and died. The biographer of your brother will be able to say with equal propriety: he wrote *Nathan the Wise,* and died." [117]

But the fact is that he didn't. After *Nathan,* and a year before his death, Lessing in 1780 published his most significant theological work, *The Education of Humanity.* Its revolutionary character cannot be sufficiently stressed. In one hundred brief paragraphs he set forth an entirely new approach to the problem of revelation: God had chosen it as His means of educating the human race. The Old Testament was a primer succeeded by the New, which was perhaps itself eventually to be left behind. Revelation and reason stood in reciprocal relation under the guidance of a divine Providence that led mankind even closer to maturity of the spirit. Reason, conceived by the eighteenth century as eternally the same and above the vicissitudes of history, was immersed in the process of becoming.[118] Each new generation possessed a higher religious truth than that which had preceded it.[119]

As Mendelssohn was unable to "understand" Kant's *Critique* since it utterly demolished the basic assumptions of dogmatic metaphysics, so he could not grasp Lessing's concept of religious progress. In *Jerusalem* he wrote:

> I, for my part, have no concept of the education of humanity.... Progress is for the individual human being whom Providence has destined to pass a portion of his eternity here on earth.... But that also the whole, humanity here below, should in the course of time ever move forward and perfect itself, this, it seems to me, was not the intent of Providence....[120]

The necessity for Mendelssohn to reject Lessing's work is apparent. If one revelation is succeeded by another bearing a higher degree of truth, then the permanent value of Torah, and hence Judaism, is destroyed. Retaining the ceremonial law becomes equivalent to having been left behind in the divine historical process; it means still reading the primer when the rest of the class has gone on to a more advanced text. Lessing made it quite clear that this was precisely what the rabbis were doing. They read more into the Old Testament than the text was itself capable of bearing and thus exercised a pernicious influence upon religious education.

Lessing's short work represented a more devastating and complete destruction of Mendelssohn's philosophy of Judaism than any individual work or historical force mentioned above, even though it came three years before the final formulation of that philosophy in *Jerusalem*. On the one hand there were the attacks on the ceremonial law by Christians and Jews, on the other the battering blows of critical philosophy, atheism, and fanaticism upon the metaphysics of rationality. But Lessing's *The Education of Humanity* attacked both at once. It relegated Judaism to the past and made reason dynamic rather than static. It was a whole new view of the world, which Mendelssohn was quite incapable of seeing.

Mendelssohn's great synthesis had been to unite Judaism with the philosophy of the Enlightenment, that philosophy of immutable reason which, because it was universal, had to make room for the Jew since he too was a human being. Tragically, his final synthesis appeared only when the rays of Enlightenment were already dimmed by a turbulently onrushing romanticism, and when Judaism was being declared an historical anachronism.

In the last days of his life Mendelssohn preferred not to gaze into the future. He would be philosopher and Jew only for the sake of enriching the present. From philosophy and from religion he chose that which he thought would contribute to felicity and virtue. In the final letter before he died, to his intimate friend and admirer Sophie Becker, he wrote:

> I choose from the systems of the philosophers always that which will make me happier and at the same time can make me better.... I rejoice in every religious custom which does not lead to intolerance and misanthropy; rejoice, like my children, in every ceremony that has something true and good for its basis; endeavor as far as possible to eliminate the false and abolish nothing until I am able to replace its good effect by something better.[121]

Mendelssohn rejoiced in the law and did not abolish it. In him the rationalism of Wolff and the law of Moses, disputed and challenged in his last days, were held together in momentary unity by the strength of his own person. But after he died the ephemeral character of the solution became all too apparent.

3

David Friedländer Dilemma of a Disciple

On the morning of January 4, 1786, the Jewish philosopher of Berlin died in his fifty-seventh year, mourned by Jew and gentile alike.[1] The Jewish community of Berlin closed stores and businesses on the day of the funeral; Ramler, the most popular German poet of his day, wrote an elegiac cantata honoring his dead Jewish friend. The tributes were deserved for Mendelssohn had occupied a unique position, prominent both within the Jewish community and outside of it, mediating between two worlds while retaining the respect and honor of each.

Upon his death there was no one in German Jewry who possessed the combination of Mendelssohn's unique philosophy of Judaism and extraordinary intellectual abilities. There were brilliant young Jewish philosophers, some of the finest students of Kant: Solomon Maimon, Lazarus Bendavid, Marcus Herz, but each of them was at loggerheads with traditional Judaism. Maimon, an adherent of the "religion of philosophy," considered himself completely outside the Jewish framework;[2] Bendavid could affirm only "the pure teachings of Moses" purged of all senseless ceremonial laws;[3] while Herz, also estranged from traditional Judaism, concentrated his interest on medicine, natural science, and Kantian philosophy. Other friends and disciples of Mendelssohn shared his concern for Jewish enlightenment, but these followers, the circle of the *Measfim*, lacked the stature of their mentor.

Of course it wasn't really necessary to find a successor to Mendelssohn. A generation earlier Enlightenment ideology had set forth the role of the exceptional Jew, which Mendelssohn had filled so well—even too well in the eyes of a Lavater. But now that role was played out. In Berlin Christians of the intellectual and upper classes had begun to mingle socially with enlightened Jews. Mendelssohn's life had shown beyond any doubt that even a Jew could be a philosopher and a man of high personal virtue. Yet the great man's death did make some wonder who would carry on his work of enlightenment among the Jews. Those who considered the question concluded there was only one logical choice: a wealthy young industrialist who openly aspired to Mendelssohn's role of leadership, David Friedländer.

Friedländer's claim to be Mendelssohn's successor was not unfounded. From the time that he came to Berlin in 1771 he had enjoyed an intimate and continuous relationship with Mendelssohn. He traveled with him, took his side in an unpleasant dispute with Solomon Dubno over the Pentateuch translation,[4] and was a chief promoter of that translation.[5] If we can accept Friedländer's own testimony, hardly a day went by when he did not spend some time with his revered mentor.[6] In 1778 Friedländer had joined with Mendelssohn and others in establishing the Free School in Berlin. He immediately became a director of the school and of the Hebrew publishing house that was established in conjunction with it.[7] The German reader which Friedländer compiled for the school created quite a sensation when it was published and, together with his other efforts to modernize and broaden Jewish education, brought Friedländer recognition as perpetuator of the cultural reform inaugurated by Mendelssohn.[8] The Hebrew journal *Ha-Measef,* dedicated to the extension of Jewish enlightenment in the tradition of Mendelssohn, issued an engraving of Friedländer titled "Founder of the Jewish Free School in Berlin."

In Christian society as well Friedländer had early made a name for himself and was there, too, regarded as Mendelssohn's heir. Shortly after his teacher's death Friedländer received a letter from the Prussian General, von Scholten, who had been a great admirer of Mendelssohn. It read:

Aside from your useful business enterprises wherein you serve your fatherland and your neighbor—and, as I know, often generously serve them—do carry on, my esteemed Mr. Friedländer, the cultivation of the humanities in which you were until now guided by the hand of so great a master.... His spirit will rest upon you and with it also his fame and the acclaim of the world! [9]

It was as the faithful student of Mendelssohn that Friedländer had made the acquaintance of some of the best minds in Europe. As his disciple he now published his first articles in the *Berlinische Monatsschrift,* a journal of the Berlin Enlightenment for which Mendelssohn himself had written some short pieces. Here the von Scholten letter appeared, very likely at Friedländer's own suggestion; and here he published, in December of 1786, a commentary to Psalm 110 as he had heard it from the mouth of his "unforgettable teacher" and which he desired to save from oblivion.[10] Within the Jewish community he strove likewise to perpetuate the name and work of Mendelssohn. He translated the traditional prayerbook into pure German printed in Hebrew characters, thus extending the goals of the Pentateuch translation to the sphere of liturgy.[11] He had prepared the translation, which appeared shortly after Mendelssohn's death in 1786, under his teacher's supervision. Like the work of Mendelssohn it represented a change of form not content. All of the traditional prayers were preserved, including those for return to Jerusalem and the reestablishment of the sacrificial cult; the word "Torah," despite its Hebrew root, was invariably translated as "law" (*Gesetz*). In the introduction which Friedländer wrote for the translation, he spoke of the purpose of prayer much in the spirit of Mendelssohn's own natural theology: prayer was intended to make the individual ponder his human destiny, to shore him up in time of sorrow and instill humility in happier times. The concept of prayer as petition was not considered at all.

In the contradiction between the deism of the introduction and the traditional liturgy of the translation, Friedländer carried forward the dichotomy of Mendelssohn—but he did so for the last time. After 1786 he moved far beyond his teacher Mendelssohn in two respects: he denied the claim of a revealed ceremonial law, which had represented for Mendelssohn the uniquely Jewish component of his weltanschauung, leaving only the naturalistic half; and he strove to extend the cultural emancipation of the Jews actively into the political sphere. Friedländer now devoted a great part of his life to propagating, theoretically and practically, the religious and political reform of Jewry. His Jewish self-consciousness in all of its vicissitudes must be seen in relation to the success and failure of these endeavors and in light of the changing milieu, both Jewish and gentile, in which Friedländer lived.

Unlike Mendelssohn, David Friedländer had been born into wealth. After the Seven Years' War his father, Joachim Moses, emerged as the richest Jew in Königsberg. In 1764 he successfully petitioned the Prussian government for a writ of general privilege, which was extended in 1775 to allow the family business commercial rights wholly equivalent to those of Christian bankers and merchants. Joachim Friedländer provided his sons with both a Jewish and a secular education, took them into his business, and secured for his children marriages into the wealthiest Jewish families. His son David, born December 6, 1750, came to Berlin at twenty-one and soon married the daughter of Daniel Itzig, the wealthiest Jew of the Prussian capital. By 1776 he had amassed sufficient funds to establish himself as partner in a new Berlin silk factory which in 1783 boasted eighty looms. Later Friedländer became an instructor at the college of manufacture and commerce, as well as an instructor, and eventually a trustee, of the school of trade. By the time he reached his middle fifties he was able to retire comfortably from all business activity. His home was sumptuously furnished, decorated with oil paintings and fine sculpture. He possessed manuscripts and first editions of Lessing as well as a valuable collection of antique coins and miniatures.[12] Within the Berlin Jewish community, where positions of power and prestige were reserved for the wealthy, he had early held the office of auditor, and at the death of Mendelssohn was already part of the governing body.[13] In view of his own financial status and his close relations with the wealthiest Berlin Jews (whom Mendelssohn had avoided), it is not surprising that Friedländer should manifest again and again a certain consciousness of class and that this awareness should significantly affect his view of both Jews and Judaism.[14]

Mendelssohn had already distinguished between Jews and Jews. But since he had come from a poor family himself and persevered in traditional practice, there was still a bond between him and the impoverished, highly observant Jews who legally or surreptitiously made their way across the Polish border and sometimes reached the Prussian capital. He too had been without money or means of support when he entered Berlin. Friedländer, however, shared next to nothing with these common Jews. His world was that of commercial and industrial capitalism, not petty money-lending; literature, art, philosophy, not Talmud. He shared the interests of the upper classes and intelligentsia of Berlin, not those of the Polish Jew.

Friedländer's class-consciousness can be seen most clearly in an article he wrote for the *Berlinische Monatsschrift* of June 1790. He was replying to a previously published suggestion that Jews give up the observance of Purim since it fomented moral corruption: when the Jew says "Persians" he probably thinks "Christians." In his anonymous response Friedländer defended the perpetuation of the Purim celebration by arguing that it has a beneficial effect: Jews who would not otherwise give to charity contribute at Purim because it is a tradition of the holiday. But Prussian Jews (who do not consider their fellow men their enemies) are to be distinguished from Jews in general. Friedländer readily agrees that the way the average Jew celebrates Purim, though not immoral, is surely disgraceful. He sits in the synagogue thinking only of the feast he will have when he comes home. "Certainly he stamps with his feet when he hears the name of Haman—because his father also did it." It's simply a matter of habit. Recognizing that the *Monatsschrift* caters especially to the upper classes, Friedländer argues that such behavior is typical of the masses—of any religious group. "The great mass of the Jews is characterized by a babbling away of their prayers, conscientious observance of religious ceremonies, and other outward piety, just like the riffraff of other religious groups." [15]

Yet for all his dissociation from lower class, orthodox, and East European Jews, Friedländer could not entirely turn his back on them. They and he both bore the name "Jew." There were only two answers: either he had to sever all identification with Jewry and turn Christian, or bring his fellow Jews more closely into line with his own status and weltanschauung. At different times in his life Friedländer moved in the direction of one or the other of these two solutions. As Mendelssohn's successor he felt an obligation to continue the reform process his teacher had begun and which he always thought he was carrying forward in his spirit. Yet, at the same time, he experienced a fitfully increasing estrangement from Jews and from Judaism.

Friedländer convinced himself that Mendelssohn had kept the Jewish law only to assure the success of cultural emancipation; he had favored religious reforms as well but had not pressed the issue.[16] In reality, of course, Mendelssohn never favored abolition of the law. At most he wanted to eliminate abuses and attribute a genuine and pure significance to the ceremonies.[17] But most of Mendelssohn's disciples could not envision reinterpretation of the law; they failed to find any value in it whatever. They accepted the point of view of the Christian community which could not understand why enlightened Jews should persist in remaining orthodox. They saw also that observance of the law stood between them and political emancipation, and of the two they were more willing to sacrifice the former. Mendelssohn had not taken practical steps to secure political rights, since for him civil equality with gentiles was not of paramount significance, as long as he could share a common culture with them. But the next generation, considering themselves already Germans culturally, now sought the recognition that they were Germans—or Prussians—politically as well.

After the prayerbook translation Friedländer moved rapidly beyond the more moderate objectives of Mendelssohn. The promotion of secular culture among Jews turned into agitation for religious reform; the plea for toleration from gentiles became an active struggle for equal rights. These religious and political objectives were intimately connected. The average Christian clergyman insisted that the principles of Judaism were directly related to moral corruption: usury and cheating resulted from affirmation of a reprehensible religion. The more enlightened argued that better treatment by the gentiles would improve the Jews and cause them to give up narrow prejudices. But even their best friends did not deny an alleged Jewish predilection for swindling and deceit, and they considered the orthodox Jew incapable of full citizenship.[18] When it came to the question of granting the Jews complete political equality there was general hesitancy. Should not the Jews first show themselves worthy and capable of the rights and duties of citizenship? Perhaps they could not be blamed for what they were; but, as Biester the *Monatsshrift* editor put it: the issue of political emancipation depended upon what the Jews themselves *could* become and what they *wanted* to become.[19]

The question was who should begin. Friedländer pressed for action on both sides. To the gentiles he argued that citizenship must be granted before one could reasonably expect reform. Despised for centuries, the Jew had actually become despicable; it was now up to the Christian who had made him so to reinvest him with dignity. At the same time, however, he urged his fellow Jews to take the initiative by proving themselves worthy of emancipation. Mendelssohn's efforts had been directed toward the ideal of the educated and enlightened, yet observant Jew. To this end he strove to bring German culture to the intellectually isolated orthodox and the Hebrew Bible back to the assimilated. His disciple envisioned only the Prussian citizen of Jewish origins and enlightened rational faith. His striving was to bring the Prussian state and society to accept the Jew as citizen and equal and to assimilate the Jew sufficiently to make him acceptable.

It is not known exactly when Friedländer himself gave up strict Jewish practice, though the process must have begun during Mendelssohn's lifetime. After his teacher died he became the declared advocate of religious as well as cultural reform. When his 1786 prayerbook translation provoked rabbinic opposition, Friedländer declared that translations into modern German would finally force Jews to realize which portions of the tradition no longer made sense.[20] He became a bitter foe of the rabbis who doggedly exerted all their influence against enlightenment. The rabbis should be leading their nation forward; instead they were holding it back. Friedländer felt constrained to tell the outside world that the rabbis did not really speak for the Jewish community; unlike Christian clergy they possessed no authority, except in the limited sphere of ritual decision.[21]

Most revealing of Friedländer's attitude toward Judaism in the years after Mendelssohn's death is a correspondence he conducted with Meir Eger of Glogau, a personal friend, business associate—and an orthodox Jew.[22] Earnestness, irony, and scorn alternate or fuse as Friedländer reflects on the Judaism of his day. When a major fire broke out in Glogau in 1789, Jewish homes, and also the synagogue, were amazingly left standing. For Meir Eger such an event could only be explained as an act of God's special favor to Israel, earned by the merit of previous generations. Friedländer, rationalist, deist, advocate of natural religion, chided his friend for his lack of sophistication; a God who interferes in history was not his God, not the God of philosophy. In Königsberg he had witnessed a fire where the only house in the street left standing belonged to a

Jewish apostate. How would Reb Meir explain that? And as for the preservation of the synagogue, was it really *worth* saving: "the synagogue where since it was built, no worshipper knows what he is praying and where three quarters of the prayers are full of blasphemy and idolatry"? [23]

To Eger, Friedländer spilled out his scorn for the rabbis who were still living in the Middle Ages, unwilling to admit what was happening all around them. Aware of the growing rift within Jewry they refused to acknowledge it. Instead of mediating between the old and the new they clung to an outworn tradition and condemned all innovation. Since their ceremonial law possessed no relevance whatever to the present, a religious revolution within Jewry was bound to come. The rabbis were losing their power; interest in the law was waning. In ten years no one in Berlin would care about fine ritual distinctions. From Berlin the reform movement would spread to Breslau, even Glogau. And he, Friedländer, hoped and wished for it more than for anything else and had vowed to work for its success. If he could only witness the beginnings of a religious improvement in his own lifetime, he claimed, he would "descend happy and contented" to his grave. But the time for a comprehensive program of religious reform had not yet come. Meanwhile, Friedländer was concentrating his attention on the second front: citizenship for the Jews of Prussia.

The political emancipation of German Jewry had already received attention in Mendelssohn's time. Dohm's open advocacy of the amelioration of Jewish civil status in 1781 set the process in motion on the theoretical level. He argued in the spirit of the Enlightenment that the Jew was more man than Jew, and that if he were treated fairly he was wholly capable of becoming a useful citizen of the state. Dohm must have had his friend Mendelssohn specifically in mind when, unlike most of those who later wrote in favor of the Jews, he did not consider keeping the Jewish law a barrier to emancipation.[24] Moral corruption among Jews was a result not of their faith but of the oppression they had suffered and the degenerative influence of exclusive concentration in commerce. Similar sentiments were expressed again in 1787 by the French Comte de Mirabeau, who shared Dohm's sanguine expectations: "The Jews will be as good as the other citizens in every state where they are given the same rights and duties." [25]

However, as long as Frederick the Great sat on the Prussian throne, there was little hope that enlightened theory would be translated into concrete political reforms. Extensive privileges were granted to select individual Jews, but no one expected that "old Fritz" would adjust the corporate character of the Prussian economic and political system to grant the "Jewish nation" equality. Like the other elements of Prussian society the Jews were regarded as a distinct entity fulfilling a particular economic function. Being Jews they were tolerated but excluded from most occupations which would produce competition with Christians or provide them with undue status. They were heavily taxed, barred from the army, and their numbers kept down through special regulations. However, when Frederick William II succeeded to the kingship in 1786, Jewish hopes for at least a lightening of the onerous restrictions and taxes seemed brighter. Soon after assuming the throne the new king showed favor to individual Jews, including a grant of general privilege to the widow and children of Mendelssohn, which had been denied by his predecessor during Mendelssohn's lifetime.[26] The Jewish community of Berlin, represented by its elders, lost no time in submitting a petition to the new king who acceded to their request for the appointment of a government commission to consider the status of the Jews. It was to work with representatives of the Jewish community in formulating a plan of thoroughgoing legal, economic, and political reform.

For the enlightened Jews of Prussia's larger cities the disparity between their level of wealth and culture and their legal status had become intolerable.[27] They were among the richest subjects of the state, associated freely with Germany's brightest intellectuals, and felt themselves more Prussian than Jewish. Yet under the law they constituted a separate and distinct entity, a collective unit subject to special restrictive and demeaning legislation. They were painfully aware of the wide gulf between what they thought of themselves and what they were considered by the state.

In the ensuing struggle for political equality, Friedländer occupied the dominant position from the first. He was selected as one of the general deputies of Prussian Jewry who, in May 1787, submitted a memorandum to the commission appointed by the king. They asked that the Jewry Regulation of 1750 be superseded by a new *reglement,* to be based on principles of human respect and toleration, with due regard for the prosperity of the state as well as for the talents and capabilities of the Jewish subjects.[28] It is worthy of note that the Jewish representatives did not seek complete freedom from special legislation—that would have been far too bold a proposal. They sought only an amelioration of Jewish status through the removal of economic restrictions and the granting of certain rights. What the memorandum stressed was the increased usefulness that the state might derive from more humane and equal treatment of its Jews. The principal appeal was not to an abstract ideal of human equality, but to the criterion of utility.

Submitted with the memorandum was a sketch outlining the economic disabilities which were imposed upon Prussian Jews: there were the regular taxes to state, province and city, the special taxes paid upon particular occasions, and the insignificant but demeaning body tax, to which even privileged Jews were subjected when traveling from one province to another. Jews were further required to purchase porcelain from the royal factory and sell it outside the country (which almost always resulted in considerable losses); they were excluded from all service to the state and from engaging in agriculture and in those crafts controlled by guilds. Even in commerce they were subjected to numerous special restrictions.

In describing the Jewish disabilities the deputies singled out two matters for special treatment: the collective liability of the Jews and the restriction of economic activity. According to the regulations then in effect, Prussian Jewry as a whole was responsible for making good the taxes of an insolvent Jew, the debts of a bankrupt, and the property stolen by a Jewish thief. That the deputies should have given this particular matter special prominence is wholly understandable in view of who they were. As the wealthiest, they were the ones who bore the main burden of making good for their less fortunate brethren; as the most assimilated, they resented the bond with less respectable Jews that this regulation imposed upon them. They justified their desire to be rid of it by condemning collective liability as morally pernicious. It led to hatreds within the Jewish community, the concealment of criminal acts, and constant anxiety by the individual Jew that the deeds of another would bring him financial injury.

Of equal concern to the deputies were the special restrictions upon economic activity. Following Dohm they argued that hatred of the Jew was the result of occupational restriction: the Jew was despised not as Jew but as merchant. They favored admission of Jews into crafts and agriculture and the elimination of special taxes and restrictions on Jewish

tradesmen. They discounted as pretext the argument that with their special talents Jews could fully take over Prussian trade; yet even if that were
so, it would only be to the benefit of the state to possess a more flourishing
commerce.

The hopes of the deputies were to be rudely disappointed. After considerable delay the government, on January 4, 1790, finally presented its
plan for reform. Although it acceded to some of the deputies' demands,
the concessions were hedged about by such a welter of special conditions
and qualifications that in fact it represented no progress at all. Moreover,
the proposal insisted that Jews accept the obligation of bearing arms, a
duty the general deputies were willing to take upon themselves but which
they were not empowered to accept on behalf of Prussian Jewry.[29]

The deputies replied to the proposal, speaking only for themselves.
Undoubtedly realizing that the Prussian government had been shaken
by contemporary events in France, they again made it clear that their
requests were made in the interest of the state, not as deductions from
abstract principle:

> Not with empty declamations nor with appeals to the rights of man have we
> importuned our beloved sovereign, but with the humble plea to impart new po-
> tential to the unused energies of true, industrious, and in gratitude obligated sub-
> jects, that through the amelioration of our civil status we might help bring about
> the prosperity and well-being of the state. [30]

The deputies' reply to the government proposal was marked by a greater
dissociation from less desirable Jewish elements than was the original
petition.[31] It stressed that Prussian Jews were on a higher cultural level
than Jews elsewhere and that most of their number would not refuse to
serve in the army. Sick or mendicant Jews from outside the country, who
would only be a burden, they thought should be turned back forcibly at
the borders of the state. But the dissociation of the deputies was not complete. Since the government was not willing to eliminate economic restrictions and collective liability for taxes, the deputies declined elimination of
the communal liability to provide for their own poor. They were still very
much concerned about the welfare of the lower class Jew who, after all,
would be the only one to take up a craft or agriculture. With manifest
disappointment the deputies concluded that unless the proposed plan be
substantially revised they would have to ask the government simply to
maintain the status quo.

Once again there was long waiting for a reply. Finally, the king yielded to the suggestion of his General Directory (which had throughout been hostile to Jewish emancipation): the whole matter was to be postponed until after the conclusion of the anticipated war with France. Eventually even the king's ardor for reform abated.[32] A new movement for comprehensive change in Jewish status was not taken up again for another fifteen years, and then under very different circumstances. The effort had produced only scattered results in individual edicts: the hateful body tax was abolished in 1787, as was the porcelain export a year later against a single payment of 40,000 Reichstaler; and in 1792 collective liability for state and communal taxes (though not for thefts and bankruptcies) was eliminated. But restrictions and special taxes remained. Politically, the Jews were still wholly outsiders, a foreign corpus in the midst of the Prussian state.

David Friedländer, the driving force behind the first reform effort of 1787–92, was undoubtedly responsible for the formulation of the various memoranda and reflections.[33] In 1793 he published the relevant documents in Berlin with a lengthy preface of explanation and justification. He was presenting the case to public opinion. This preface is most important for an understanding of Friedländer since it stresses two of his most basic contentions: that the Jews are not responsible for what they are, and that, given the opportunity, all their distinctive traits will fall away.

For Friedländer Jewish history was passive: the Jew had been shaped against his will into a human being possessing such faults of character as reflected his treatment; his religion had come to stress messianic redemption and return to Palestine because he was denied a home in Europe. Dohm and other Christians had of course said the same thing; the point is that Friedländer and Jews like him accepted the thesis and so came to see the present state of both Jew and Judaism as a misfortune of history, a condition to be eliminated or at least radically corrected. Centuries of barbarism had made the Jew what he was; enlightened, humane treatment would reverse the process and bring him back into the human community.[34] In recent years certain Jews had begun to undo the effects of their history: they simply responded in accordance with what was offered them. If Jews were given fully equal rights and privileges they would become exactly like everyone else: "physically stronger and more stupid." [35] The initiative must come from the side of the state and the society in which Jews lived before inner change could be expected.

But once on the way the Jews would prove themselves worthy. They would free themselves from the shackles of a tradition which represented only an enslavement to the past.

Over the centuries the word "Jew" had acquired derogatory connotations. It had become a designation of base character, a word the masses used in derision. Friedländer wanted to be rid of it entirely. Like every other Jew he was grieved by the common use of the appellation, but when applied to him it was doubly wrong. He not only thought himself free of the character traits associated with the word, but also of what he knew to be a perfectly correct usage of the term: the unassimilated orthodox. He could not envision a reinterpretation of the word—it had to be abandoned. The reply to the government proposal suggested that state documents henceforth refer to Jews simply by their names, adding only where especially relevant "of Old Testament faith." Naively, Friedländer believed that a new name could dislodge the old prejudice.[36]

To the preface Friedländer attached three appendices. The last of these was supposed to show how low the crime rate among Jews really was. The other two were intended as evidence that at least certain families in Prussia were willing, capable, and worthy of the rights of citizenship. One of these documents was a letter sent to the General Directory by the Itzig family upon receipt of a royal patent of naturalization. It expressed their willingness to subject themselves to the laws of the state in all matters except those of a purely ceremonial character. The other was a request for naturalization by the descendents of David Friedländer's father, stressing that members of the family were never accused of usury or doubtful dealings, and that they had been and could continue to be of great value to the state. In the printing of these two documents the element of "some Jews and other Jews" was again present. Even if all Jews were not worthy of emancipation some certainly were. These at least would have to be considered.

During the emancipation effort a number of writings appeared which must have had a disheartening influence on Friedländer. In 1792–93 Solomon Maimon, the Jewish Kantian philosopher, published his memorable autobiography. It was avidly read by German intellectuals who developed their concepts of orthodox Judaism from it.[37] In this popular work Maimon took over Mendelssohn's conclusion that Judaism meant the keeping of the law. He condemned those Jews who remained within the community because of family ties or personal interest while they violated its laws. Judaism was a theocratic "state" which imposed laws on its members. Only the individual who left this state and adopted paganism or the religion of philosophy (as Maimon himself had done) was free of the law. Maimon's analysis excluded the possibility of a non-legal, purely confessional Judaism.[38]

In 1793 Johann Gottlieb Fichte, one of the founders of German nationalism, came to the same conclusion and drew political consequences from it: since the Jews constituted a state within the state, they could not be given Prussian citizenship.[39] Shaken by the French Revolution and afraid the emancipation efforts of the Jews might succeed, other writers hostile to the Jews raised their voices. And even in the Jewish camp there were those among the orthodox who had no desire to take over the duties of citizenship.[40]

As the eighteenth century drew to a close Friedländer had met with double frustration. Inner reform seemed a scant possibility.[41] Outside the larger cities Jews remained stubbornly orthodox; in centers like Berlin they often became atheists or hypocritical Christians. At the same time the great effort for political emancipation had died its slow death. There was no immediate prospect of revival. For himself Friedländer had gained the rights of citizenship on the naturalization patent granted his father-in-law Daniel Itzig, but his petition to gain the same rights for the entire Friedländer family had been rejected. Over the years his estrangement from Judaism had grown. Now, in 1799, Friedländer turned his back on both campaigns. Together with a few like-minded friends, heads of Jewish families, he addressed an anonymous open letter to William Abraham Teller, provost and head of the Berlin consistory of the Protestant Church.[42] Mendelssohn's disciple offered to become a Christian, having concluded there was no other way.

Friedländer's letter to Teller has generally been taken as a renunciation of Judaism; in fact the epistle is largely an apology for it. Judaism is found devoid of any unique value which would make its preservation worthwhile. Yet a residual identification with Judaism remains, a need to defend it, and a great hesitancy about exchanging it for Christianity. This document of willingness to leave Judaism behind provides abundant testimony of a lingering, ineradicable Jewish self-consciousness.

Certainly Friedländer could find no value in the ceremonial law and the concept of a personal messiah, but nonetheless he felt constrained to explain how these two characteristic features were grafted onto a pure patriarchal tradition; and how even such additions had done far less to vitiate true religion than Christian dogma had. Friedländer was at pains to point out that nothing in traditional Judaism in any way ran counter to genuine morality. The duties of one human being to another are as sacred to the observant Jew as to the most enlightened moralist. The principal texts of Judaism—Bible, even "many fragments of the Talmud," Maimonides—constitute rich sources for individual morality and sense of duty.[43] The ethical consciousness of the Jew is at least as advanced as that of the Christian; he lags behind only in the development of his creative powers. Immorality among Jews is more frequently the result of *discarding* the Jewish tradition—throwing away the kernel of eternal verities necessary for the moral life along with the husk of the ceremonial law.

The defense of Judaism as a morally beneficial religion was qualified by Friedländer's assertion that orthodox observance did prevent the Jew from performing the duties required of a citizen—a point at variance with what Friedländer had said in the documents of 1793 but his private opinion all along. Certainly for his own circle the laws of orthodoxy had lost all religious value. As Mendelssohn's student and avowed successor, Friedländer must have been well aware of his teacher's contention in *Jerusalem* that these laws were commandments revealed by God Himself on Sinai. But the disciple frankly admitted that they had become encumbrances to life in society and even objects of embarrassment in the presence of gentiles. He had to find a rational argument to support their rejection. In justification of his position Friedländer took recourse to a concept which Lessing had used but Mendelssohn rejected: historical evolution. He bound the law to time. Despite his Enlightenment philosophy Friedländer did not fail to appreciate the succession of ideas in world history, and in this respect he was more the disciple of Lessing than of Mendelssohn.

In distinct but unstated contradiction to Mendelssohn, Friedländer contended that the ceremonial law was not given by God but by Moses. The wise lawgiver, who had inherited the pure truths of religion from the patriarchs, saw the necessity of providing these truths with a suitable vehicle for their preservation in the midst of the people. They were a sensual (*sinnlich*) people and required an authoritative system of commandments to keep them from idolatry. In Friedländer's words one can hear the echo of Lessing: "They were not yet capable of any other kind of education upon the level where they then stood." [44] The ceremonial law had a purpose at a particular point in time and for a particular people. Moses had wisely devised the laws to promote the well-being and morality of ancient Israel. But they were a means to an end not an end in themselves; once the society in which they functioned was destroyed their role also should have ceased. When the laws were nonetheless perpetuated outside their original context they lost their intended significance and became wholly inane. For Mendelssohn there had still been an organic relationship between ceremonial law and religious truth. For Friedländer that relationship ceased with the destruction of the Temple: "Customs are the body whose spirit is the doctrine. If the soul has taken flight, of what value is the stripped-off husk? The butterfly has escaped, the empty cocoon remains." [45]

Through the centuries outside pressures had made Jews cling to the ceremonies and the hope of messianic redemption. Now a more favorable treatment was lessening their attraction, especially in Central and Western Europe. Friedländer proclaimed on behalf of this small group of family heads that they had completely given up ceremonial law and belief in a personal messiah. Had they therefore given up Judaism? Yes and no. They had become totally estranged from Judaism as it existed in their own day; with rationalist disgust they termed it "mystical." But again and again Friedländer insists that in retaining the basic religious truths, available to all mankind, they were remaining true to the original Judaism. In this respect his thought is in complete agreement with that of Mendelssohn who had also argued that there was no contradiction between Judaism and natural religion. [46] The family heads claimed that their devotion to what they considered essential in their religion was as sacred to them as their very lives. But the law was not essential; Moses the lawgiver would himself have demanded its abrogation had he lived in the modern age. Friedländer's epistle thus sounds again and again like a proposal for reform, a return to the pristine Judaism, not an abdication of what he believes to be its true spirit. Yet in the end he asks in all seriousness for acceptance into the Christian Church.

At no point in the epistle is Christianity described as a more noble religion than the original faith of Israel. In the Middle Ages it had sunk to a lower spiritual level than the contemporary Judaism. Its supernatural dogmas were an affront to human reason and moral sense. But in the modern age enlightened Christians were divesting themselves of dogma while at the same time enlightened Jews were leaving behind the ceremonial law. The two faiths were moving toward one another; they shared natural religion. Mendelssohn had emphasized the existence of this common ground, but his own adherence to the ceremonial law and Christian persistence in dogma had obviated any effort at a unification of religions. Now Friedländer thought he saw in Teller a dogma-less Christian and knew himself to be a non-practicing Jew. He was enough of a realist to know that a separate sect of the enlightened was not a practical or desirable possibility, nor did he fail to see that religion needs forms of expression as well as theoretical content. But this recognition still did not exclude the possibility of reformed, enlightened elements persisting within both religious groups. There really was no religious or moral reason for an enlightened Jew to become an enlightened Christian. There was, however, a practical reason: the political and economic handicap of the Jew. Since no doctrinal differences existed between the two, was it fair that one should suffer manifold disabilities while the other enjoyed all the rights of the state? Friedländer thought not. Conversion would mean only a change in name not an actual change in religion. He now inquired of Teller how such a conversion might be accomplished. Utterly refusing to accept any Christian dogma or submit to any ritual that would compromise his intellectual integrity, Friedländer nonetheless asked for admission into the Church. Christianity was to be purely a matter of form not belief. In Judaism he had rejected the ceremonies as inadequate receptacles of religious truth; in Christianity he hoped to find nobler vessels, but not nobler truths.

In a deeper sense, therefore, Friedländer did not propose conversion at all. He desired only a change of name in return for the acceptance of a few rituals. It was a step taken in the spirit of Mendelssohn in that it dramatized the universal bond of natural religion. In Friedländer the logic of Mendelssohn came to its necessary conclusion once the attachment to the ceremonial law was lost—its neglect justified through its humanization and the concept of historical progress. For Mendelssohn the law had been precisely what made Judaism unique, its reason for continued separate existence. Friedländer did not find a new unique content to replace the law.

He thus had no more basis for a religious expression of Jewish identity than, in view of his social position, he had for an ethnic expression through the concept of Jewish solidarity. Since there was no good reason for the preservation of Judaism, why should the Jew continue to suffer all manner of disabilities on its account? All political and economic rights were to be gained by conversion; if it could be done without an abdication of integrity nothing stood in the way.

The line of thought reflected in Friedländer's epistle was not novel. As early as 1793 another member of Mendelssohn's circle, Lazarus Bendavid, had published a work characterizing contemporary Jewry, which—though it did not propose conversion—manifested a very similar point of view. For the outmoded ceremonial law Bendavid wanted to substitute a Biblical Judaism which he considered coterminous with natural religion.[47] An anonymous Jewish reviewer of Bendavid's pamphlet went even further. He saw no reason why Jews should maintain themselves as a separate entity. They should mingle with the native population and assimilate spiritually and physically. The reviewer prefers the religion of Jesus to that of Moses since the latter, he feels, is inextricably tied to the ceremonial law.[48] Perhaps Bendavid himself came to prefer Jesus to Moses, or, more likely, Kant confused reviewer with author when in 1798 he praised Bendavid for proposing to accept the religion of Jesus, and declared that pure moral religion with the abandonment of all teaching of the law meant the death of Judaism.[49] Like Mendelssohn—and Friedländer—Kant saw Judaism as unique only in the ceremonial law. Mendelssohn's conception of Judaism had served to shape thinking on the subject by Jew and Christian alike.[50]

In the year before the epistle Wolf Davidson, a physician in Berlin about whom we otherwise know very little (but who may well have been one of the participants in the letter to Teller), published a pamphlet on the amelioration of Jewish civil status.[51] He defended the Jews against accusations of usury and deceit, proudly listing those who had achieved prominence in the arts and sciences. In Prussia, thanks to the *Aufklärung,* his brethren had been enabled to make great strides forward, leaving behind their outworn tradition. As the final goal of this remarkable progress Davidson envisioned a complete union of Christians and Jews. To further this process the state should freely allow intermarriages without conversion. If Christians would only abandon their lingering hatred of Jews a total unification of both religious groups could eventually come about.[52] Although Davidson does not suggest exactly how the union is to be achieved, Friedländer's train of thought is already present here and manifest in other earlier writings as well.[53]

The choice of an addressee for the epistle was easy and logical. William Abraham Teller was a theologian of the most highly enlightened views. He wrote articles for the *Monatsschrift,* was a friend of Mendelssohn, and was highly respected and trusted by Jews. He had clung to rationalism in theology even when, for a time after the death of Frederick the Great, it had become dangerous to do so. In 1792 he wrote two religious works with which Friedländer was familiar; and in neither of them did he mention Jesus as the son of God. Teller thus seemed the ideal person to whom to address the epistle.

The Berlin Provost's public reply [54] has been variously interpreted, anywhere from a definite rejection to the warm welcome of a missionary.[55] In fact it was neither. The enlightened Teller did not want to discourage the family heads, but neither did he feel compelled to save them for the Church. Probst Teller was not a Lavater. Thirty years earlier, when the Zurich theologian had issued his challenge to Mendelssohn, Teller thought it an act of intolerance. He was not of the opinion that every good Jew must become a Christian. That Mendelssohn had not converted was to the good since it enabled the Jewish philosopher to work for the improvement of his own people. Had Mendelssohn changed his religion he would have lost all influence. Recognizing the beneficial effect that Mendelssohn and his disciples (including Friedländer) have had upon the Jewish community, Teller now wonders why the more enlightened Jews are not satisfied to continue this work they have begun. They have already purged their Judaism of its dross, leaving only the "pure gold" of the "original Israelite religion." He is really asking them why they do not reform Judaism instead of fleeing to Christianity, since for Teller the reform of Judaism is as much in the spirit of Christ as conversion. He cannot assure them that they will gain the rights of citizenship simply because they have given up the Jewish law, but he is convinced that they have thereby removed the major obstacle. Up to this point the reply is certainly a rejection, but Teller goes further: if nonetheless they want to enter into a purified Christianity he will gladly extend them his hand.

Teller does not demand that the authors of the letter adopt Christianity in its entirety. His faith consists of fundamental doctrines (*Grundwahrheiten* or *Grundlehren*) and dogmas; they need accept only the former. The latter category includes theological statements about the trinity and the sonship of Jesus. The former, however, may be compressed into a single teaching which he insists the family heads must accept if they are to be called Christians: "that Christ, chosen and sent by God, was the founder of a better religion than all of your erstwhile service through ceremonials was or could be; that he is the lord and head of all who choose him as their model in the true worship of God and who follow his instruction." [56]

What Teller refused was to allow the Jewish heads of families merely to give up the ceremonial law and remain deists under a new name. He insisted they acknowledge the historical superiority of Christianity, that it represented a more elevated faith than Judaism. If they would agree to this he was personally prepared to make special allowances. A different confession of faith could be substituted for the usual trinitarian formula of baptism. They were free to reinterpret the Christian rituals—as enlightened Christianity itself had done. But, Teller admitted, the relationship between their conversion and the rights of citizenship was beyond his jurisdiction.

Teller's reply was not a rejection of the epistle. It was his honest answer to the question Friedländer had posed: what would he require of them to become Christians? But the demand he made was too high.[57] Friedländer and his friends were not seeking a *religious* conversion, only a nominal one, and not even the most enlightened of Christian theologians was willing to accept that.

The epistle to Teller and his reply provoked lively public interest. Within the year they both went through three printings. Pamphlets and articles, most of them anonymous, were circulated expressing all shades of opinion and reaction.[58] Their tone ranged from utmost seriousness to sarcastic humor; they took the form of essays, letters, dialogues—even one novel. Although these writings did not mention Friedländer his authorship was widely known.[59] Certainly Teller, who also exercised the function of censor in Berlin, knew to whom he was replying. By and large the reaction was unfavorable. Orthodox Christians used the occasion to decry the religion of reason in both camps.[60] Others denigrated the proposal as a selfish act done only to secure economic and political privilege.[61]

Of all the reactions, by far the most interesting, and next to Teller's reply likely the most profound in its influence on Friedländer, was a pamphlet in the form of letters authored anonymously by the young theologian Friederich Schleiermacher.[62] This proponent of romantic religion, who that same year delivered a mighty blow to Christian rationalism with his epochal *On Religion,* was not at all eager to gain more indifferent adherents for the faith. He clearly recognized that the epistle did not flow from a deep religious feeling, and that its authors would never become serious Christians. Moreover it was inevitable that they would bring something of Judaism along with them. Recognizing religion to be much deeper than the intellect, Schleiermacher perceived what most of his contemporaries did not: that, for example, in the moral defense of orthodox Jewry and the polemic against Christian dogma the epistle revealed a residue of Jewish identity that would accompany these Jews into Christianity. Once one has really adhered to a faith—and the epistle made the point that its sponsors had all grown up in orthodox homes—its influence could never be fully expunged. Schleiermacher favored rejection of the epistle not because conversion would make its authors citizens, but because "quasiconversion" would not be in the interest of Christianity. By indiscriminately denying rights of citizenship to the Jew the state not only acted inhumanly vis-à-vis the Jews, but also injured the Church by driving them to insincere conversion. Schleiermacher's solution was that the state grant full civil equality to any Jew who would give up belief in the messiah and those ceremonial laws which conflicted with the duties of a citizen. Since the senders of the epistle had indicated they were willing to do this much, they should therefore remain Jews, but constitute a special sect within Judaism.

Such a proposal must have given Friedländer cause for reflection. But the greatest effect undoubtedly came from what Schleiermacher said almost at the very beginning of his pamphlet about the contrast between this approach to civic rights and the noble efforts of the past decade. Its irony must have stung the fighter for Jewish emancipation and sorely shamed the disciple of Mendelssohn.

How deeply hurt especially the admirable Friedländer must be! I am eager to see whether he won't come forward and raise his voice against this betrayal of the better cause; he who with such high hopes—so it seemed at least—once departed the battlefield, who—more genuine disciple of Mendelssohn than this one here—did not even want to consider an abolition of the ceremonial law, but rather asserted decidedly that Jewish orthodoxy constitutes no obstacle to citizenship for his people.... Reason demands that all should be citizens, but it does not require that all must be Christians. It should therefore be possible in a number of ways to be a citizen and yet not be a Christian....[63]

The Jewish reaction to the epistle was no more favorable.[64] Of course the orthodox were opposed, but so were more enlightened Jews. In the September 1800 issue of the *Neue Berlinische Monatsschrift* there appeared a letter to the authors of the epistle by a "Dr. Schönemann of the Jewish nation."[65] It was the first (and only) published response by a declared Jew.[66] Schönemann charged the family heads with not taking into account the consequences of their action. They thought only of themselves, not considering the effect their step must have on those who remain Jews. Orthodoxy will triumphantly point to the converts as necessary consequences of any enlightenment. Educated Jews, alone capable of spreading light among the people, will follow their example. Skimming off the leadership will put the Jewish nation back centuries in culture. "I ask you yourselves," writes Schönemann, "can one commit a greater sin against a nation than to take away its instructors and guides?"

Against such a reaction Friedländer withdrew back into Judaism. He could not convince himself to accept the kind of conversion proposed by the enlightened Teller, much less by the others. Teller, Schleiermacher, and Schönemann had raised the painful question why he did not continue the noble tradition of his teacher Mendelssohn, working from within for the religious and political improvement of his fellow Jews. Friedländer had started out to do just that but in the face of despair had abandoned what seemed a hopeless path; the unexpected, negative reaction to the epistle now set him back upon it.[67]

For a long time after the failure of the initial effort hopes for Jewish emancipation in Prussia remained dim. From 1803 to 1805 a nasty pamphlet war raged on the issue. Grattenauer, Paalzow, and others like them decried Jews as foreigners, a caste of usurers, and the bearers of a hateful tradition. But then in October 1806 came the crushing Prussian defeat at Jena followed by the humiliating Peace of Tilsit the next year. Vast territories were yielded to the victorious Napoleon. The Prussian leadership at last came to realize the need for thoroughgoing social, economic, and administrative reform. Stein, Hardenberg, and their associates moved

Prussia toward a national regeneration. Untapped energies were drawn into the service of the nation; the peasantry was emancipated; a modern bureaucracy established. The time was ripe for a reconsideration of the Jewish question as well.

The initiative now did not come from the Jewish community but from the government.[68] Emancipation of the Jews became an integral part of the overall plan of reform. The Prussian leadership recognized that the national interest coincided with the yearnings of the Jewish community. Once again it was Friedländer who served as liaison between the government and Prussian Jewry. He remained its acknowledged representative, although his role in this final successful struggle for emancipation was not as great as it had been earlier. As the edict went through its preliminary formulations Friedländer made his views known in various ways, and twice the edict was submitted to him for his comments.[69]

Friedländer still enjoyed enormous influence. His letter to Teller had not cost him the respect of the Berlin Jewish community. In 1806 they elected him elder, a post which he held for six years.[70] At the same time he occupied a prestigious civil position in Berlin. According to the Stein municipal ordinance of 1808, cities in Prussa were granted a considerable degree of self-government. Friedländer, who had gained municipal citizenship in Berlin as early as 1792, was now elected to the governing council of the city. Simultaneously holding two positions of authority and influence, he was the logical representative of the Jews to the government.

The various proposals formulated by the government were sent back and forth through the bureaucracy for more than three years, until they at last resulted in the well-known edict of March 11, 1812.[71] In its final form, under the influence of Hardenberg, the edict embodied the French concept of complete equality.[72] It declared the Jews natives and citizens of the Prussian state. Special taxes and occupational restrictions were abolished. Jews were given the right to occupy academic positions and were made subject to conscription. Only the admission of Jews to state offices was left undecided. In one stroke the legal and political status of Prussian Jewry had been radically transformed. The Jewish elders of Berlin hastened to express their humble gratitude to Chancellor Hardenberg for this long awaited proclamation of citizenship.

But this new status, conferred upon the Jews by the government, now had to be harmonized with their own religious and educational system.

The last paragraph of the edict provided for deliberation on those decisions which would have to be made regarding adjustment of Jewish religious life and the improvement of education. It suggested that leaders of the Jewish community who enjoyed public confidence should be consulted and their opinions heard.

Here at last was Friedländer's opportunity to declare openly his views on Jewish religion and education. He rushed into print with suggestions he thought suited the new situation.[73] Immediately he sent copies to the king, to Hardenberg, and to the Minister of Religion and Education. His pamphlet, which he published anonymously, was concerned first of all with revision of the religious service. Since the Jews were now recognized as citizens, prayers for the return to Palestine were totally out of place. As long as they had been oppressed, as long as they were considered foreigners, the hope of return to a land of their own was significant. But for Prussian citizens such prayers should be eliminated. At the outset Friedländer symbolized the new change in status by a change in language. No longer should there be reference to a service of God (*Gottesdienst*) in the Jewish synagogue, but to a "worship of God (*Gottesverehrung*) in the temple of the Israelites."

Friedländer described what he considered the degeneration of the liturgy over the centuries both in content and in style. The utter lack of relationship of the religious service to the present day had emptied the synagogues. Few still knew enough Hebrew to understand the prayers. Yet there was a need for Jewish worship, worship befitting the modern man, the rationalist: a sensible tribute to God in a language understood by all. Friedländer proposed a liturgy based on the Bible and a service conducted entirely in German, except for perhaps a few Biblical selections in Hebrew by the reader. Its exact outlines he would leave to someone with more expert knowledge.

Integrally related to the revised service was to be the new education. Friedländer saw no reason for the average Jewish child to learn Hebrew, much less to study in the Talmud a legal system no longer relevant. But he did see a great need for a Jewish textbook to teach the revised Israelite religion. Such a book should single out the truths of the faith, based upon the Bible, and present them in a systematic manner. The Holy Scriptures represented for him a kind of treasure house (*Fundgrube*) from which this book of doctrines might be drawn and the liturgy constituted.

Friedländer urged those Jews who agreed with him to join in bringing

about the reform. Keeping in mind the king's dislike of religious innovation, he stressed that all segments of the Jewish community—even those
who disagreed with his proposals—were united in their veneration for the
Scriptures and that no sectarianism would result.

The brief pamphlet was intended for presentation to the government,
but directed to the Jewish community. It was written in a hopeful moment, when it seemed to Friedländer that emancipation would now at last
bring about reform. Rejecting the images of both Jew and Christian, he
had come to identify himself with a new concept: the Israelite. He now
wanted the rest of Jewry to become Israelites as well. That meant complete assimilation except in worship and religious education, the latter to
be based exclusively on the Old Testament. But what was this reformed
faith to be? Though Friedländer left both prayerbook and textbook to
be worked out by experts, it was clear that to be an Israelite meant simply
to draw natural religion—a religion of mankind—from the pristine source
of ancient Israel.

Friedländer was not to have the opportunity of putting the proposal
into effect. Although his ideas were welcomed by Hardenberg and also by
some of his fellow Jews,[74] the bulk of Jewry was opposed.[75] The assimila-
tors had already converted; those that remained were more conservative.
They objected to the proposed elimination of Hebrew from the worship
and from Jewish education, and they feared a split in the Jewish community. In January 1813 the Jewish community of Berlin held an elec-
tion to select two deputies who would aid the government in formulating
a plan of religious and educational reform.[76] Of course Friedländer was
among the candidates, but this time he was not chosen. Those elected
received 229 and 230 votes respectively, Friedländer only 84. Thirteen
years earlier the letter to Teller had not deprived Friedländer of his honored position in the Jewish community. That proposal, after all, was a
personal matter. But the concrete suggestions which he now offered would
affect everyone. His radical assimilationism went too far for most of those
who still wished to remain Jews.

Friedländer's tasks as the representative of Prussian Jewry had ended.
Emancipation had been gained; on reform there was no agreement. He
now associated himself with that portion of the Jewish community which
shared his own views. He wrote sermons [77] which were delivered by
younger men at the reform services then established in Berlin by Israel

Jacobson [78] and Jacob Beer. Most of these sermons lacked any Jewish character; they could as well have been given in a church. One is a lesson in natural theology: highly abstract, devoid of imagery, assuring the congregation that man's soul is immortal and his destiny self-fulfillment. Reason is the ultimate criterion of truth, God's way of speaking to the human being.

The worshippers at these services consisted mostly of the upper-class Jews of Berlin, the merchants and manufacturers. Friedländer offered this class a capitalist ideology in religious terms. In a sermon entitled "On Trade and Wealth" he defended the striving for material gain as a noble pursuit, if its fruits were wisely and generously used. In an almost Calvinistic spirit he preached against the bad use of time, and exalted the man who used every minute in productive endeavor. Of course, along with this justification of wealth went a doctrine of noblesse oblige. Having fulfilled his obligations to himself and his family the virtuous man had then to fulfill his duties to his fellow human beings. [79]

The attitude to Judaism in these sermons is ambiguous. As before, Friedländer is still unable to find any value in most Jewish customs and ceremonies—at least in their present form. While religious truth is based on eternal verities, the laws are bound by time: "Whosoever gives up the former ceases to be an Israelite and a virtuous human being; whosoever leaves the latter unobserved can perhaps become an Israelite in a higher sense and a better human being." Yet, at the same time, Friedländer, having decided to remain within the Jewish community, has only contempt for those who convert. Perhaps there is a hidden envy in these words; certainly they must have sounded strange to anyone who remembered Friedländer's epistle fifteen years earlier:

But let us not, on the other hand, go astray in our religion on account of the scorn, mockery and derision of the frivolous; not leave the teachings of our fathers because people ridicule our customs, language and manners. What man, what woman of conscience, who possesses a feeling of *true* honor, can change his religion without conviction, for reasons of fashion and vanity or base selfishness, like one changes his clothing or the time of a meal; change it for the sake of a certain degree of comfort or for advantages that are transient and vain. No! Let us not thus desecrate the holiest possessions of man: peace of conscience, integrity, and love of truth. [80]

But nothing was to come of the reform services in Berlin. According to the historian Jost, who was himself a member of the governing body, the flat, insipid character of the services became apparent even to some of the leaders.[81] In 1823 the orthodox finally convinced the government to abolish them on the pretext that they fomented sectarianism. In a book he published that same year [82] Friedländer called attention to this failure of reform among his fellow Jews. Already four years earlier he had reavowed the principles of his epistle to Teller; now he returned to them completely. Indeed this last published work was addressed to the disciples and friends of Probst Teller and the other Christian theologians of the Enlightenment. Once again Friedländer could find nothing in Judaism to make it worth preserving as a separate faith. He favored a "complete fusion" of Judaism and Christianity in which the former would totally lose its identity. Jewish religious services should be organized along Christian lines—"since where else should my co-religionists take their model from?" In the last years of his life Friedländer unswervingly regarded reformed [83] Judaism as an intermediate step on the road to enlightened Christianity.

Friedländer lived on to the age of eighty-four, a living fossil preserved from the eighteenth century. He joined the Society for Culture and Science among the Jews but his voice, in the midst of this group of young men animated by a new spirit, sounded like the hollow echo of an age gone by.

From time to time he wrote an article or a pamphlet: suggestions on the emancipation of the Jews in Poland,[84] a defense of the Jews against calumnies,[85] reflections on the reading and translation of Scripture.[86] But his active years were over. Plagued with the gout, he was often confined to his home. With a few friends of his own generation he would pass the time in nostalgic reminiscence of the Enlightenment, the age of Lessing and Mendelssohn. In the course of his long life he had become acquainted with some of the great men of his time: Kant, the Humboldt brothers, Chancellor Hardenberg. The German popular philosopher J. J. Engel even dedicated the edition of his works to Friedländer, his "noble friend." [87] Through his hobby of collecting coins and miniatures he came into correspondence with Goethe,[88] but was quite unable to appreciate his literary genius.

Friedländer had lived far beyond his time. German nationalism had replaced the cosmopolitanism of the Enlightenment; romanticism was the fashion in literature and theology; historicism had gained increasing prominence since Herder first launched the movement a generation before; and in politics the defeat of Napoleon had ushered in a period of darkest political reaction. Friedländer no longer wanted to live in a world so totally unfamiliar. In 1825 he confided to his young friend Leopold Zunz that he was ready to die.[89]

What sustained Friedländer in his last years was his reaffirmed conviction that he was the genuine disciple of Mendelssohn.[90] He put out a new edition of the *Phaedon* [91] and recommended his famed teacher as an example for the Jewish youth.[92] All he had wanted to do, he still claimed in 1823, was to spread the teachings of Mendelssohn.[93] Late in his life the aged Friedländer wrote ecstatically in his diary:

> Mendelssohn, palm of Israel, cedar of Lebanon! Thus you grew up, thus you overcame a thousand obstacles, which bodily stature, religion of your fathers, the constitution of the state, placed in your way. In your pleasant shade even I, a tiny plant, was suffered, sheltered and nurtured. It is a wonderful feeling to have been close to a wise man, true ecstasy of the soul the remembrance that a noble man honored my childlike attachment and loved me like a father. Even in old age your memory is as alive in me as fifty years ago.[94]

When Friedländer died on December 25, 1834, his tombstone was inscribed, not unexpectedly, according to his wish:

> Burial place
> Of David Friedländer, born in Königsberg, December 6, 5511
> The son of Joachim Moses Friedländer,
> True disciple and friend of the philosopher
> Moses Mendelssohn,
> Died December 25, 5595.[95]

For his contemporaries he had become "the good old honest Friedländer." For later generations he was to be the object of both virulent contempt and incommensurate praise.[96] To himself he was always simply the devoted disciple of Mendelssohn, carrying on the work his master had begun. He did not seek the preservation of Judaism, but the ennoblement of the Jew, the Jew as human being—as Lessing had seen him. Unable to find in Judaism a message of its own, he bore it as an unwanted burden. Fleeing, returning, fleeing again but never completing the flight, Friedländer struggled with his own Jewishness until in the winter of old age he fastened his eyes only backwards, on Mendelssohn and the past. Ever ambivalent in his Jewish identification, Friedländer had lost his mentor's warm regard for the tradition-oriented life, and he died having found nothing in Judaism to take its place.

4

Rationalism and Romanticism Two Roads to Conversion

In March of 1797 Sara Grotthuss, née Meyer, the daughter of a wealthy Jewish merchant of Berlin, wrote a letter to Goethe, her much admired idol. She included a reminiscence of her youth, which she insisted was the absolute truth:

> I was in my thirteenth year [she wrote] when I had a tender romance with the son of a Hamburg merchant, a very handsome, good and educated young man. One day he sent me that consolation of star-crossed lovers, the divine *Werther*. I devoured it and sent it back to him with a thousand underlined passages and a very glowing *billet*. This dispatch was intercepted by my dear father and I was confined to my room. Mendelssohn, who was my tutor, appeared and reproached me bitterly as to how I could forget God and religion, and to add to the absurdity, took the dear W., the innocent *corpus delicti,* and (after doughtily giving me a piece of his mind on every underlined passage) flung it out the window.[1]

Whether or not the episode occurred just as Sara related it, the image of Mendelssohn as a decided opponent of Sturm und Drang emotionalism was a true one. The lifelong friend of Nicolai and Lessing could only regard Goethe's *Sorrows of Young Werther* as moral and literary degeneracy. He was not alone in his opinion; in Berlin and Northern Germany *Werther* was at first more despised and mocked than admired.[2] The enlightened Jews of his own generation, his disciples, and the larger portion of the next generation shared Mendelssohn's verdict. Their libraries invariably displayed the works of Lessing, which they felt almost obligated to read. *Nathan the Wise* was, in the words of the young Ludwig Börne, the "book which every Jew who makes any pretense to culture reads a few dozen times and praises to the skies as the most beautiful work of art, even if he doesn't understand a word of it, and is thoroughly bored." [3]

Though Mendelssohn's own adherence to rationalism and clarity in philosophy and literature is largely explained by the intellectual climate in which he matured and to which he himself contributed, the persistent predilection of German Jewry in the next generation for Enlightenment thought and expression warrants further explanation. As the *Aufklärung* came increasingly under attack at the close of the eighteenth century, leading Jews were among its staunchest defenders. Some, like Friedländer, not only clung to the older literature, but even remained true to the philosophy of Leibniz and Wolff. More frequently, the younger men became convinced of the untenability of the old school of thought and made the move from Leibniz to Kant. In so doing, however, they only traded a defunct dogmatic rationalism for a more acceptable critical one. To become a Kantian meant to continue in the Enlightenment tradition. The metaphysical basis of the old natural religion crumbled away only to be replaced by an equally rational faith grounded in the moral imperative. Feeling and fantasy were banned from religion as much by Kant as by the *Aufklärung*.[4]

The Jewish commitment to rationalism had its roots in the intellectual tradition of the rabbinic literature and in the medieval Jewish philosophy so much admired by Mendelssohn and Solomon Maimon. It may have been nourished by the Jew's centuries-long activity as merchant and moneylender, carefully and hard-headedly calculating his own advantage. The Jewish man of business, harassed by burdensome taxes and regulations, ever taking great risks, had to think rationally to succeed. A prosperous Jewish banker of Berlin who was also a mystical enthusiast—while not impossible—would have been a gross incongruity. But the most significant factor contributing to the Jewish preference for philosophical rationalism and literary clarity was the conviction that political emancipation could come only from a universalistic weltanschauung, one that stressed the inherent similarity of men rather than their differences. Whether they openly subscribed to the principles of the French Revolution or whether, like Friedländer, they appealed to Prussian paternalism, the spokesmen of an assimilating German Jewry were at one in their rejection of any permanent individuality that might be attributed to the Jewish people. There was no Jewish soul, no irrational tribal bond which united the Jews. Together with Mendelssohn and the Christian intellectuals who adopted his view, they regarded Judaism as law. Like Bendavid they expected their fellow Jews eventually to abandon the Jewish law and subscribe to the religion of reason in its Kantian form. Judaism had lost its raison d'etre, since it possessed no unique eternal content. For the cultured Jew the faith into which he was born represented only an outmoded form which produced an unpleasant and unnecessary separation between himself and his gentile environment.

The conception of Judaism as a dying remnant of the past led the Jewish rationalists variously to a religious service modeled on that of the church, an indifference to all organized religion, or a token acceptance of Christianity. The irresoluteness of David Friedländer, the disciple of Mendelssohn, on the issue of reforming Judaism or leaving it has been described in detail. Highly similar in attitude to Friedländer were Mendelssohn's own three sons. Of these Joseph, the oldest, was the only one to remain a Jew throughout his entire life. His father had paid particular attention to his education but had been less successful in arousing interest in Jewish studies than devotion to general philosophy and literature. It was for Joseph that he had originally prepared his last philosophical work, *Morgenstunden* (*Morning Hours*).

Although Joseph never developed a serious interest in Judaism, he did actively identify himself with the progressive segment of the Jewish community. Toward the end of the century he became one of the founders of a "Society of Friends" in Berlin, consisting of Jewish young men interested in the enlightenment of their fellows, mutual aid to one another, and friendly sociability.[5] At the first meeting of the society, in 1792, Joseph was the principal speaker. In his address he referred to the benefits that had accrued to the Jewish community from thirty years of enlightenment. As was to be expected he praised reason in matters of religion and rejected the authority of the intransigent orthodox. Although the members of the society were originally all Jews, the organization engaged in no projects of a specifically Jewish nature, beyond giving money to the Jewish Free School of Berlin. However, it did see fit to devote much of its effort in the early years to fighting the orthodox on the old issue of immediate versus delayed burial.

In later years Joseph Mendelssohn, then a banker of considerable wealth, devoted his leisure hours to extensive intellectual pursuits. He studied mathematics and wrote critical works on literature and economics. An active interest in his father's life and writings prompted him to write an introductory biography for the first major edition of Mendelssohn's works, edited by Joseph's son, Professor G. B. Mendelssohn. But Joseph never did develop an interest in Jewish literature or a firm attachment to the Jewish religion. His younger son Alexander became the last of the family to remain a Jew, while the aforementioned elder son, after leaning for a time toward Catholicism, in 1823 became a Protestant with full seriousness and conviction.[6] It is not known how Joseph reacted to this conversion, although apparently it did not alter the friendly relations between father and son.

Mendelssohn's second son, Abraham, only nine years old when his father died, could hardly have profited from his influence. Like his older brother Joseph he became a banker, was an officer of the Society of Friends, and maintained broad intellectual interests. Unlike Joseph he had his four children baptized, added the name Bartholdy to distinguish his branch of the family, and eventually was himself baptized together with his wife Leah Salomon. Philosophically a religious skeptic, Abraham was no more able to accept the dogmas of Christianity than was Friedländer, but unlike the disciple, the son was apparently able to overcome intellectual compunctions. He readily admitted his own agnosticism and his view that Christianity, like Judaism, was only a timebound form. In a Christian age society demanded the adoption of the Christian form as it did the language, manners, and habits of the majority. In 1820, two years before his own conversion, Abraham expressed these sentiments in a well-known letter to his daughter Fanny on the occasion of her confirmation in the church.[7] Having not yet himself decided to convert, he suggests that in content religion is essentially reducible to morality. Parents and children, even when they belong to different faiths, still owe one another the essentially religious duties of filial devotion and loyalty.

It is a curious irony that Abraham's famous son Felix should have possessed the profound religious consciousness that his skeptical, often pedantic father lacked. While Abraham tried to mask his origins with a change of name and religion, but could evoke no more deep religious attachment to the new faith than to the old, his son was both less ashamed of his Jewish origins and more sincere in his Christianity. When on an

English concert tour in 1829 Felix seemed reluctant to use the name Bartholdy, his father—now long converted—felt it necessary once again to justify raising his children as Christians:

> Naturally, when you consider what scant value I placed on any form in particular, I felt no urge to choose the form known as Judaism, that most antiquated, distorted and self-defeating form of all. Therefore I raised you as Christians, Christianity being the more purified form and the most accepted by the majority of civilized people. Eventually I myself adopted Christianity, because I felt it my duty to do for myself that which I recognized as best for you.[8]

In changing name and religion Abraham even contended that he was following the lead of his father, who supposedly had changed his name from Moses Dessau to Moses Mendelssohn to mark his break with ingrown orthodoxy. As Moses *Dessau* could not be a philosopher, Abraham argued, so Abraham—or Felix—*Mendelssohn* could not be a Christian. "If Mendelssohn is your name, you are *ipso facto* a Jew." Like Friedländer, Abraham saw his father as the originator of a movement which was destined to go beyond him. Moses had bridged the intellectual insularity of Judaism. Possessed of the majority culture Abraham was intent on breaking free of his origins entirely.

Of Nathan, the youngest son of Moses, relatively little is known. Like Abraham he also converted, and presumably for similar reasons. None of the three sons made any contributions whatever to Judaism. Well educated and highly intelligent as they all were, none—not even Joseph—to the best of our knowledge carried on even an intellectual interest in the Jewish tradition. They were typical of most of the educated and wealthy Jews in the generation after Mendelssohn. They were industrious in business, outstanding in their mental abilities, and the bearers of a highly rationalistic philosophy which saw both Judaism and Christianity as mere forms of a universal moralism. They did not possess a deeper religious consciousness which might burst through the iron laws of intellect. Perhaps it would have been too incongruous with their activity in the world. But unlike them, two of their three sisters, Dorothea and Henriette, became serious and enthusiastic in their Christianity. These two daughters of Moses Mendelssohn, along with other prominent German Jewesses of the day—notably Henriette Herz and Rahel Varnhagen—were, like their brothers Abraham and Nathan, destined to leave Judaism—but not out of religious indifference. The cultured Berlin Jewesses were to find in Christianity, Catholic or Protestant, not merely a new form but a vital faith. Their

religious consciousness rejected Enlightenment rationalism for the un-
structured depths of romanticism.

Unlike the late Enlightenment, romanticism was not at all congenial to
Judaism and Jewish strivings for emancipation. Kantianism emphasized
a duty-imposing, ethical imperative which, from the point of view of
human needs and passions, was just as external and demanding as the
commands of a revealed religion.[9] A Jew raised in the conception of religious commandments could feel quite at home in Kantian religious
philosophy. But the romantics firmly rejected any externally imposed obligation. They insisted upon sundering religion from morality and metaphysics and making it an autonomous attitude flowing from the feelings
of the human being and cultivated in the depths of his individuality. Religion was not the driving force toward moral improvement and the enlightenment of mankind, nor was it reducible to philosophical proposi-
tions. Religion grew differently, out of the inner, subjective experience
of each personality. Not rational, and hence not fully transmittable, romantic religion could not be used as a tool in the struggle for Jewish
equality. There were no longer three principles—God, Providence, and
immortality—which automatically made all subscribers to them religiously
one. Each man, each nation, was uniquely possessed of an indissoluble genius; each represented mankind in its own way. There was no single norm
for all humanity. For the observant Jew, an adherent of the Mosaic law,
the personality-centered romantic religion represented the counterpole of
a faith based upon demands externally imposed by God. For the assimilating Jew, yet unwilling to convert, a philosophy that stressed individual
differences rather than similarities had to be viewed as a major obstacle
to complete social integration. Those Jews who were attracted to romanticism—almost all of them women—correctly recognized in it the antithesis
of both the old commandment-centered Judaism and the new Friedländer
variety. Like the Jewish rationalists they wanted to assimilate, but none
of them could regard Christianity as merely a form that one took over because society demanded it. Religion was a necessity of their souls which
Judaism seemed particularly unable to satisfy.

Among the young men whom Mendelssohn instructed in natural religion during the early morning hours in the last years of his life, was his
son-in-law Simon Veit. He was an eminently good-natured, moral and

generous young man, a banker by profession. His moderate wealth and fine traits of character recommended him to Mendelssohn as an ideal choice for his eldest daughter Brendel. A few months after the wedding in 1783 Mendelssohn wrote to Herz Homberg, "She is living with her incomparable Veit in a happy marriage, happier than if the son of the richest man had generously condescended to marry her." [10] But the happiness of the couple—if it ever existed at all—was short-lived. Possessed of a youthful, independent spirit, a powerful intellect, and a highly emotional temperament, Dorothea, as she already called herself in 1794, found her marriage to the pleasant but unspirited Veit lacking any inner bond. The bourgeois orientation and mode of life of the businessman were abhorrent to her. Her mother, Fromet, had been satisfied to play the role of housewife and mother. Dorothea wanted more from her life. She was drawn to the conception of womanhood of the young romantics, a conception radically at variance with that of both the Enlightenment and traditional Judaism. By the canons of the Romantic movement a woman was expected to be spiritually and intellectually independent of her husband, to challenge him, spur him on, stimulate and complement the development of his character. The wife was her husband's equal partner and was obligated to care for the cultivation of her own personality as much as he for his. The mature, talented, educated woman, not the undeveloped pretty young girl, was admired. All of this Veit simply did not understand, but he left his wife the freedom to pursue her own interests.

Dorothea was early intent upon developing herself, upon understanding her thoughts and feelings. Activity in the world was not as significant as probing to the interior of her own personality. What bliss it was to sit in one's own room "head cold and still, heart warm and responsive to every feeling." [11] Only a few years after her marriage Dorothea had this advice for her younger sister Henriette:

> Never cease to perfect your own self, improve steadily, and do not tire to extirpate flaws which you notice in yourself. Believe me, the only way to happiness is always to improve yourself; everything else is outside of us and can make us happy only so long as it is new to us. Accustom yourself to write down faithfully every evening not only what you did and what you encountered, but also what you thought and felt.[12]

Finding no response to her own personality in her husband, Dorothea turned to the sensitive, bright young men who had visited the house of her father or whom she met in the circles of Henriette Herz and Rahel Levin. For a time she was enamored of the genial adventurer Eduard d'Alton.[13] Later her interest turned to the youthful Wilhelm von Humboldt whose infatuation with Henriette Herz was just wearing off. Humboldt highly esteemed and sympathized with this *femme incomprise,* though, already devoted to his future wife Caroline von Dacheröden, he was unable to return her love.

> She is indescribably unhappy [he wrote to Caroline]. If you knew her husband— there is no expression for such shallowness and inanity, crudeness and effeminacy! And with this husband her feelings for me can only grow. She loves me in every sense of the word.... For me she presents the liveliest picture of the wanton destruction of a beautiful, splendid blossom. Whenever I see her, admiration and pity alternate inside of me.[14]

Unlike her close friend Henriette Herz, the red-haired Dorothea was neither beautiful nor gracious. There was something masculine about her appearance. She was heavy-set, rather bony, and her face, at least in one pastel portrait, bore remarkable resemblance to that of her father. Caroline Schlegel found her rather Jewish-looking:

> She has a national, *c'est à dire* Jewish appearance, mien, etc. She does not seem pretty to me: the eyes are large and fiery, but the lower part of the face too slack, too plump.... Her voice is the most tender and feminine thing about her.[15]

But there was really very little that was Jewish about Dorothea. In the manner of Jewish girls at the time she apparently received no extensive Jewish training, although according to Henriette Herz her father had personally taken an interest in her general education. In the Veit household the major holidays were celebrated,[16] but there is no indication that Dorothea's observance of the Jewish tradition was anything more than perfunctory, if indeed she did not already despise it. Her father's definition of Judaism as "revealed legislation" served to make Judaism a non-religion in her eyes. For this young woman who thought, acted, and felt out of her own self, an externally imposed code, like a loveless marriage, had to seem a weighty, senseless yoke, a kind of "slavery." Yet in a quite different, romantic sense Dorothea was religious: she possessed an inner life, creativity of the spirit, and a feeling for the universe. It was in this sense that Friedrich Schlegel could write of Dorothea shortly after meeting her: "Her entire being is religion, although she herself doesn't realize it." [17]

Dorothea met Friedrich Schlegel, the fiery enthusiast of the Romantic movement, in the salon of her friend Henriette Herz. In him she saw all the qualities that Veit lacked: an unconfined masculine spirit, intensity, originality, the vigor of youth—and endless plans for the future. Schlegel, for his part, found in Dorothea his ideal of womanhood: educated and mature, with a sense for love, poetry, wit and philosophy. The acquaintance with Schlegel dealt Dorothea's marriage to Veit its final blow. She had borne her husband four children of whom two sons had survived. Despite her intellectual and emotional energy, she was a good and concerned mother, with a great maternal love for her children. Nonetheless, the attraction of Schlegel proved too great; she resolved to divorce Veit although the children would be given into his custody. Her efforts to secure a divorce were mediated by both Henriette Herz and the Protestant theologian Schleiermacher. According to the ethos of the young romantic circle, to which Schlegel and Schleiermacher both belonged, a marriage not based on love was inauthentic and should, if necessary, be dissolved. On the basis of this conception, Dorothea's divorce from Veit was wholly justified, although Veit was guilty of nothing more than the limits of his own personality.[18]

In January of 1799 the divorce was completed. Veit generously permitted Dorothea to take her younger son Philipp with her to a house on the outskirts of Berlin where she now took up residence, and where she was visited regularly by the young Schlegel. He was her idol, this "divine Friedrich," this "rich abundance of spirit, soul and life."[19] In those first years of freedom the love of Friedrich captured her whole being; it allowed for nothing more. Her greatest desire in life was to serve her beloved. "There is no other man," she wrote to Rahel, "to whom one can so completely entrust one's soul and salvation."[20]

Schlegel gave poetic expression to his relationship with Dorothea in a novel that appeared the year of the divorce, entitled *Lucinde*. Its repudiation of all the canons of literary form and coherence and its free treatment of sexuality caused a considerable stir. It was widely branded an anti-novel and the height of immorality. What Schlegel tried to portray in this odyssey of the emotions was the quest of a young man to achieve a unity between sensual and spiritual love. In highly disjointed form, Schlegel described the sometimes sordid love affairs of a certain "Julius," which at length culminate in the purified, reciprocated love of Lucinde. The heroine symbolizes the romantic woman whose entire life is love, and in whom all womanhood is reflected. Schlegel called *Lucinde* a "religious book," despite, or indeed because of, its sensuality. Religion for Schlegel could not be morality in the common sense of abiding by an ethical code. Nor could it be metaphysics. Trying to prove the existence of God was for him only "a relatively uninteresting game." Religion meant freedom, inner development, being true to oneself. It was closely tied to the romanticist ideal of *Bildung,* cultivation of the personality. In the periodical *Athenaeum,* which he edited with his brother, Schlegel gave a definition of religion as anti-Jewish as it was anti-Kantian. It appeared in an essay entitled "On Philosophy," dedicated to Dorothea. A person is religious, according to Schlegel, if he

> thinks and creates and lives divinely, if he is full of God; if a breath of devotion and enthusiasm is poured out over his whole being; if he no longer does anything on account of duty, but everything out of love, only because he wants it; and if he wants it only because God says so, namely the God within us.[21]

In the fall of 1799 Dorothea with her son Philipp moved to Jena, then the center of the Romantic movement. She lived with Friedrich in the house of his brother whose gifted, impetuous wife Caroline at first welcomed the Jewess from Berlin. Here Dorothea helped Schlegel with his literary work and in 1801 published her own novel *Florentin*.[22] With characteristic modesty and self-effacement before her revered Friedrich, she let it appear anonymously with only Schlegel's name as editor mentioned on the title page. Although the impetus to write the novel had originally been financial, it turned out to be of considerable literary merit, and was regarded by later criticism as possessing more creative power than Schlegel's poetic works.[23] Influenced both by Goethe and by the romantic writer Ludwig Tieck, *Florentin* is much more conventional than *Lucinde.* It has neither the sensuality nor the formlessness of Schlegel's work. Set in a pleasant idyllic countryside, *Florentin* deals with the feelings of a sensitive, artistic youth who is unhappy in love. Love and marriage, Dorothea is saying through this novel based on her own experience, do not necessarily go together; nor do religious feeling and organized religion. It is characteristic of her low opinion of any religious externals in this period of her life that her hero has only the utmost contempt for Catholic institutions: he speaks of monks as a "hated class."

For more than five years after her divorce—in Berlin, Jena and Paris —Dorothea lived with Schlegel, though not officially married to him and nominally still a Jew. Serving as priestess at his altar, she gradually let her own being flow into him. Her once independent spirit humbled itself before Friedrich's spewing, fragmentary genius. He filled her horizon completely. Schlegel, seven years her junior, had from the first been willing to marry Dorothea though he doubted whether he could remain faithful to her. What had prevented the marriage was Veit's stipulation that Dorothea could keep her son Philipp only as long as she did not marry Schlegel. It was not until April 6, 1804, after they had lived in Paris for two years, that Dorothea was converted to Protestantism and the same day married to Schlegel. This conversion, which Dorothea laconically recorded in her diary, had little permanent influence, though afterwards she recalled strangely having seen a vision of her father at the very moment she received the holy baptism.[24]

The eldest daughter of Mendelssohn had contemplated changing her religion for some time. In the first Jena days when Friedrich was her whole life, she had brushed off Christianity as merely a vogue among the romantic circle. It was *"à l'ordre du jour,"* and she did not take it very seriously.[25] Impressed with Catholic painting and music, she toyed with the idea of a conversion to Catholicism, but there is no indication that at this time Dorothea felt a real desire to change her faith. It was only in post-Revolutionary Paris that she began to think seriously of Christianity. She had never possessed the spirit of a libertine, and the profligacy she encountered here repelled her. She wanted to set apart her own illicit relationship with Schlegel from what she saw around her. It seems that in Paris for the first time she experienced a feeling of guilt about her behavior toward Veit and needed the sanction of some higher authority. She condemned the French society as immoral: *"Liberté?—*No; rather *Libertinage."* [26] As an antidote to her surroundings she began to read the Bible in Luther's translation. Her family, because they were unwilling to accept her relationship with Schlegel—or perhaps because they were unwilling to give her financial support—were branded philistine Jews. Her brother Abraham she called an "unfeeling barbarian ... not one wit better than any Berlin Jew, except that he has even finer underwear and even coarser arrogance." [27] To her old friend Schleiermacher she wrote a confession of faith that was both repudiation and affirmation:

I am attentively reading both testaments and find, according to my own feeling, Protestant Christianity indeed purer and to be preferred to the Catholic. For me the latter bears too much resemblance to the old Judaism, which I very much abhor. But Protestantism seems to me quite the religion of Jesus and the religion of culture; as far as I can determine from the Bible, I am in my heart wholly Protestant....[28]

Yet despite her words to Schleiermacher, Protestantism for Dorothea was only a station along the way. The romantic circle was moving steadily in the direction of Catholicism. The talented Novalis had marked its course with his idealization of the Middle Ages and his attack upon Protestantism as the source of all evil in the modern world. Then in 1805 Ludwig Tieck became a Catholic in Rome; others followed him. In Paris Schlegel's thought, as well, was inclining toward Catholicism. For some time already he had been of the opinion that the arts had blossomed in medieval Germany but had decayed on account of the Reformation. In Paris he and Dorothea enjoyed the company of Catholics, particularly the brothers Sulpiz and Melchior Boisserée who were boarders in their home. They were impressed by these two intelligent and devoted Catholics from Cologne, and in 1804 accepted their invitation to move to the Rhineland city.

In the shadow of the magnificent Cologne cathedral, in the company of Catholic friends who treated her with great kindness, and in the frequent absence of her husband, Dorothea felt an irresistible attraction to Catholicism. There was much that entered into her regard for the Church: its close association with the arts, the aesthetic appeal of the service, its venerable age, its opposition to all that she regarded as bourgeois, egotistical, frivolous—and Jewish. It was the antipode of the *Aufklärung* with its presumptuous reliance upon reason. In 1806 she wrote, "From my heart I hate this Enlightenment of our time; nothing good, no nothing, has yet come of it. Simply because it is so very old I prefer Catholicism. Whatever is new is worthless." [29] But it would seem that dominant in Dorothea's increasing attachment to the Catholic Church was the persisting need for a transcendent authority and justification for her life. Her attachment to Schlegel had not disappeared, but he was no longer her god. To avoid the despair of loneliness she began to attend mass regularly at the Cathedral. She could see her life following a divinely ordained pattern: the break with Veit, the illicit romance with Schlegel, all culminating in a final consecration to the Church. In the beauty of the mass she could submerge her identity as she had done earlier in the genius of the young Friedrich. Without belief in a higher power the world seemed a wilderness. What she required was faith: "Whether I have faith?—That I do not yet dare to assert, but I know that I truly have faith in faith." [30]

Catholicism granted Dorothea a new transcendent perspective on her life and the history of her time. While the Napoleonic wars were evoking strong sentiments of patriotism, she could remain entirely detached.[31] There was no "my country" and "your country" for her, only the providential action of God and his universal Church; her fatherland was wherever Catholics lived.[32] Those who did not share her perspective she condemned. Her wealthy brothers she again branded gross materialists: "*Anch' egli filistri!*" she wrote of Abraham.[33] Of Schleiermacher, who had become an ardent Prussian patriot, she now wrote, "I never really trusted this Calvinist." [34] And Goethe, whom she had once admired and emulated, she now decried as a pagan.[35] After two years in Cologne it was she who urged the hesitant Friedrich not to delay his conversion. Four years after she became a Protestant and married Schlegel, they were accepted together into the Catholic Church. Catholicism became a new life for Dorothea: daily she entrusted herself to the saints; she made herself a little prayer alcove in a corner of her room and adorned it with crucifixes, rosaries, relics, and pictures of the saints. "How shall I describe to you the incalculable wealth which has been revealed to me in the treasures of the Catholic faith," she wrote to her husband a few months after their conversion.[36]

It now became Dorothea's mission to draw her friends and relatives to the true faith. She was particularly concerned about her sons whom Veit, with unwonted strength of will, had insisted remain Jews. The children above all had to be saved. With a fanatical singleness of purpose she intrigued to win her sons for the Church. The elder son Jonas had studied with Abraham Mendelssohn to become a man of business, and was presumably educated in the rationalist tradition. Philipp the younger son, raised by his mother, had taken over his mother's sympathy for Catholicism from the very first. Yet even Jonas, who shared his brother's interest in art, was soon won over after a short period the two brothers spent together. In 1810 they traveled to Vienna, where Dorothea and Friedrich were now living, and both were baptized that summer. In succeeding years these grandchildren of Mendelssohn were to be among the leading figures of the Nazarene school of painting.[37] Their father Simon Veit, shocked by the additional blow of his sons' conversion, accommodated himself to it with his usual good-natured pliancy. He continued to pay for their support and seek their friendship. In a letter he wrote to Philipp on October 25, 1810 he expressed his feelings. Like the letter of Abraham Mendelssohn to his daughter Fanny ten years later, it is typical of the Enlightenment Jewish tradition, of a world diametrically opposed to that of Dorothea and his sons:

> Let us draw a veil over what has happened between us and commit it to oblivion. I shall not cease to love you both and to do my best for you, even if we are not of the same opinion in regard to religion.... My dear son, as long as we differ only in religion and are at one in our moral principles, a division will never fall between us. Only do not believe, once you have gone over to another religion, that the millions of people who have other religious principles are poor sinners and hated by God, that they can have no part in eternal salvation. This belief has often separated friend from friend, father from child, the happy husband from his beloved wife, and has wrought nothing but harm.[38]

In the later years of his life Veit made great efforts to overcome his cultural inadequacies. In order to better understand his sons, he strove to develop an appreciation of art and studied poetry and literature with great assiduity. It became more and more apparent that Veit was no longer a man of narrow practical interests. Over the years the progressive revelation of Veit's depth of character intellectually—but even more, morally—created a severe dilemma for Dorothea. Had Veit been wholly a boor, had he been cruel or at least miserly, Dorothea could easily have justified leaving him and drawing their sons away from his influence. But she could not comprehend Veit's steadfastly remaining a Jew while behaving just like a "Christian." So she took the sin upon her own shoulders, humbled herself before him and asked his forgiveness. She had come to believe with consummate certainty in the inherent sinfulness of all mankind and the error of reason.[39] Now she wrote to Veit in 1819, shortly before his death, with all the relish of a martyr, "You are guilty of nothing." She had erred and was responsible, but finally she had recognized "the light of the true faith." [40]

In the years after she became a Catholic Dorothea's piety grew ever more intense. The romanticist who had rejected the bonds imposed on the spirit by Jewish law and narrow rationalism now recommended regularly scheduled prayer even when there was no disposition toward it, and the subjugation of the soul to a higher will not its own. Salvation for herself and others became her dominant concern. Yet she did not have the repulsive characteristics of a bigot. Rahel and Henriette Herz, who both spent time with her after she became a Catholic, were quite taken with Dorothea. Rahel wrote of her in 1817, "She is full of sincerity and cheerful kindness, prepossessed with her faith in a way that is honest and which one gladly respects: thoroughly amiable, and quite clever; I love her very much!" [41]

As she grew older Dorothea tried to draw nearer to her family. She corresponded with all of them and was concerned for their happiness in this world and in the world to come. When her mother, who had never forgiven her, died a Jewess in 1812, Dorothea asked her son Jonas, now Johannes, to pray for the soul of his grandmother. Her younger sister Recha became a special object of her attention. This middle daughter of Mendelssohn [42] was the only one of the three to react negatively to the romantic circle—and to remain a Jewess. Schlegel called her the "unutterably mean sister" when she opposed his affair with Dorothea.[43] She had been married to Mendel Meier, son of the court factor in Mecklenburg-Strelitz, but after the union failed she returned to Berlin where her daughter Betty was married to the banker Beer. This sister and her family were apparently part of the rationalistic circle of Friedländer, Simon Veit, and the Mendelssohn brothers. In 1821 Henriette Herz wrote scornfully of Recha to her young friend August Twesten:

> She is just as you knew her, only that she loses more of the outer world without gaining any of the inner. Betty is the mother of a son whom she has allowed to be made that which he will never become, i.e. a Jew. The "rational" education which he will receive is, according to the common opinion, also to protect him inwardly against becoming a Christian—and thus will make him a pagan.[44]

After Recha's death in April of 1831, Dorothea noted that her sister died "quite suddenly, but nonetheless after many years of illness and great physical suffering—alas, alas without being a child of the holy Church." [45]

The youngest sister Henriette was the least attractive of the three. Like her father she was short and slightly deformed, but like him also she was favored with a keen intellect. She was the only one of her brothers and sisters never to marry, although at various times she enjoyed close relationships with Bernhard von Eskeles, Varnhagen von Ense, and especially August Wilhelm Schlegel, the brother of Friedrich and also a leader of the Romantic movement in Germany. A governess by profession in Vienna and later in Paris, she at first had more sympathy for the rationalistic disposition of her father than the pietism of her eldest sister. Varnhagen, who was her frequent visitor in Paris during his stay there in 1810, later noted, "Fräulein Mendelssohn paid homage exclusively to reason and decisively rejected all other sources of knowledge. Her love for Frau von Schlegel was dimmed from the time that the latter, together with her husband, had become a Catholic." [46] In Paris Henriette enjoyed the company of some of the outstanding figures of the day, who all admired the well-educated, amiable Berlin Jewess. Madame de Staël, Benjamin Constant, and Wilhelm von Humboldt were among her regular guests. But as the years went on Henriette grew progressively more dissatisfied with her life. By 1810 she had become subject to despair,[47] and in that same year she considered becoming a Christian. The rituals and dogmas of the Catholic Church were still repugnant but, as she wrote to August Wilhelm,

> Until now I have followed no strange light—yes, I have closed my eyes—and nonetheless there grew inside of me what I regard as Christianity and the essence of Christ: resignation, courage and faith, not in those outward things, but in a divine love and justice.[48]

Two years later Henriette joined her sister Dorothea in the Catholic Church. Although for a while after her conversion she hung between doubt and belief, she finally became just as pious. Like Dorothea she gave herself up to a higher authority, though she was never plagued with the same feelings of guilt. Rahel Varnhagen, whose individuality remained precious to her throughout her entire life, pierced the false security of such self-abnegation when she wrote in her diary: "Whoever gives himself up completely is praised: that is the way we are supposed to be. That is what will happen to Jette [Henriette] Mendelssohn. But if she will only let herself suspect that there is still a Jette, the bliss will be over." [49]

Shortly before her death in 1838, Henriette met Dorothea again in Dresden after many years of separation and the two sisters found themselves entirely in inner accord. When Henriette died she left behind a testament which indicates how very far she had come from her earlier universalistic rationalism. She thanked her relatives for their friendship toward her and for not hindering her in the practice of her religion, so that I must blame myself if the Lord God has not vouchsafed unto me the Grace of drawing my family into the Catholic, genuinely saving Church. May the Lord Jesus Christ hear my prayer and enlighten them all with the light of his Grace. Amen! [50]

These were the paths of Mendelssohn's children: two Jewish, two Protestant, two Catholic. Of Recha and Nathan we know little. Joseph and Abraham, who both subjected religion to reason, became respectively a nominal Jew and a nominal Protestant. Dorothea, whose spirit found the bonds of reason too narrow, was swept up into the Romantic movement and finally into the Church, while Henriette catapulted directly from rationalism into Catholicism. It still remains to explore further this antithesis which romanticism presented to Judaism, through a consideration of two extraordinary "salon Jewesses" of Berlin: Henriette Herz and Rahel Varnhagen.

Marcus Herz was already thirty-four years old when he married Henriette de Lemos, the beautiful fifteen-year-old daughter of the chief physician at the Berlin Jewish hospital. Unlike Simon Veit, Marcus was not a businessman but a physician like his father-in-law, and highly accomplished in philosophy and science. Their childless union was happier than that of Simon and Dorothea, though it too lacked an inner harmony. Henriette later described it as a "happy relationship ... not really a happy marriage." [51] The seventeen years that separated Marcus and Henriette represented more than a mere division in age: he was entirely a child of the Enlightenment, she of romanticism. Neither was wholly able to understand or sympathize with the other.

In their well appointed home in the Neue Friedrichsstrasse, the Herzes were almost daily hosts to the aristocracy of birth and talent that lived in or visited the Prussian capital. Among their frequent guests during the early 1780's was the sculptor Gottfried Schadow, who did a noteworthy bust of Henriette. Recalling his visits he described the Herz salon as in fact two salons. In one room Marcus, an inveterate smoker, sat with young physicians and visiting scholars. In another sat his pretty wife surrounded by young men of a quite different type—artists, writers, poets —reciting, discussing, and criticizing the most recent works of literature.[52]

The world of Marcus Herz was that of the older Berlin, the city of Biester and Nicolai, Engel, Teller, and Mendelssohn. Born into poverty he had first studied for the rabbinate and then undergone a brief apprenticeship in business. Both these earlier pursuits gave way, however, before a growing interest in medicine and philosophy. He studied with Kant in Königsberg before finally settling down in Berlin as assistant and later successor to de Lemos at the Jewish hospital. He became a close friend of Mendelssohn and of those around him, and he shared their intellectual and literary prejudices. Characteristically, he rejected any writer who did not possess the clarity of Lessing. When David Friedländer once asked him to explain a passage in a poem of Goethe, Herz promptly referred him to his wife. Schlegel's *Lucinde* he considered a combination of smut and nonsense and was convinced that Novalis, the very personification of romanticism, did not himself understand what he allowed to appear in print.[53] Herz's personality was typically rationalist: he was witty but never emotional. His wife later complained that when she tried to express her love for him he dismissed it as mere childishness.

Henriette, by contrast, grew out of the enlightened Jewish atmosphere of her parents' home into a world very different from that of her father and her husband. As a girl she was attracted to theater, music, and dance; with her friend Dorothea she avidly read the sentimental novels of her day and they had a profound effect upon her. Later, as Herz's wife, she drew into her circle the younger generation that stood in revolt against the still dominant tradition: Ramler in poetry, Mendelssohn or Kant in philosophy, Nicolai in criticism, and Iffland or Kotzebue on the stage. The young men who became her acquaintances regarded the Enlightenment tradition as dry and shallow. Although they still venerated Lessing it was for his iconoclasm, not his drama, that they paid him homage. He had cleared away the rubble of the past, but in the clarity of his vision he had lost all sensitivity for the ambiguities of the whole.[54]

This salon of Henriette Herz was considered the most brilliant and sparkling of Berlin. In an age when the official functions of the aristocracy were insufferably dull and the burgher class had only the most limited cultural horizons, Jewish homes were unique in offering informality combined with stimulating intellectual discussion. As one contemporary remarked, only *there* was literature "really discussed."[55] And conversation was the very hallmark of this period in Prussian history, before military defeat at the hand of France turned talk to action and cosmopolitanism to fervid patriotism.

The young Jewish women possessed a strange fascination. They were educated, open-minded, sometimes of easy virtue, often intelligent, and occasionally, as in the case of Henriette Herz, very beautiful. Born into bourgeois Jewish families, but in revolt against both the perfunctory religion and practical business orientation of the older generation, they were exceptionally sympathetic to the new world of the inner personality unveiled to them by the young romanticists. Their enthusiasm for Shakespeare and the yet unestablished Goethe, their freedom from convention, and their position as Jews on the edge of "proper" society lent them an appeal with few exceptions unmatched by the more conventional Christian women. By contrast to Berlin, life was dreary in a city like Jena, where there were few Jews, only "lots of dull Christians, nothing piquant, not a single head of black hair." [56]

In the possession of a staff of servants and without children, her duties as mistress of the house took little of Henriette's time. She could devote herself to reading, the study of languages, and the cultivation of her emotions. Since Marcus hardly sympathized with her sentimentalities, she turned to the young men of her acquaintance. Together with Dorothea she joined Carl La Roche and Wilhelm von Humboldt in a "society of virtue." The members agreed to bare their souls to one another and hold back no secrets. Jew or gentile was of no consequence in their rebellious but chaste fraternity. The aim was to make one another happy through love; they rejected all merely conventional restraints and sought to partake of every pleasure compatible with moral perfection.

Wilhelm von Humboldt, then in his late teens, was particularly attracted to the beautiful Henriette. He fell passionately in love with her and sent her sentimental, intimate letters, written for secrecy in the Hebrew script she had taught him. It was not long, however, before the young Humboldt began to recognize in Henriette's letters a quality of personality that her contemporaries remarked on again and again: a kind of affectation, a display of emotion which was not really genuine.[57] He eventually rejected her artificially manufactured sentiment as somewhat ludicrous and began to regard the society in the same way.[58] Humboldt had been educated in the Enlightenment tradition: Engel was his tutor in philosophy and he had enjoyed the personal acquaintance of Mendelssohn.[59] For a time attracted by the intense feeling of Lavater and Jacobi, he finally absorbed something of both traditions into a harmonious, rather more classical than romantic personality. In succeeding years, though he judged Henriette harshly, he retained a certain devotion to this love of his youth. As a Prussian statesman he became one of the most outspoken and least self-interested proponents of Jewish equality. Regarding his defense of a particular Jewish cause, he once remarked that it was the last spark of his loyalty to Henriette—except that by this time (1814), Humboldt noted, she had practically become a Christian.[60]

The religious transformation of Henriette Herz began in 1796 with the arrival of a serious young theologian who had been appointed chaplain at the "Charité" in Berlin. Introduced to the Herz household on a short visit two years earlier by his close friend Count Alexander Dohna, Friedrich Schleiermacher now became a regular guest. He established a close, but entirely passionless, relationship with the mistress of the house that was to last to the end of his life. The two of them read Shakespeare together; she taught him Italian, he taught her Greek; and they "spoke to one another directly out of their inmost feelings about the most important things." [61] Her Jewishness was insignificant to the young preacher, since beneath this surface distinction he thought he detected an emotional kinship which made her essential for his spiritual growth: she provided the necessary complement to his own feelings. There was something in his nature, Schleiermacher admitted to his sister, that inclined him to seek the companionship of women rather than men; the latter seldom understood him completely. Unlike Schlegel he was not seeking the almost masculine, intellectual assertion of the young Dorothea, but rather the more passive, feminine understanding which characterized Henriette. During the period of their closest relationship, Schleiermacher wrote his first significant work: *On Religion: Speeches to its Cultured Despisers,*[62] which he finished in the spring of 1799. As sections of it were completed, he sent them to Henriette for comments and reactions; the two were in almost daily contact. For Henriette this acquaintance with Schleiermacher became the great good fortune of her life. She admired, respected, and in her own way loved him—and she became devoted to his interpretation of religion.

Addressing himself to the intellectuals of his time, Schleiermacher presented them with a concept of religion which excluded the dogma of orthodoxy they so despised, yet took no refuge in the postulates of natural religion. Differentiating religion sharply from both morals and metaphysics, to which it had become subservient, he assigned it an autonomous existence. Religion was defined as an emotion, feeling, or disposition of the soul, a surrender of the self to the Infinite and Eternal. In marked contrast to the Enlightenment, Schleiermacher thus removed religion entirely from the cognitive realm, making knowledge and religion two different departments of life. True piety could not be learned or constricted into a system; it could only grow out of the personal experience of the individual human being. The marked object of his attack was the application of rational criteria to religion and the sameness which was produced: that universal *Vernunftreligion* which he regarded as no religion at all. Thinking of Mendelssohn—or perhaps of Kant—he wrote, "With the God of existence and command, religion has nothing to do." [63] Against orthodoxy, he regarded the sacred texts as monuments of the heroic epoch of religion, but not as indisputably authoritative. They represented only the religious experience of a past age; God revealed himself anew to each generation and each individual. Therein lay the true nature of religion: the individual's consciousness of the Deity in the self and in the world.

For Schleiermacher Christianity represented the highest, purest expression of this true religion. By contrast Judaism, once a living faith, was long since dead: "Those who yet wear its livery are only sitting lamenting beside the imperishable mummy, bewailing its departure and its sad legacy." Its conceptions were primitive and childlike, the belief in the messiah its highest product. When its sacred books were closed, it breathed out its spirit. All that remained was "that very unpleasant phenomenon, a mechanical motion from which life and spirit have long vanished." [64]

Her friend's view of Judaism as no longer a religion in the true sense became Henriette's own opinion, if indeed she had not inclined in that direction earlier. In the memoirs of her youth, which she wrote in 1823, a few years after her conversion, Henriette described her observant home and her Jewish education which—unusual for a girl—extended to reading the Bible in Hebrew together with several commentaries. In a significant, though necessarily self-justifying, passage she outlined the transformation from empty forms into equally empty rationalism which Judaism had undergone:

> The children, particularly the girls, were not at all really instructed in the faith of their parents, but were constrained to observe its *forms,* i.e. they had to keep all of the countless customs which it—or rather the rabbis—prescribed. Girls had to

pray in the Hebrew language, without understanding what they were praying. I remember well occasionally having thus prayed with devotion and fervor, especially when there was a thunderstorm, which always frightened me a great deal. Then I would say lots of prayers—any ones at all—quickly one after the other. Now, of course, Jewish children don't do this any more, since the prayers have been translated into German—but they are no more pious on that account. Their parents, who were still raised in the old way, threw aside the onerous observance of the Jewish customs (in which alone their religion consisted) as soon as they became their own masters. Nothing took its place, and so they lived on without thought of God, except—at most—in times of distress. The children were now raised in the same way. Their parents didn't want to teach them what they themselves did not believe, and so they were and are raised in no faith—no devotion fills their soul, and they cannot pray to God when their heart is oppressed and frightened by immense affliction. Reason, which the more cultured take as their help and support, does not suffice to sustain them in severe suffering. Happy is he for whom, at least later in life, the beautiful light of faith dawns inside, and he is permeated by that elevating, blissful feeling of devotion before his death. By the Grace of God this happiness has also been mine.[65]

For the young Henriette, Judaism was indeed only onerous and senseless forms. Admittedly very vain in her earlier years, she resented having to cover her beautiful black hair with a wig, as prescribed for married women by Jewish law. Yet she had great admiration and respect for her orthodox father and for Moses Mendelssohn. She thought her father was imbued with the "tenderness and love of Christianity," just as the generous Simon Veit possessed "Christian virtues." Contrary to the opinion of Friedländer, she held that Mendelssohn did not keep the commandments only to retain influence with his fellow Jews, but rather from sincere conviction. She wanted to set Mendelssohn apart from his deistic disciples. Unlike them, he had possessed God in his heart; insufficiently acquainted with Christianity, he had sincerely sought God through Judaism.[66]

Despite the close relationship with Schleiermacher that persisted from 1796 onward, Henriette did not convert until more than twenty years later. Out of filial piety to her orthodox mother she remained nominally Jewish until a few months after her mother's death in 1817.[67] After Marcus passed away in 1803, she served for a time as English teacher in the Berlin residence of the Duchess of Courland. Later she became tutor to the children of Charlotte von Kathen on the little island of Rügen in the Baltic, and finally undertook the instruction of a group of middle-class girls in

Berlin. She never remarried, though her old friend Count Dohna remained attached to her for close to twenty years.

Her flight from real life—the escape from herself—became more obvious to Henriette's contemporaries in the years after her husband's death.[68] She was always making plans for the future, always engaging in some physical or mental activity. She learned one foreign language after the other until she had some knowledge of no less than eleven. When Humboldt came upon her one day in 1810 she was busy translating Voltaire from French into Spanish.[69] As her great beauty began to wane, she surrounded herself with young people and dressed as if she were herself still a girl. She had long preferred the uninvolved relationship of "mother," "sister," or confidante to that of beloved. Insecure in her existence, she lacked any appreciation for the silly, the pleasantly stupid, or the intemperate. She frequently sought company, since what mattered to her most was the approbation of others. Rahel remarked of her insightfully, "Madame Herz spends her life all dressed up, without realizing that one can get undressed, and what one feels like then." [70]

When she could no longer play young, and as the future in this world became ever shorter, Henriette began to look more and more to the afterlife, although she dreaded the thought of actual death. In 1817 she was finally baptized a Protestant in the little town of Zossen by an old friend, the Pastor Wolff, and almost immediately thereafter set out on a trip to Rome. There, fervid in her new faith, she was responsible for the attachment of a Protestant chaplain to the Prussian embassy; she had become as avid a Protestant as Dorothea was a Catholic. Like Schleiermacher, she had no respect for those Jews who became Christians without conviction. The now converted Ludwig Börne, once passionately in love with her when he had been a student and boarder in the Herz home, she chided with: "Still so godless, Louis?" [71] Schleiermacher, her ideal of the true Christian, was ever before her eyes in the long years of old age until her death in 1847. A loyal daughter of the Protestant Church, she found in a "religion of the heart" the support that society no longer offered her.

For Henriette, as for Dorothea, Christianity represented the consolation of a higher order which transcended the individual self and its futile attempts at rational explanation. They both considered themselves fully Christian, and one listens in vain for echoes of a vestigial Jewish consciousness. Such, however, was not the case with Rahel Varnhagen who, more painfully sensitive than the others, could never overcome the consciousness of having been born a Jew, but who, like them, became a devoted and convinced, believing Christian.

Unlike Dorothea and Henriette, Rahel never fled from her self. She never gave up her being to a Church or disguised it by assumed postures; throughout her life she remained uniquely Rahel. Retention of originality she regarded as the greatest virtue, hypocrisy or cowing to authority the gravest sin. She recognized herself as a Jewess and saw in this fact of her birth a great personal tragedy, but also a magnificent opportunity to perceive the unveiled truth. Yet, like Dorothea and Henriette, she considered the religion of Judaism shallow and meaningless; her salvation lay in her own highly personalized form of Christianity. In the failure to find religious significance in Judaism, the three women were at one.

Rahel's Jewish education was apparently even more sparse than that of her contemporaries. Her father, a relatively prosperous, somewhat despotic Jewish businessman, let Rahel grow up with little formal education of any kind. "An ignoramus," she later called herself, though not without some degree of irony. For Rahel, favored with a keen mind and wide interests, had managed through her reading to feel quite at home in the literature of her time and, even more, to penetrate its depths and make it her own. She developed a particular fondness for Goethe whose praises she sang to all her friends. She felt that this as yet not fully recognized writer had understood like no other the motivation of the human spirit. In her garret room on the Jägerstrasse, Rahel spoke of literature and life with the prominent young men of Berlin society: Prince Louis Ferdinand of Prussia, the Swedish ambassador Gustav Brinckmann, and many others. In Rahel they found wit, sparkle, and charm, but most of all a freshness, honesty, and truthfulness that were rare.

A large part of Rahel's fascination grew out of her being Jewish. How she hated this fact of her "infamous birth." How she complained to her young friend, David Veit, that one cannot escape the fate of Jewishness.[72] Yet the young Rahel would not consider conversion for the sake of complete assimilation, as did a number of her friends.[73] When Veit converted in 1796 he was much admired for giving up his Judaism, but to an eye like Humboldt's he still revealed "his circumcision in every fingertip." [74]

Rahel was too aware that the world would regard her as a Jewess no matter what she did. She also recognized in her youth, and from time to time later in her life, that Jewishness was an indispensable part of herself.

Being a Jew meant for Rahel standing at the edge of society, freed of its pretenses and lies because one was not really a part of it. It enabled one to perceive things to which others were blind. As a Christian she might have become all too commonplace; as a Jew she was unique. She had learned to value the compensations of the outsider that made up for his social unacceptability. From Paris in 1801 she wrote to her family in Amsterdam:

> So with the Jews things here are supposed to be so bad?! It's their own fault. For I assure you I tell everyone here that I am one; *eh bien! le même empressement*. But only a Berlin Jew can possess the proper disdain and demeanor in his insides—I don't say that he *has* them. I assure you, being from Berlin and a Jew really gives one a kind of *contenance* even here, at least it does me....[75]

Of course to be a Jew meant to suffer. It meant always having to re-legitimize oneself, never being completely at one with society.[76] Especially as a woman it meant the fear that you were being used rather than loved, only a source of thrills. But suffering for Rahel was a blessing in painful garb. In the spirit of romanticism, she believed that not to have suffered was not to have truly lived. She almost reveled in tormenting her soul, in driving each experience to the height of inner agony: "I should comfort myself? God forbid: I don't *want* to at all. *That would be the most abominable.* I want to feel pain with real intensity, like a large *torn open* wound." From the fires of affliction one emerged purified and more ardent. Rahel admitted she could find interesting only the person who had himself known unhappiness. She derided Henriette Herz precisely because her friend never allowed herself to descend to the depths of genuine suffering.[77]

Despite her salon, her many acquaintances, and romantic relationships, Rahel's final concern was always her own inner life; in the last analysis, her friendships were only explorations of her own personality. Veit noted that she could get along quite well without her friends since they were, after all, just modifications of herself.[78] Yet there was nothing artificial about Rahel's emotions; she did not fabricate them to suit the occasion and fearfully keep her true self unexposed, as did Henriette. Instead she let life "rain down" upon her. She sought *leben* and *erleben,* to live and to experience to the fullest. Above all, she cherished her freedom from all societal constraints. "Marry you say," she wrote to Brinckmann, "I cannot marry, because I cannot lie."

As Dorothea had come particularly under the influence of Schlegel, and Henriette under that of Schleiermacher, so Rahel was particularly drawn to the philosophy of Johann Fichte. In him she found a kindred spirit and an expression of what she had long felt. To her brother she wrote in 1807, "Hail, hail to Fichte! With tears I read that in Paris you are reading our honored teacher, that most consummate man! He has drawn out the best in me, fructified it, taken it in troth; called out to me: 'You are not alone!' " [79] In the fall of that year Rahel and her brother attended the romantic philosopher's lectures together in Berlin.

Fichte preached a doctrine of the almighty *"ich,"* the self independent of a world which was only its pale reflection. To the mechanism of nature he opposed the world of freedom in the human personality. Not the loss of the self in the Universal, as in Schleiermacher, but the Fichtean assertion of the self appealed to Rahel. However much she might be rebuffed and rejected by the world, there would remain to her that rich inner life of the spirit upon which no outside forces could impinge. She called Fichte "my dear lord and master" [80]—and through him she came finally to Christianity. To Fouqué she wrote in 1812, "To whom else but to Fichte would you direct the adult who wants to grasp the message of Christ? That adult am I." [81]

Although Rahel ambivalently hated and prized the *status* of Jew, she simply could not take the Jewish law seriously at all. *"Imaginez,"* she wrote to Veit a couple of years after the death of her orthodox father, "yesterday...on the Sabbath in bright daylight and in a royal carriage I drove to the opera rehearsal at half past three in the afternoon; no one saw me; I would have, would, and shall deny it to everybody...." [82] Judaism seemed to her as dead as the Christian intellectuals pronounced it. In an age of great artistic and intellectual creativity, it consisted of irrelevant customs and restrictions. Even at its source, in the Bible, Judaism was unable to satisfy Rahel's religious yearnings, which had long inclined toward the mystical:

> I feel as if there were knives cutting away inside of me when people speak so impudently of God as of a county magistrate and consider those who are mute and over-filled with Him (Him!) as estranged. Now again in the Bible, all of the

speeches and laws in the desert have produced the same sentiments. I become totally alienated from my nation—even though I have to allow Moses the justification that it was a necessity with a childlike people of six hundred thousand. It is certainly written and presented horribly. As far as I've gone, it is pleasing only up through the story of Joseph.[83]

Rahel assuredly had no religious reason to remain a Jewess, and as the years went by the special status of the pariah also began to lose its luster. As early as 1806 she wrote with characteristic insight to Rebecca Friedländer, "Even being a *Jewess* does not harm you; it only *has* harmed you when you are old." [84] In 1810 she took the first step to escape her status: she changed her name from Levin to Robert, as her brothers had done earlier. Then, four years later, she had herself baptized and married the diplomat and writer Varnhagen von Ense. From a religious point of view, her conversion did not represent a significant break; she had long celebrated the Christian holidays and considered herself in the broadest sense religiously a Christian. The timing was due entirely to the practical consideration of facilitating her marriage.

In Varnhagen, fourteen years younger than she, Rahel did not find a passionate love, but an admirer who cherished her personality and preserved its freedom. Basically an observer and spectator of life rather than one who forges his own way, Varnhagen recognized in Rahel the example of a genuine life and made it his devoted task to preserve that life for posterity. He collected all of her letters and wrote down practically every apothegm that dropped from her lips. Rahel appreciated his flattering attention. His youth allowed her to forget her increasing age and saved her from the loneliness of a Henriette Herz.

Rahel would have liked to possess all that marriage offered her and yet to have remained the same inside. Had Vernhagen not explicitly promised to place no restrictions upon her, she could never have married him: "Freedom, freedom! especially in a closed-off condition like marriage. Ah-a! the old Rahel! Ah!—" [85] Yet in spite of the full liberty Varnhagen allowed her, life as the respectable wife of a member of the nobility was "constraint and ennui." What she had never been as a Jewess, she was now—"bored to tears." [86] She recognized that at last she was only playing a role and to do that was not to live at all. No one could better understand her feelings than her old friend Pauline Wiesel, the once beautiful and admired mistress of many men, who was in her own way as much of an outcast as Rahel had been. Only she could understand what Rahel had given up. To her Rahel wrote that one could not be free if one had to represent something in society: a wife or, even worse, the wife of an official.[87] As a Jewess she had suffered, and through her suffering plumbed the depths of her soul. As the wife of Varnhagen she was too protected, too cut off from the anguish of life.

In quest of a higher meaning, she explored her new faith. She, who wanted above all to preserve her own freedom and uniqueness, was necessarily repelled by Christian orthodoxy. Unlike Dorothea, she found no sympathy for a doctrine of original sin, nor could she ever—in contrast to both Dorothea and Henriette—decry human reason. She intensely disliked dogmatic, authoritarian religion; attempts to prove logically the truth of a particular faith only made her angry. But she felt that somehow the human soul itself was by nature Christian,[88] and the Christian mystical literature exercised a particular fascination upon her. She loved the writings of Lavater and Saint-Martin because she felt that they "emerge with their ideas as out of a religious ocean." [89] Her favorite religious writer was the seventeenth-century mystic Angelus Silesius, a strikingly original figure whom the Enlightenment had wholly neglected. Rahel always kept a copy of Angelus near at hand, sent copies to her friends, and in 1822 together with Varnhagen issued a collection of his sayings. In Angelus Rahel found an audacious assertion of the individual soul which actively seeks the *unio mystica*. Unlike most Christian mystics, Angelus did not passively offer up his soul to the embrace of God or the Cosmos. He found God in the soul itself—as did Rahel. Commenting on one of his couplets, she wrote, "As soon as one rightly thinks about it, one immediately finds the true God in oneself: that which is not of one's own making; the creative imagination; the great splendor; the eternal wonder." [90]

Rahel's religion was highly personal, but couched in the imagery of Christianity.[91] With the Romantic movement she believed in the revelation of God to each individual and in prayer as the pouring out of the soul to an ineffable Deity. Long before her conversion, she had felt the need of God as a ground for her own existence; repeatedly through her life she had dreamt she lay upon a corner of His mantle.[92] The Judaism of her day did not offer Rahel the framework for such an individualized religious consciousness. She became convinced that traditional Judaism was for *Kindermenschen,* people with an underdeveloped religious sensitivity, while the Christian message alone was a philosophy for thinking human beings. Reform Judaism, as it then existed, was even more repugnant to her; she disputed its entire basis. Religion was not something that could be shackled to reason. Although she recognized the role of reason in religion, the cold, dignified reverence of the Jacobson services could have no appeal to Rahel's mystical soul.[93]

As she had never felt any religious identification with Judaism, so too Rahel was entirely removed from any identification with the lot of her fellow Jews.[94] She was almost totally indifferent to the strivings for political emancipation which so possessed Friedländer and his circle. Being a Jew was for her above all a *personal* fate, not one that she bore as the member of a people. When the post-Napoleonic reaction in Prussia brought on riots directed against the Jews, Rahel was appalled. But she did not react out of a Jewish sympathy—she was ashamed for Prussia and for Christianity. To her brother Ludwig she wrote in 1819:

> I am boundlessly sad, and in a way that I have never been before—on account of the Jews....I know my country! Unfortunately!...The hypocritical new love of the Christian religion (God pardon my sin!) for the Middle Ages, with its art, poetry and atrocities, incites the people to the *only* atrocity to which it still, reminded of old sanctions, lets itself be incited: assault on the Jews!...It is not a matter of religious hatred: they don't love their *own* religion; how can they hate that of others!...The preachers, the ministers, the servants of religion should speak out.[95]

Though she could identify with neither Jews nor Judaism, Rahel carried to the end of her life a feeling that her hated Jewish origins had been a blessing in disguise; the sorrows they brought upon her had elevated her spirit. Shortly before her death she spoke to Varnhagen the often cited words:

> What a history!...A fugitive from Egypt and Palestine, and here I find your help, love and care!...With sublime rapture I think back upon these, my origins and this whole web of destiny, by which the oldest memories of the human race are connected with the latest circumstances, and the greatest distances of time and space are bridged. What for such a long period of my life was my greatest shame, my bitterest suffering and misfortune—to have been born a Jewess—I would not now have missed at any price.[96]

Rahel was glad she had been born a Jew. But what those writers who have tried to make her in some way "Jewish" [97] have usually neglected is the end of the same passage. Tearfully and near death, Rahel spoke to Varnhagen:

> Dear August, my heart is refreshed in its inmost depths. I have thought of Jesus and cried over his passion; I have felt—for the first time so felt it—that he is my brother. And Mary, how she suffered! She saw her beloved son suffer but did not succumb; she stood at the cross! That I could not have done; I would not have been that strong. Forgive me God, I confess how weak I am.

Dorothea, Henriette, Rahel—different as were their personalities and the course of their lives—were at one in giving up Judaism for Christianity. In its traditional form they found their ancestral faith an inhibiting, meaningless law, its modernized variety dry, sterile rationality. For none of the three could religion be merely the form of a universal moralism. Possessing the need for personal religious experience, they found it in romanticized Christianity. Born Jews in a romantic age, they could draw spiritual sustenance only from foreign wells.

5

Religious Reform and Political Reaction

The image of the post-Mendelssohn generation in Germany would be grossly distorted if David Friedländer, the Mendelssohn children, and the salon Jewesses of Berlin were taken as typical. These exceptional individuals represented but a small segment of German Jewry, characterized by extraordinary intellect, beauty, or wealth. Either on the very fringe of the Jewish community or beyond it entirely, they bear witness to the fate of a Jewish self-awareness forced into the mold of a rigid rationalism or rejected in the intense introspection of an antinomian romanticism. They were the few who chose the extreme paths that led away from Judaism in opposite directions.

Less well-known outside the Jewish community, and neither as wealthy as Friedländer nor as sensitive as Rahel Varnhagen, were the numerous young men who assumed the task of both carrying on the Mendelssohnian enlightenment and at the same time saving their generation from the shoals of indifference and conversion. They became educators in modernized Jewish schools, authors of Bible translations and interpretations, editors of journals directed toward the enlightenment of their brethren, and preachers in newly formed temples. They sought to give Judaism a new dignity and provide it with a theoretical basis; when it became necessary, they defended it against the hostile opinions which marked the post-Napoleonic reaction. Most of them are unknown except to the specialist

—they were not intriguing personalities and they made no outstanding single contributions—but it is to them that we must turn if we would venture from the outskirts back into the center of the Jewish community.

For the Maskilim, the young enlighteners who gloried in the fame of Mendelssohn,[1] the principal task in the last decades of the eighteenth century seemed that of countering the intellectual and social isolation of all but a relatively small number of their fellow Jews. They made their chief vehicle a journal devoted to the Hebrew language which bore the title *Ha-Measef* (*The Gatherer*). In its first three years in Königsberg (1784–86), this monthly periodical was devoted principally to Biblical exegesis, the revival of the Hebrew language in both poetry and prose, and the education of the Jewish youth; it presented brief biographies of the heroes of the Jewish past and reported the literary or political events affecting Jews in the present. Following the suggestion of the admired Hebraist Hartwig Wessely,[2] the editors scrupulously avoided offending the orthodox. Yet for all its conservatism, there was something revolutionary about the journal from the very first.

Although the rabbinic tradition was not attacked in those early years of *Ha-Measef*, its absence was conspicuous. Responding to the classicism of their day, the *Measfim* reached back beyond the Talmud to the Bible for their principal object of concern. They strove to purge the Hebrew language of its later impurities and regain the pristine style of psalmist and prophet. The Hebrew language, to which they were devotedly attached, became for the Maskilim an object of both grammatical analysis and aesthetic appreciation. Despite their firm adherence to the Masoretic text and avoidance of controversial issues,[3] the use of Hebrew and not Judeo-German for all subjects, profound and trivial, the focus upon Bible and not Talmud, and the introduction of scientific and aesthetic criteria in the treatment of traditional materials set the early Maskilim apart from most of their fellow Jews.

After *Ha-Measef* moved to Berlin in 1787, it took on a more obviously radical complexion. Hebrew language and literature were no longer central. Significantly, its sponsors had transformed themselves from the "Society for the Study of the Hebrew Language" into the "Society for the Propagation of Goodness and Virtue." The emphasis was shifted from the inner world of the Biblical literature to the outer world of physical and biological science and to the changing political status of the Jew, especially in France. In an article favoring the secular education of Jewish youth, Mendel Bresslau, one of the original editors, addressed the rabbis and leaders of Israel urging them to awaken to the realities of the day. It was a time, he insisted, when the nations were desirous of entering a new covenant with Israel; the gentiles must not be allowed to think the Jew unresponsive. He envisioned the pursuit of secular knowledge as an integral part of Judaism. Natural science is the ladder between heaven and earth and it is the will of God that "we serve Him with our intellect and our understanding." [4]

The third phase of the journal's life began in 1794, after publication had been interrupted for four years. In contrast to its previous policy, *Ha-Measef* now did not merely seek broader horizons but waged aggressive warfare upon the obscurantist orthodox. The new editor, Aaron Wolfssohn, saw fit to employ a rather effective device to discredit the rabbinic opponents of enlightenment. Instead of an essay he chose the form of an imaginary conversation in the Hereafter among three individuals: Maimonides, Mendelssohn, and a nameless rabbi who had been an opponent of the latter.[5] The scene opens upon an uncommunicative conversation between Maimonides and the rabbi. The rationalist Rambam obviously has no sympathy for the rabbi's superstitions and mystical leanings, nor for his excessive piety and fear of secular knowledge. He finally mutters under his breath, "I pity the generation whose leader you are! Oh, people of God, how you have fallen and been horribly degraded!" Quite cleverly Wolfssohn has chosen Maimonides, by virtue of his legal works the great hero of traditional Judaism, as his spokesman against the orthodox. When Mendelssohn arrives upon the scene amidst great splendor and escorted by the archangel Michael, Maimonides goes out to greet him and immediately they are at one. Says Rambam to him, "Call me no longer 'my instructor' and 'my teacher'; call me 'my brother,' for we are brothers. Have we not one mother? both of us were born on the lap of wisdom and suckled the blessings of her breasts...." Wolfssohn's point is clear: the true Jewish tradition runs in a line from Maimonides to Mendelssohn, not to the nameless rabbi. In the end the two Moseses are ushered into the presence of God while the poor, befuddled rabbi, variously depicted as childish, obstinate, and rude, remains standing alone.

However, in its effects, Wolfssohn's sarcasm proved more disastrous for *Ha-Measef* than for the rabbinate; his aggressiveness had gone beyond what his readers were willing to tolerate. The journal found itself without a public; those who still read Hebrew were the conservative elements in the community, the very ones who were offended by Wolfssohn's attack. As a result, in 1797 *Ha-Measef* died, unable to muster more than 120 subscribers. When it was finally revived in 1809 under new editorship, it had returned to its original conservative policy and concern with Biblical exegesis. As its subscriber list shows,[6] it was directed to a new wave of Jews breaking out of the ghetto, now to a large extent in the south and east: in Prague, Posen, and Glogau.

For a long time the German word *Aufklärung* and its Hebrew equivalent *haskalah* remained the slogan of the followers of Mendelssohn. The obscurantism of the rabbis was condemned in the name of *haskalah*. But it gradually became apparent to the Maskilim that an overdose of enlightenment was as pernicious as an utter lack of it. They could not shut their eyes to the opportunistic conversions, the licentiousness, and the scorn for everything connected with Judaism that increasingly characterized the younger generation, especially in the larger cities.

As early as 1792 or 1793 Isaac Euchel, one of the original editors of *Ha-Measef,* wrote a comedy entitled "Reb Henokh" in which he characterized, far better than he might have done in an essay, the growing rift between the generations and its dire results.[7] The central figure of the play, Reb Henokh, is pictured as a strictly orthodox paterfamilias with all of the distasteful characteristics that Euchel thought he saw in the older generation. Henokh is superstitious, opposed to all secular studies—including Hebrew grammar—and more punctilious in the ceremonial law than in his moral conduct. As a result, he and his wife reap the devastating consequences in their own children. The eldest daughter, Elke (Elizabeth), is a crass effigy of the Berlin salon Jewess. Though married, she falls in love with a member of the German nobility who cannot take her seriously. He characterizes her thus: "Vanity, loathing for her own people and a quasi culture which she fancies to find in our company constitute her entire existence. She no more loves me than I her." The other children are no better. The eldest·son, Herzkhe (Hartwig), has become a gambler and a cheat while the youngest, Samuel, is revealed as a pious hypocrite, continually mumbling psalms to cover up his illicit love affair with the gentile maid. The moral of Euchel's tragicomedy is all too clear. One of his characters makes it explicit when he says to Reb Henokh in a prophetic tone: "You are not the only unfortunate father; there are many like you; and it will not be long before they will see the sad consequences." That is Euchel's conclusion: the ceremonialism of the old generation is directly responsible for the corruption of the new.

What is needed is not just a revolt from orthodoxy. A sharp break can produce only Herzkhes and Elkes. A distinction must be made between enlightenment and "true enlightenment." A physician, the drab hero of the play, is made to embody this genuine *haskalah*. To him Herzkhe, now repentant, confesses: "We took frivolity for enlightenment and arrogance for freedom.... Unfortunately we call religion what is really nothing but observance, in which neither the head nor the heart participates." If Herzkhe had only been subjected to the proper influences earlier, he would now be genuinely enlightened like the doctor.

Euchel's play marks the beginning of a growing fear of the consequences of unbridled enlightenment, even among the Maskilim themselves. Well into the nineteenth century, educators, reformers, and preachers consistently take pains to point out that what they advocate is "true enlightenment," to be distinguished from "pseudo-enlightenment" (*After-Aufklärung*) on the one hand and religious fanaticism on the other. The Maskilim come to see themselves as mediators rather than rebels. Shalom Cohen, who revived *Ha-Measef* in 1809, claimed that the old journal was too radical; the new series must restore the balance by a return to the traditional literature.[8] Said Jeremiah Heinemann, editor of the Jewish pedagogical journal *Jedidja*: "Formerly [the task] was to promote enlightenment among the Israelites. Now, in contrast, it is to teach Israelites to differentiate true enlightenment from false."[9]

Mediation between tradition and assimilation was the avowed purpose of a new Jewish periodical—the first in the German language—that began to appear in 1806.[10] Founded by Joseph Wolf and David Fränkel, both Jewish educators in Dessau, it was significantly entitled *Sulamith,* a feminine name from the Hebrew root meaning to be whole and hence at peace. Through the many years of its existence—Fränkel carried it on until 1848—the *Sulamith* again and again played upon the theme of moderation and anti-extremism. The editors were convinced that the transformation of Jewry must be a development originating within the community; they wanted to "enlighten the Jewish nation out of its own self." [11] The greatest danger lay in seeing enlightenment as an outside force incompatible with Judaism or, for that matter, with any particularism. Far from rabid assimilationism, Wolf, the more profound of the two editors, recognized that every people has its own needs, capabilities, and national characteristics which cannot be entirely reduced to universal human ones.

Mediation within the Jewish community was to be matched by mediation between the community and the outside world. The title vignette of the journal bore the figure of the "wise woman" who in the Biblical narrative saves her city from destruction by Joab, David's general (II Samuel 20:16–22). To avoid war, she persuades the inhabitants of the city to deliver up the head of Sheba, the traitor hiding in the city, and thus preserves the peace. According to Wolf, the new journal was to be like this Biblical figure: "Like her it too steps forth out of the midst of an oppressed nation and appears as mediator and peacemaker between this nation and its opponents, who erroneously think it aids and abets the enemy of mankind in its midst." [12] The thinking of the editors was that if the enemies within, "the superstitious additions and distortions," were exposed and destroyed, peace and harmony with the gentiles would be the certain result.

The *Sulamith* carried through its self-appointed task by pursuing a "golden mean." On the one side it launched out against those Jews who had made a religion out of rationalism and as a result had led the orthodox to equate enlightenment with irreligion.[13] On the other, it attacked what seemed to the editor the orthodox practices most offensive to his religious and aesthetic sensibilities. For this purpose the *Sulamith* introduced a special column entitled: "Gallery of pernicious abuses, unseemly customs and absurd ceremonies among the Jews." Included were the monetary transactions involved in arranging betrothals, the boisterous celebrations at circumcisions, and the old matter of early burial. As a contrast to the average rabbi and an example worthy of emulation, the *Sulamith* singled out the enlightened rabbi Joseph David Sinzheim, President of the Napoleonic Sanhedrin;[14] and later it called attention to the three progressively oriented rabbis of the Westphalian Consistory.

The goal of all this mediating effort was, of course, political, economic, and social integration. But few Maskilim were willing to accept the principles of the Berlin rationalists and favor religious integration as well. Judaism was to be de-nationalized, but not made to disappear. Yet if the Jew was to retain his identity, purged of all national characteristics, a new *religious* identity had to emerge. Mendelssohn, the hero of the Maskilim, had laid no foundation for such an identity, and the results were now everywhere manifest: "They have destroyed the old structure and built no new one in its stead. The child knows how to despise the old customs but doesn't know how to live a moral life...." [15] The product was a generation that simply could not see what it meant to be a Jew once the ceremonial law was abandoned. The new generation was seen pleading in vain with the old: "Father, give us a faith in something that we might know Whose we are!" [16]

Jewish consciousness had once stemmed from and involved the whole of life. It was sustained by customs, traditions, considerable legal autonomy, and by the hostility of the gentile world. But when in the last years of the eighteenth century European society showed itself ever more ready to integrate the Jew, the price was always elimination of incongruous prerogatives and pecularities. It was a price the more acculturated elements were perfectly willing to pay. For them the old Judaism resembled an all-encompassing shell which now felt strange and confining. Yet if the shell were cast away, what was left? Was one any longer a Jew? What did it mean to be a Jew when one no longer recognized every law and custom as possessing divine sanction?

The answer the Maskilim gave to these questions was that Judaism constituted a religion, not a nationality—yet was more than mere deism. Like other faiths, it bore certain features which set it apart. Nations are separated by language, customs, and manners, but faiths by tenets and dogmas. And so, despite Mendelssohn's dictum that Judaism has no dogmas, it was gradually realized that if being a Jew meant subscribing to the Jewish *religion,* the essence of that faith had to be made clear. The Maskilim therefore undertook the task of transforming a total Jewish consciousness in which religion was intertwined with every act into a religious consciousness which could be formulated into articles of belief. Such a creed would make Judaism comprehensible to gentiles and could be taught to a new generation whose Judaism was no longer integrally woven into their lives.

The attempt to restructure Judaism through dogmatization was first undertaken by a most unusual figure whose significance has been recognized only in recent years: Saul Ascher (1767–1822).[17] Perhaps in his youth an acquaintance of Mendelssohn, Ascher lived in Berlin as a bookdealer [18] and devoted much of his time to political journalism. A man of uncommon daring, he expressed his opinions on political matters so frankly that in 1810 he was for a time imprisoned as "a restive and refractory citizen." [19] As early as 1788, at the age of twenty-one, Ascher published his views on the current issue of whether Jews should serve as soldiers in the Austrian army.[20] The Maskilim had glorified Joseph II, and Wessely had strongly urged that Jewry in the Austrian empire carry through the political and educational reforms of the benevolent monarch. Unlike them, Ascher had no illusions and he refused to fawn over a monarch whose motives for emancipation he regarded as dubious. Joseph, Ascher claimed, had decreed that Jews be drafted because he was waging an expensive war upon the Turks, and not because he wanted to grant the Jews a special honor of citizenship. Under the influence of the social contract theory, especially in the Hobbesian formulation, Ascher argued that the Emperor had no right to draft the Jews since he has not yet fulfilled the obligations he owes them. Since Joseph had not allowed the Jews to enjoy full privileges of citizenship, he could not demand they discharge the duties of citizens. Rather than force enlightenment upon a backward Austrian Jewish community, the Emperor should guide them by his own enlightened conduct. Unlike so many of his contemporaries, Ascher, by no means an orthodox Jew himself, recognized very early that a forced assimilation could have no beneficial effects.

Ascher set forth his own philosophy of religion and Judaism in a work titled *Leviathan, oder Ueber Religion in Rücksicht des Judenthums* (*Leviathan, or On Religion with Respect to Judaism*. Berlin, 1792). Though verbose and muddled in its presentation and of no apparent influence upon the Jewish community, the work is of extraordinary interest: it is the first attempt to carry through a systematic revolt against the Mendelssohnian dichotomy of natural religion and revealed law, and to established a unified basis for a redefinition of Judaism as religious doctrine. Ascher stands at the beginning of the modern trend to find a dogmatic content or, more broadly, an essence of Judaism.[21]

Ascher was the first to seek a substitute for the revealed law as the distinguishing feature of Judaism. Against Kant and Fichte, he argues that Judaism basically is as pure a religious faith as Christianity and not, as they would have it, merely a political constitution.[22] Unlike Friedländer, with whom he takes issue,[23] Ascher insists that there must be some difference between Judaism and pure natural religion, and he claims to find this distinction in certain dogmas which constitute the essence of Judaism and the sole reason for its preservation. Ascher contends that the false equation of Judaism with law is responsible for its widespread rejection by the enlightened:

> Disobeying the law came to be regarded as complete apostasy from Judaism, and since those who dared to violate it publicly were despised by their coreligionists, they did not bother any more about the remaining, important points of Judaism. This is still occurring with daily increasing results so that we are threatened with the complete ruin of our faith, a faith whose form is so inspiring, so uplifting, and can bring people such happiness.[24]

Those Jews who have refused to consider the law essential to Judaism have been unable to find a substitute. "All one has to do is ask the adherent of Judaism the character of his religious faith—he will soon betray his embarrassment." [25]

The great error has been to regard the law as end rather than means, and hence of eternal rather than temporary validity. It resulted in an erroneous conception of Judaism which made it seem incompatible with surrounding society. Before the civil status of the Jew can be improved a wholesale reformation must take place in Judaism. Using the image of Judaism as an edifice—a figure common in his generation [26]—Ascher calls for a complete renovation, not a mere patching up here and there. Judaism is to be "purified," the dust of centuries removed and the firm, sturdy foundation laid bare.

After a lengthy theoretical interpretation of religion, Ascher arrives at fourteen dogmas of Judaism. Ten are properly dogmas in that they express beliefs; the other four are commitments to certain observances. The Jew is to believe in the one God of love, who revealed Himself to the Patriarchs, rewards and punishes, and guides the world for the best through His divine Providence. The law, though revealed at Sinai, is specifically rejected for the present day: "We believe that the observance of the laws was holy for our ancestors and that it kept them upon the way which we now travel in the pure belief in God and his prophets." The

last of the dogmas of belief, apparently influenced by Maimonides' thirteen articles, expresses the hope of messianic redemption and even the
resurrection of the dead. Finally, the practice of circumcision, the observance of the Sabbath and holidays, and seeking God's favor through atonement are made essentials of the faith. Arbitrary as the formulation is, it
is significant as an attempt to overcome the dichotomy between universal
religion and particular observance which was the heritage of Mendelssohn.
In these dogmas universal and particular are merged into a new unity
which is deemed the eternal content of Judaism.

It would be a mistake, however, to exaggerate the novelty of Ascher's
approach to Judaism. A careful analysis of his religious philosophy leaves
little doubt that he was a man of the Enlightenment who cannot significantly be linked to romanticism.[27] Like Mendelssohn, he was a strict rationalist trying to justify remaining Jewish. The function of religion for
Ascher, as for the eighteenth century, is still to bring happiness (*Glückseligkeit*) to the individual. Such a eudaemonism relegates religion itself—
and not just the revealed law—to the position of a means: it leads man to
the moral and hence the blissful life. Like Lessing, Ascher conceives of
revelation as a preliminary to rational comprehension. Religion based on
revelation is therefore a necessity only because of the difficulty our reason
has in apprehending ultimate truths. And so too "Judaism is a religion,
and therefore likewise a means for filling that gap, a means we can replace only with effort through speculation or dialectic." [28] What finally
distinguishes Judaism from other religions is that its dogmas, unlike those
of Christianity, do not disturb freedom of thought and action. Thus, despite the loud attack upon Mendelssohn, Ascher's dogmas are not of the
type that Mendelssohn rejected as confining human reason. His Judaism
becomes, as Wiener has correctly pointed out, a mere "variation" of the
religion of the Enlightenment.[29]

An overall evaluation of Ascher's work discloses that his principal concern was the transformation of Judaism from what he considered a political constitution into a religion. His purpose was to "present Judaism in
such a way that any enlightened man might embrace it, that it might be
the religion of a member of any society, and that it would have principles
in common with every religion." [30] Judaism was to be a member of the
family of religions, with its own peculiarities to differentiate it from the
rest. Its essence might be expressed through "dogmas," some universal,

some particular, none in conflict with reason. By acknowledging these dogmas, these tenets of the faith, the enlightened Jew, it was hoped, might replace the decaying corporate identity with a purely religious one. Though they may not have read Ascher,[31] the Maskilim in succeeding years took up this same task of confessionalizing and doctrinizing Judaism. They did so by squeezing it into the dominant form of religious education, the Protestant catechism.

During the last quarter of the eighteenth century the need for a manual of religious instruction was expressed with increasing frequency. In its second year *Ha-Measef* announced a forthcoming German translation of the sixteenth-century *Leḳah Tov,* a Jewish catechism by the Italian rabbi, Abraham Jagel.[32] The translator argued that it had been a grievous error to leave the path of Maimonides and Bachya, who had given Judaism clear formulations. The Jewish child simply does not know how to explain his religion; he cannot render account of it to himself or others. A catechism in the German language would enable him to carry the principles of his religion on the tip of his tongue; moreover, a gentile reading such a catechism would be prompted to exclaim, "What a wise and sage people this great nation is!"

By the end of the second decade of the nineteenth century, numerous Jewish catechisms had appeared.[33] It seemed that this approach, since it was the way the Christian religion was taught, was the way all religion should be taught [34]—and Judaism was now to be conceived as within the genus religion and bearing only the differentiae of species. The catechisms were authored by the educators in the modernized Jewish schools and utilized in religious instruction or as part of the confirmation ceremony, first introduced in 1807. They are strikingly similar. Employing the method of question and answer, they often put into the mouth of the student religious conceptions beyond his range of understanding. Nearly always the ten commandments and the thirteen principles of Maimonides or the three of Albo were made the basis of the catechism. Very popular also was the arrangement in terms of a threefold classification of duties: to God, to oneself, and to one's fellow man. Under the last rubric there was generally a reaffirmation that the Jew was completely loyal to the state and that there was nothing in Bible or Talmud that conflicted in any way with that loyalty.[35]

Although the catechisms retain the traditional conceptions of Judaism and a few even dwell upon the ceremonial law, their purpose is not to stress Jewish distinctiveness. No attempt is made to indicate to the child why he should remain a Jew; never a single word to specifically differentiate Judaism from Christianity. Their desire to gain political acceptance by the state and religious acceptance by the gentile community prevented the catechists from stressing any unique value which Judaism might possess and Christianity lack. Instead they dwelt upon what both faiths had in common. The chosenness of Israel was either passed over in silence or limited to the past.[36] And yet, desirous of maintaining Judaism at least as a separate confession, they cast about in search of some reason for its preservation. As the following section from a catechism by the Frankfurt teacher Joseph Johlson indicates, they were unable to supply the child with any motivation for remaining Jewish but the harsh admonition of the Bible. The section is entitled: "Can we be indifferent about which religion we confess?" The answer Johlson gives (obviously influenced by Mendelssohn) could hardly have satisfied his students:

> No, it is rather the most sacred duty of every Israelite to remain true to the religion which our fathers most solemnly received and avowed for themselves and their posterity. Accordingly, we cannot in any way absolve ourselves of the religion of our fathers without breaking the covenant and calling down upon ourselves the curse which the entire people declared before the Eternal (Deut. 27:26). Therefore in the religion we were born into we must also die....[37]

The catechisms and textbooks replaced the traditional practice of immersing the student immediately in a text of which he had no conception either why it was studied or what constituted the religion based upon it. By and large, these didactic works reiterated the natural theology of the eighteenth century, reconciling it as best they could with the Sinaitic Revelation. The main purpose remained that of pointing out Judaism's compatibility with citizenship. As one of the typical textbooks would have it, the principal task of the religious instructor of Jewish youth is "above all to teach them that the Jewish religion in its purity is not only reconcilable with the obligations of man and citizen but that the former constitutes the basis of the latter." [38]

To balance the picture, however, it must be noted that some of the educators rejected the catechism as foreign to the spirit of Judaism.[39] While a confession of belief was necessary to make the natural man into a Christian, a Jew was a Jew by birth. He might be taught the principles of his religion or undergo a special ceremony of confirmation, but the formal declaration of faith did not suddenly provide him with Jewish identity.[40]

When it was not thus formulated into principles of belief, Jewish consciousness was often put into the broad terms of a general religious consciousness or simply a humanistic one. Almost always, though not consistently, the term Judaism was replaced by "Mosaic religion" and the term Jew by "Israelite," thus explicitly disavowing the particularistic rabbinic tradition. Although for some this Mosaism involved a recognition of the Biblical legislation (or at least a portion of it) as divine,[41] for others, such as Peter Beer and Aaron Wolfssohn, it was simply natural religion.[42] But it was left to Gotthold Salomon, preacher at the Hamburg Reform Temple, to give Jewish identity the most universal formulation of all: "The summons to be an Israelite," he insisted from the pulpit, "is the summons to be a human being." [43]

One looks in vain during this period for any expression of Jewish nationalism [44] or for the romantic notion of a Jewish spirit; both of these were only to manifest themselves later. What does come to the surface is a nostalgic longing for the solidarity once present in the Jewish community and now, in the wake of enlightenment and emancipation, fast vanishing. Typical is Salomon's remark:

> It is highly desirable that with ever increasing (in part false) enlightenment among the Israelites the communal spirit (*Gemeingeist*) should not disappear. It was able to achieve so much that was good and pleasing in the sight of God. Unfortunately this beneficent spirit has here and there been shoved aside by its stepsister!!! [45]

In the later literature of the period one even finds a yearning to resurrect the pre-enlightenment Jewish family, for it was much easier to break with the past intellectually than emotionally.[46] Faced with students whose homes were devoid of any religious atmosphere, the Jewish educators could only regret that the traditional Jewish home was fast disappearing. No longer was the orthodox household pictured as a revolting den of hypocrisy, the way Euchel had described it in "Reb Henokh." Now, as a counter to rampant, religion-deriding false enlightenment, it was idealized, even romanticized. Moses Philippson (1775–1814), a teacher at the Dessau Jewish school, had once spent time in such an idyllic religious home. His biographer writes:

> Here in this house, Philippson often told me, he quite clearly realized what a beneficial influence religion is able to exercise upon its adherents. When...Herr Wertheimer would come home from synagogue on the eve of the Sabbath or one of the other holidays and step into the brightly lighted room, his family would gather lovingly about him and, in accordance with the old Jewish custom, beg for his blessing. As he tendered the blessing to them with a joyous heart, he seemed to resemble more an angel of light than an earthly creature; a heavenly joy radiated from his eyes and in those blissful moments he would certainly not have exchanged his heaven-ordained lot with the richest and greatest of men. Peace and contentment reigned undisturbed in his heart and in his house, and in every circumstance of life he found in his faith the mightiest of supports. False, so-called enlightenment has unfortunately driven this heavenly bliss from many a family....[47]

The men who became the teachers in the Jewish schools that sprang up during this period were born into such orthodox homes. They all had received traditional educations, but at some point had broken away from an intended career as rabbi or scholar of the old type and begun—almost always on their own—to acquire a secular education. They read the pedagogical works of Campe and Pestalozzi and determined to reform Jewish education in accordance with their theories. Very likely these young men (many were under twenty when they began to teach) had little alternative but to choose the profession they did. Coming from poor families they lacked the necessary capital to go into business, and as Jews they were afforded few other opportunities for making a living. In part because their work demanded that they avoid giving offense, almost all of them—even an extremist like Bendet Schottlaender, who had his children converted for the sake of their careers [48]—scrupulously kept the dietary laws.

The vocation of teacher was not an enviable one: it yielded neither honor nor wealth; even after years of service a teacher's social and economic status remained low. Despite all of their obvious differences from the old Polish *melamdim,* the teachers of the new type enjoyed little better treatment from the average Jewish householder. Parents were reluctant to give their daughters to them in marriage; they were excluded from the elegant world of the wealthy Jews and from contact with prominent Christians. Their salaries were pitifully low,[49] and they usually had to take other jobs to supplement their income. A visitor in the home of the Dessau instructor Joseph Wolf described it in these terms:

> The entire family lived in one and the same room. His wife and children were there; he gave private lessons there, worked on his sermons and his writings, on petitions and other written documents for the Jewish community, all using a large rectangular table which simultaneously served as dinner, coffee and work table. The furniture was most simple: the weak and always sickly man had no sofa or easy chair on which he could comfortably relax. Most of the linens were as a rule in the pawn shop.[50]

Nor was the educative task of these men an easy one. Because they advocated secular studies, they were denounced as heretics by the strictly orthodox, while the out-and-out assimilationists would have nothing to do with *any* institutions furthering Jewish education. The educators, for their part, waged continuous warfare on the remaining *hadarim* which they felt hindered the process of emancipation and social integration. Here they were aided by the various German governments, which issued decrees eliminating these remnants of the traditional Jewish education.[51] At the same time the educators complained bitterly of those parents who provided their children with no Jewish education whatever. They claimed that a child from such a home grows up alienated from the Jewish community: "The Jew is for him and he for the Jew a strange creature. And if he enters a society of Christians, he is often out of place there too. He is thus everywhere an unseemly creature, everywhere an unfortunate in-between thing!"[52]

The religious education of Jewish girls had been particularly neglected by both the orthodox parents and the enlightened. Little wonder, therefore, that the feminine sex spent Sabbaths and festivals reading sensual novels instead of the Bible.[53] To combat the increasing moral laxity, efforts were made to bring Jewish girls into the new schools and into the synagogues. The ideal of the educators lay somewhere between the passive, averagely educated wife of Moses Mendelssohn, Fromet, and her brilliant, philosophically adept daughter, Dorothea. While the former type was considered "insipid and dull," the latter was "irksome and annoying."[54] For a time the *Sulamith* carried a regular series of articles for the edification of the feminine sex. Written by the young Gotthold Salomon, it was entitled "Letters to a respectable young lady of the Jewish religion."[55] It appears, however, that most of these young ladies preferred the popular romance literature of their day to Salomon's moralizing and rather dull Bible stories.

The new Jewish schools that sprang up in Berlin, Dessau, Frankfurt am Main, Breslau, and other cities differed vastly from traditional Jewish institutions. Instead of occupying nearly all of the students' time with the Talmud, as had been customary, the new schools limited the study of traditional texts to a varying, but generally quite small portion of the weekly schedule. Instead of constituting the core of the Jewish child's education, rabbinic literature became one subject among many. The principal reason for including Judaism in the curriculum at all was the same as that advanced for the inclusion of Christianity in Christian schools: it was felt that only through religion could a child become an honest, useful, and happy person. The words "religious" and "moral" were hyphenated into the single adjective *religiös-moralisch* to describe the kind of education that made for happiness.[56] The classes in Judaism, where catechisms were frequently employed as tools of instruction, stressed morality above all. The children were to gain through their study of selected Jewish sources a belief in God, a love of neighbor, and the desire to be a good citizen. Religion was seen as the basis for the duties of the human being and the patriot.

Though it was still generally accepted in this generation, as it had been by Mendelssohn, that reason was the great unifier of men,[57] here and there traces of romanticism crept into the educational theories of the Maskilim. The aversion to passion and mysticism persisted but, for all of their catechizing, they realized that religion involved more than the learning of formulas. Religious instruction should begin out in nature, some of them suggested, where the child would more readily gain an appreciation of God's creation than in a musty, dismal room.[58] Because the religious rationalism of the Enlightenment had flowed into channels of indifference or even atheism, this generation, unlike that of Mendelssohn, sometimes found it necessary to exalt religion above reason to preserve it; or at least to widen its scope so that reason would not exhaust it.

In an article in the *Sulamith* specifically on enlightenment, Salomon, then still a teacher in Dessau, wrote in a vein that leaves no doubt he had at least read the Christian romantics:

> *Religion* means to us the holy awe and reverence with which the Infinite fills us, which surrounds us on all sides, revealed to the eyes but ever hidden from the

understanding; it means to us that conviction and that way of thinking with which the human being expresses his own relation and that of all finite beings to the entire All of Creation with which he feels himself closely bound up. Religion means to us a clear surmise of the Most Holy, the Unseen, the Incomprehensible, who cannot be *grasped,* but only *experienced,* only *felt.* Therefore the seat of true religion is in the heart of the earthly creature—inside of him; for visible signs can never proclaim the invisible. We can only *feel* the Infinite, *believe* and not perceive: man shall not see Me and live.[59]

Such a statement is striking because it is so rare in the Jewish literature of the period; it is the exception to the rule. A pronounced contrast is afforded by the following words of the same author, Gotthold Salomon, taken from a sermon which he gave twelve years after the *Sulamith* article:

Let the educated and the uneducated set forth in a thousand sophisms that reason has neither the right nor the capability to raise its voice in regard to matters of faith—God Himself taught us otherwise! The essence of our religion is no incomprehensible mystery, but rather a discernible truth; it is an object of reflection; it need not shrink from examination or fear the verdict of reason. *Reason is its element! Learn* and *know, perceive* and *examine!* its teachers call out to us. Its greatest truths are to be *perceived, grasped, understood.* Go ahead and play with the word *faith*—for us there is no *faith* without *perception;* play with the word *feeling*—for us *feeling* without *discernment* is no certain guide; assert that there is no religion without *reverie*—*reverie* without understanding fashions dreamers and fanatics.[60]

Generally there was some attempt to work out a compromise between faith and reason. Due largely to the influence of Kant, the role of mediator was given to morality. It was commonly recognized that although religion could not be fully comprehended by reason, the latter was to be its guide. Religious feeling, directed by reason, was then itself conceived as the product of the moral consciousness,[61] and the function of prayer seen as the raising and ennobling of this primal morality.[62] Like the Christian theologians and educators of the late Enlightenment,[63] their Jewish counterparts were of the opinion that religion must above all be edifying. For them as for Ascher, religion, and hence Judaism, remained subordinated as a means to the goals of the moral life and human happiness.[64]

The conception of Judaism as a religious confession was given concrete practical expression in the transformation of its two principal institutions, the school and the synagogue. It has already been pointed out how in the schools of the Maskilim Judaism came to occupy only one niche in the curriculum and how it was taught according to the Christian model. Hand in hand with the reformation of Jewish religious education went the attempt likewise to adapt the worship service to the new requirements of enlightenment and emancipation. The classic example of the endeavor to reshape Jewish institutions in Germany systematically is the experience of the Jewish Consistory of Westphalia, which lasted from 1808 to the end of 1813.

The need for some kind of government-supported authority to achieve reform had been recognized by Jews themselves as early as 1804. At that time Wolfssohn wrote that it was necessary for the state to take over the work of inner reform since the Jews would never reform themselves. He thought it the duty of the state not merely to emancipate the Jews politically but also to be concerned with their moral welfare.[65] After the Napoleonic Sanhedrin in France, David Fränkel was even more convinced that reform must come from above: "Only a synod authorized from the throne, thanks to its authority and inner strength, can be in a position to achieve good results in making Israelite coreligionists aware of their *true* religious and political duties and in encouraging them to carry out these duties." [66]

In January of 1808, under the rule of Napoleon's brother Jerome, the Jews of the newly formed kingdom of Westphalia became heirs to the civil emancipation which French Jewry had enjoyed for nearly two decades. But, as in France, the price here too was centralized organization of the Jewish community under state control. The purpose of the Westphalian Jewish Consistory was to direct the Jewish community and to further its integration into society. The government appointed as its president the wealthy, enlightened, somewhat autocratic Israel Jacobson, who in turn selected three rabbis of a mildly progressive stamp and two laymen, David Fränkel and Jeremiah Heinemann (both educators), to serve along with him.

Under the Consistory's guiding hand, Jewish education was transformed from the study of Talmud to the kind of balanced curriculum advocated by contemporary educational theorists. The school which Jacobson had earlier established at the little town of Seesen prided itself on being able to supply an acceptable education to Christian children as well as Jewish.

Along with the schools, the rabbinate of Westphalia was made an instrument of the Consistory. Orders went out to the rabbis prescribing their duties. These included: exemplary moral conduct, giving edifying sermons regularly (if possible in German),[67] advocating Jewish military service, and conducting confirmations.[68] The Consistory made it perfectly clear that it expected its orders to be obeyed. In ordaining that pulse was to be acceptable food on Passover, the Consistory added ominously that any opposition would be regarded as "the action of a man neglectful of his duties and unwilling to prove himself worthy of the Consistory's confidence."[69]

Jewish religious services in Westphalia were regulated by the Consistory according to an order of September 24, 1810.[70] The changes and deletions which it ordained had little to do with theology. The principal interest was to bring order and solemnity into the service; consciously or unconsciously the example of the dignified Protestant service was the criterion and model. First of all, a proper setting was necessary: everyone to be dressed as cleanly and neatly as possible; children under four excluded entirely and the older brothers and sisters kept under the watchful eye of parents; and a ban on all announcements regarding secular matters. Given the right atmosphere, the second consideration was that all excessive emotion, confusion, and unaesthetic elements of the service be eliminated. Many parts of the liturgy which previously involved congregational participation were now given exclusively to the cantor. Customs that seemed undignified were either restricted or eliminated entirely. Carrying the *lulav* on Sukkot and the Torah scrolls on Simhat Torah was an honor given only to the officials and leaders of the congregation. Noisemaking during the reading of the Scroll of Esther on Purim was outlawed entirely. All was to be solemn and worshipful—without any of the "horrible-sounding *Schreien* which so often disturbed quiet, true devotion." Finally, the service was to be shortened by the elimination of inessential, little-understood, late accretions to the liturgy. Yet none of the prayers—with the exception of that for the king—was required to be said in German. According to the forty-third paragraph, complete obedience was expected so that the Consistory not be required to employ "unpleasant measures of force."

The highlight of the five and a half years that the Consistory functioned was unquestionably the dedication of the "Jacob's Temple," located next to the school in Seesen. Construction on the classical edifice had begun as early as 1805, but completion was delayed by the organ, which was made ready only after repeated delays; [71] like a church, the building also boasted a clock tower with a bell that chimed the hour.[72] The dedication, which finally took place on July 17, 1810, was a gala event of symbolic import. In solemn procession and to the sound of the temple bells, Jacobson, the leaders of the Consistory, the children of the school, and numerous invited Protestant and Catholic dignitaries marched into the new building. As they entered, the temple organ and sixty to seventy singers greeted them with an inspiring German chorale. The service was conducted with all dignity by Jacobson himself, who also gave the principal address. There followed a festive dinner in the schoolhouse with the finest food and champagne. The costs of both building and dedication were borne by the proud, ecstatic Jacobson; it was the high point of his career. In his speech he summed up the purpose of his own reform efforts and those of the Westphalian Consistory: a near union of Jew and gentile brought about by a reshaping primarily of the forms rather than the content of Judaism. Addressing the Jews present, he reminded them that their "true and progressive enlightenment, the cultivation of their spirits in genuine religiosity as well as their future increased political welfare" depended upon first steps to eliminate differences. In a final prayer Jacobson summed up his sanguine hopes:

> Above all let us vividly recognize that we are the *brothers* of all the adherents of other faiths, the descendants of one race which honors Thee as its common father; brothers who must instruct themselves in love and gentle tolerance; brothers, finally, who under Thy guidance stride toward a common goal, and in the end—when all of the fog has vanished from our eyes, all errors retreated from our spirit, all doubts been removed from our understanding—shall meet each other upon the same path.[73]

Only three and a half years later the Kingdom of Westphalia was dissolved and along with it perished the Jewish Consistory, all of its decrees, plans, and hopes. Jacobson himself settled in Berlin where, without government authority, he attempted some of the same reforms. But the glory that was Westphalia had vanished, to be grievously mourned by the erstwhile leaders of the Consistory for years thereafter.[74]

The Prussian capital of 1815, where Jacobson now opened a private temple in his own home,[75] was a far different place from the Westphalia of

1810. The French government had encouraged and authorized ritual reform; the increasingly reactionary Prussian regime frowned upon any tampering with tradition. Yet, for a time, Jacobson's endeavors in Berlin achieved a considerable degree of success. When the room in his house proved too small, a new temple was arranged in the home of the wealthy banker and elder of the Jewish community, Jacob Herz Beer; at one time the temple membership reached a total of 435 families and single individuals.[76] Like the reforms of Westphalia, those in Berlin were limited to externals and were dominated by aesthetic considerations. The services lasted only two hours every Saturday morning and were enhanced by organ music, a German sermon, German prayers, and impeccable decorum.[77] Although men and women continued to sit separately, the changes were quite sufficient to arouse the ire of orthodox elements in the community, whose repeated complaints to the government at length succeeded in closing the temple permanently in 1823.

Somewhat more deliberate and systematized was the program undertaken at the end of 1817 by a reform-minded group of Jews in the old Hanseatic city of Hamburg. Like the entire early Reform movement, the efforts in Hamburg were an attempt by laymen to *adapt* Judaism as an only alternative to its rejection. The rabbis had done nothing to prevent assimilation except deliver exhortations and condemnations. In their response they insisted that customs were not subject to change. They believed, as one scholar has put it, that "Judaism must be made to rise above the exigencies of life and submit to no change or modification whatsoever."[78] The result in Hamburg, as in Berlin, had been to make the younger generation leap from one extreme to another. Such was the nature of the reformers' accusation against the three rabbis of Hamburg:

> Is it not time to act for God? They have voided His covenant! ... Hear O teachers, is this commandment not upon you? ... Look and see: our sons and our daughters grow up, a generation with heart and spirit unfaithful to God; they know not the God of Jacob or the Holy One of Israel.... Is it not your doing? ... These three men in our midst, will they save our sons and daughters?! [79]

Spurred by the young, devoted Eduard Kley, who had been a preacher in the Beer Temple in Berlin, a "Temple Society" was formed in December of 1817 with its stated purpose "to revive the nearly atrophied inclination for the venerable ancestral religion." [80] Within a year's time the group built a house of worship which, following the precedents of Seesen and Berlin, they called "temple," but which the orthodox persistently termed a mere "place of edification" (*Erbauungslokal*). For the religious services a special prayerbook was created by two members of the board of directors.[81] The Hamburg Temple instituted changes of form similar to those that had been adopted in Seesen and Berlin: a number of prayers to be recited in German; omissions to shorten the service; the use of the Portuguese rather than the German pronunciation of Hebrew; passages to be sung by a choir to organ accompaniment; and, of course, a German sermon.

Of greater significance is the theological point of view which underlies—albeit inconsistently—certain changes in the Hamburg liturgy. The God of the new prayerbook is undiminished in might: He revives the dead; He created the world in six days. But He is no longer the God who especially favors Israel. The Adoration, with its exclusivist tendency, is omitted from the Sabbath service; in the High Holiday services, where the full Hebrew text is retained, the German translation excludes pagans but not Christians from divine blessing.[82] The reformers' God did at one time command animal sacrifices, but He now desires only prayers and sacrifices of the heart.[83] In place of a *Messiah* to lead Israel back to Palestine He will send *redemption* to Israel—and to all mankind.[84]

The new service aroused the most violent opposition on the part of the three rabbis of Hamburg who unsuccessfully tried to involve the city government on their side. The Rabbinate felt its position and authority threatened, but was unable to persuade the government to take steps against the wishes of a large—and wealthy—segment of the Jewish community. Failing in their political endeavors, the rabbis gathered a collection of responsa from all over Eastern and Western Europe, each one condemning the new temple.[85] As the three cardinal sins of the reformers the rabbis listed: changing the prayerbook, using a language other than Hebrew, and accompanying the Sabbath service with an organ. Afraid that the slightest concession might unleash a landslide, the rabbis could only condemn.

The responsa collection of the orthodox in turn provoked polemical writings from the side of the reformers.[86] Both parties invoked proof texts from the Bible and Talmud. But beneath the specific issues of language, music, and liturgy lay the far deeper problem which is encountered repeatedly in this post-Mendelssohn generation: "Is there any basis for Jewish identity once the isolated existence of the ghetto is abandoned?"

What is to bind the children to the fathers? No one saw this essential element of the Hamburg dispute more clearly than the traditionally inclined, but eminently fair-minded, Lazarus Riesser.[87] In an epistle to his coreligionists,[88] both orthodox and reform, Riesser argued that the inner enmity produced by the controversy was a far greater sin than the non-observance with which rabbis charged reformers. How could respect be maintained for a religion which fostered such internal dissension? Orthodox parents gave their children a worldly education and then naively expected them to honor a Judaism that was strife-torn, intolerant, and loveless. Unlike the orthodox, Riesser refused to condemn the Temple. He preferred to see it as a partial return to Judaism of those who were on the verge of losing all Jewish consciousness. Instead of raising a clamor against the Temple— and thus increasing the rift between generations—traditional parents should encourage their children to attend. Finding an acceptable form of Jewish expression there on a Saturday morning, they might eventually return to the pervasive, traditional Jewish life. To the Temple members, who indeed had already eliminated an extremist group from their midst,[89] he counseled greater adherence to the customs of their fathers. Unlike the Rabbinate, Riesser wished to view the Hamburg Temple as a bridge rather than an abyss.

In the temples of Seesen, Berlin, and Hamburg and in all of the new Jewish schools of Germany, Judaism had become a religion, and Jewish consciousness, at least in its explicit formulation, a broad religious consciousness of universal character. It was a transformation that fitted well into the years of its conception, the days of German *Aufklärung* and French *égalité*. But by the time of the founding of the Hamburg Temple, intellectual Germany had come to scoff at the Enlightenment and denigrate everything that was French. Under attack from an outside world, which had once seemed so set upon the right path but now was becoming increasingly hostile, the German Jew was more than ever compelled to ask himself whether being a Jew was worth it. And, if so, why?

Although Jewish emancipation in Germany had provoked loud opposition almost continually since Dohm first earnestly proposed it in 1781, it seemed over the succeeding thirty years that the course of history—though winding tortuously—was leading toward complete political and social acceptance for the Jew.[90] Events in France, Westphalia, and finally even in

Prussia strengthened the impression. When Prussia granted the Jews emancipation in 1812, it appeared as if the millenium were at hand. Conversions from Judaism declined, and it was felt that now all that was needed was for the Jews to prove themselves worthy. Few Jews understood (or at least they did not express it openly) what a sympathetic gentile came to realize as early as 1807: the more Westernized the Jew became the more he was hated; the average Christian preferred the "dirtiest orthodox to the cultured man." [91]

Already during the period of Napoleon, young German intellectuals began to rebel against the cosmopolitanism of the eighteenth century and its ideal that men were first of all human beings and only secondly members of a particular nation and religion. It had been that ideal which first created a place for a "virtuous Jew" in the intellectual world outside Judaism. Now it was ever more seriously called into question. In 1811 the romantic writer Achim von Arnim formed a society in Berlin called the Christian-German Eating Club (christlich-deutsche Tischgesellschaft) which included some of the most prominent intellectuals of Berlin: the University syndic Johann Eichhorn, the philosopher Fichte, the writers Kleist and Brentano, the political theorist Adam Müller, the musician Zelter, the architect Schinkel, and the legal philosopher Savigny. Composed also of members of the nobility and the military aristocracy, the society established rules which excluded women, philistines, and Jews from its membership.[92] At one of the meetings, it was rumored, a member read aloud from the writings of the seventeenth-century Jew-baiter Johann Eisenmenger.[93] As a group, these highly respected men resented the penetration of the emancipated, enlightened Jew into the inner sanctum of the German spirit. Arnim himself would have nothing to do with the Jewish salons of Berlin. In his play, Halle [94]—with Lessing obviously in mind—he introduced a character named Nathan. But the Nathan that Arnim pictured was not "the wise" of Lessing; he was the old stereotype of the avaricious moneylender, wholly devoid of any virtue. Already before the defeat of Napoleon, Germany was turning in upon itself, and among the patriots even the noblest Jews were no longer welcome.

But the Jewish community, at least judging from the literature, was blithely oblivious to the change in sentiment. Looking ahead, they knew they would soon have an opportunity to show what loyal sons of the fatherland they really were. When Prussia entered the war against Napoleon in 1813, the Jews did not wait to be drafted; hundreds of them volunteered.[95] Although they owed their emancipation indirectly to the French, they were only too eager to show their feelings for the *Vaterland*. Fifty-five Jewish officers fell at the battle of Waterloo; from 1813 to 1815 seventy-two Jews were awarded the iron cross; in Mecklenburg the percentage of soldiers from the Jewish community even exceeded that of the gentile population. In the Prussian capital, Kley and Günsburg issued a call to the colors:

> O what a heavenly feeling to possess a fatherland! O what a rapturous idea to be able to call a spot, a place, a nook one's own upon this lovely earth.... There upon the battlefield of honor where all hearts are animated by one spirit, where all work for a single goal: for their fatherland; there where he is best who submits most loyally to his king—there also will the barriers of prejudice come tumbling down. Hand in hand with your fellow soldiers you will complete the great work; they will not deny you the name of brother, for you will have *earned* it.[96]

Very few possessed the insight to see that the defeat of Napoleon would bring the Jews not the welcome given a brother but the rejection accorded an intruding stranger.[97]

Resentment of the Jew was one element of the powerful political, economic, and intellectual reaction that swept Germany in the second decade of the nineteenth century. With the fall of Napoleon it gained momentum. The cosmopolitan ideal sank beneath the tide of German nationalism. Once admired, the French conception of the state based upon law was now decried as shallow and mechanical. In its stead German political romanticists created the conception of state and society as a single unified organism. Citizenship, culture, and religion were no longer separable realms. To be fully a German meant to be a patriot, a product of German culture, and a Christian; Christianity was conceived as the "holy bond" of the society. A precedent was found in the long-neglected Middle Ages which were characterized by reciprocal obligations of class, a markedly religious orientation, and a pre-capitalist economy. The Enlightenment was condemned for destroying this organic harmony by its rationalism, its cosmopolitanism, and its reliance upon abstract principles.

In the struggle to piece together a unified German society out of a torn political fabric, the Jew became the symbol for all that frustrated the effort. He was the cosmopolitan, the remnant of the Enlightenment, the capitalist, the parasite feeding upon the German organism into which he could never be absorbed. Beginning in 1815 a portion of the romantic reaction was directed openly against the Jew. Political rights, which had been gained only with the utmost effort, were pared down or taken away entirely. On all levels of society voices were raised against the Jews; professors, demagogues, and playwrights joined in the chorus.

In 1815 a war of words broke out on the Jewish question and remained heated for more than two years. For the problem of Jewish identity its significance lies in the reimposition of the old definition of the Jew from the outside and in the reaction of enlightened Jewry to the destruction of its carefully cultivated image.

The two most prominent figures that directed writings against the Jews were both professors. The one, Friedrich Rühs, occupied a chair of history at the new University of Berlin; the other, Jacob Fries, was a philosopher and natural scientist at Heidelberg. Rühs triggered the controversy with an article regarding Jewish claims to citizenship, which was reviewed favorably and at length by Fries.[98] Rühs's essay received a wider circulation as a pamphlet in 1816; Fries's review, also reprinted, was read aloud in the public taverns.[99]

Rühs's basic contention, uttered by Fichte years earlier, was that Judaism did not constitute merely a creed or confession, as its enlightened adherents claimed, but a nation and a state. The religious laws of the Jews were the laws of a state, their rabbis the legislative power. It was a peculiar contradiction for the citizen of a Jewish state to want to be part of a Christian one as well. Like the Germans, the Jews possessed their own *Volkseigentümlichkeit,* their own national peculiarity. They should be proud of their distinctiveness, Rühs suggested, and even wear a special ribbon to distinguish themselves—as a sign of honor. Judaism could not be called a religious denomination. Any Jew who called it that and denied its character as a state was neither Jew nor Christian but something in between, the adherent of a "fully untenable natural religion, a moral religion of convenience and advantage put together in foolish arrogance, a sect of its own which recognizes no state and only enjoys a tacit toleration." Nor would Rühs allow the distinction between Jew and Israelite that was so dear to Friedländer and the reformers. Rühs, Fries, and the other writers of the romantic reaction insisted on calling the Jew all those things he claimed he was not. They insisted he could not be a German without also being a Christian since religion was not just one subject in a curriculum or one aspect of society; it was the very basis of society. While Rühs preferred conversion as the only way to integrate the foreign corpus, the less Christian Fries suggested outright expulsion.

The basic reaction of enlightened Jews to Rühs and Fries was one of deep shock. They simply could not or would not see that the intellectual climate had profoundly changed. Not realizing what had prompted the attacks upon them, they engaged in the futile task of refuting individual contentions. In reply to exclusivist passages from the Talmud used by their enemies, they quoted universalist ones; against instances of usury on the part of Jews they cited instances of love. They insisted that Rühs and Fries were isolated in their opinions, that they were out of harmony with the zeitgeist, and were merely instruments of a few remaining obscurantists. The truly cultured—and above all the governments—they thought were still on their side. So Michael Hess, teacher at the Jewish school in Frankfurt, could conclude his defense on a hopeful note:

> Let us, my co-religionists, not be led astray by this clamor. With zeal let us carry forward the task of amelioration we have begun as much as it is in our power to do so. And let us await the determination of our fate, consoled by the noble insights of our statesmen and the wise enactments of our princes.[100]

Faced with the rejection of their new Jewish identity, the defenders simply reasserted it more loudly: "The Jews are absolutely not a *people;* nearly everywhere they speak the language of the country; with the exception of their religious customs, their manner of life is like that of all the other inhabitants.... They are to be regarded only as a *confession.*"[101] Once again Judaism was pictured as a religion which commanded love of Christian as well as Jew. If here and there the behavior of certain Jews still left something to be desired, it was the result of those many years of oppression and economic restriction. If Jewish youth were provided with a proper education and diverse occupational opportunities, there was no reason why they could not be absorbed into German society. If they were not forcibly isolated and squeezed out they would soon be hardly distinguishable from the rest of the populace. Give the Jews fifty years and only then, if they had not rid themselves of their faults, might it be said with justice: "The Jews don't fit into civil society."[102] To the teachers of his school in Dessau David Fränkel, in 1817, could suggest only more enlightenment, more improvement of the Jews as an answer to the reaction.

He insisted that the teachers should not allow themselves to be led astray by the consideration that here and there efforts were being made to re-isolate them socially, but rather they should continue to teach virtue, the fulfillment of duties, and obedience to the laws of the state.[103] Thus almost the entire Jewish community wished to see in the romantic reaction only a temporary ebb in the flowing tide of *Aufklärung* and *Humanität*.

Once again it was Saul Ascher who presented the exception. Just as he had been alone in seeing the problems in Mendelssohn's religious philosophy as early as 1792, so he was now the only one of the Jewish defenders that had a clear grasp of the underlying mood which prompted Rühs and Fries.[104] He dubbed it "Teutomania." With unusual insight Ascher saw this phenomenon as an attempt to devise a counterweight to the "Gallomania" of the previous generation and as an ideological tool to overcome the political division of Germany and the split between Catholics and Protestants. He even discerned the close connection between the fusion of German character with Christianity and the transcendental philosophies of Fichte and Schelling. To propagate their ideas effectively among the masses, the Teutomaniacs victimized the Jews. As Ascher put it, "Fuel has to be gathered in order to maintain the fire of enthusiasm, and our Teutomaniacs wanted to see in the little heap of Jews a first bundle of twigs to spread the flame of fanaticism." [105]

Although Ascher penetrated to the underlying cause of the new attacks upon the Jews, he was no more able to cope with them than his fellow defenders. Like Hess, Weil, and the others he put his hope in the princes: they were still free from the "miasma of Teutomania." Like them, he could regard the romantic reaction only as retrogression and primitivization; he lacked any appreciation of its new grasp of history and its literary achievements. Vainly he hoped that Rühs, "the picture of a true Teutomaniac," might return from his Teutomania to the cosmopolitanism which the professor had espoused in his youth. For all of his perspicacity Ascher, too, had no response to romanticism, except to re-utter the ideals of the Enlightenment.

Despite the persistent sanguinity of the Jewish leaders, the national-Christian reaction took ever deeper hold in the years after Napoleon. The *Burschenschaften,* a league of student organizations devoted to "Christian-German development by every spiritual and physical force for the service of the fatherland," increased its strength.[106] On October 18, 1817, the fourth anniversary of the battle of Leipzig, it held a general assembly at the Wartburg near Eisenach. There followers of the arch-nationalist *Turn-vater* Jahn erected a huge bonfire and burned the books of unsympathetic writers, among them Ascher's pamphlet *Teutomania*. Then, in the summer of 1819, a series of riots broke out against the Jews. Prompted by famine and the increased impoverishment of German craftsmen suffering from English competition, the pogroms lasted until October of that year and spread all over Germany.[107] To the cries of "Hep! Hep! Down with the Jews!" the mobs looted Jewish houses and stores and burned synagogues. In response, the Jewish journal *Sulamith* adopted an official policy of not mentioning the riots:[108] if ignored, this demon from the Middle Ages would surely disappear. But it did not disappear. Conversions increased once again.[109] Among others, Abraham Mendelssohn decided at this time that Judaism was simply not worth the aggravation. After his son Felix was accosted by a royal prince with the words "Hep, Hep, Jewboy!" he had his children converted that very year.[110] It seemed as if the careful work of political and religious reform had all been in vain. A new conceptualization of Jewishness, more in keeping with the age, had become a necessity.

6

Leopold Zunz and the Scientific Ideal

Every age has its dominant intellectual motifs, which find expression in a characteristic vocabulary. The age of Enlightenment gloried in being "philosophical" and enthroned on high the universal ideal of "humanity." Thus Mendelssohn's fame rested upon his remarkable talents in philosophy and upon the eighteenth-century desire to find bearers of humanity in every nook of society. Mendelssohn himself and those who wanted to follow in his footsteps attempted to apply these ideals to Judaism and the Jewish community; they strove to reconcile the Jewish religion with reason and to bring the spiritually isolated Jewish community back into the mainstream of humanity.

These ideals of the Enlightenment found their apotheosis in the French Revolution, an application of universal reason to political reality. While at first the events in France evoked a chorus of praise from across the Rhine, the increasingly radical character of the revolution, the reign of terror, and the conquests of Napoleon turned European intellectuals away from the ideals which had nourished the cataclysm. In England Edmund Burke as early as 1790 decried political action based on abstract principle, and insisted that continuity and tradition be principal considerations of government. In Germany a rabid nationalism was the response to French domination, while the European states, controlled by Metternichian diplomacy and under the aegis of the Holy Alliance, set their sights backward to a restoration of the old, pre-revolutionary society.

In nineteenth-century Germany, philosophy and humanity were no longer the brightest stars in the intellectual firmament. Kant's *Critique of Pure Reason* had destroyed on the intellectual level the confidence in metaphysical postulates that the outcome of the French Revolution shattered in the political realm. Attention was drawn away from the "eternal verities" of metaphysics toward the individual and empirical facts of history. Philosophy was employed to explain the course of human events since it was realized that it could never explain the ultimate nature of the physical universe. Gradually, philosophy became absorbed in a new and more comprehensive ideal, and one at the same time better suited to a conservative age: the ideal of *Wissenschaft*. The German term means much more than empirical science, although it includes it; it makes room for speculation but tempers it with historical fact. As the eighteenth century made of philosophy far more than an intellectual discipline, so the new century raised "the pure idea of *Wissenschaft*" to the role of society's guiding light. Wilhelm von Humboldt, the founder of the University of Berlin, saw it as a distinct moral force: "The *Wissenschaft* that stems from inside oneself and can be implanted inside another transforms the character...." Where *Wissenschaft* is pursued for its own sake, a healthy intellectual and spiritual life is assured.[1]

The shift from philosophy to *Wissenschaft* was accompanied by the transformation of the cosmopolitan ideal of humanity into the particularist ideal of the nation. It is Herder who stands directly at the midway point in this process. For him the highest value was still humanity, which he considered the ultimate aim of human nature. Yet he broke radically with the cosmopolitanism of the Enlightenment. Instead of stressing the essential similarity of all men he chose to emphasize the unique qualities which constituted the *Volksgeist* of each nation. Though he was not a chauvinist, Herder's ideal of humanity was mediated by the nation: mankind consisted of nations, not autonomous individuals. His conception represents a transitional stage in the process of transformation, what may be termed a "humanitarian nationalism." [2] With Fichte's *Speeches to the German Nation,* published in 1808, a further step is taken. The individual is submerged in the group; the old Germanic sense of duty is revived. The child must receive a specifically *national* education, not a universal one. The German people is an *Urvolk,* a nation with deep roots in the past which must be made aware of its common heritage and destiny. As the emerging national ideal grows increasingly particularist, the exclusion of

foreign elements from the national organism becomes ever more imperative. As we have seen, by 1815 Rühs, Fries, and others had conceived the
national welfare as incompatible with political and social integration of
the Jew. They had been answered by Jews of a generation raised in the
Enlightenment tradition who either failed to perceive the demise of the
humanitarian ideal or refused to acknowledge it. But now a new generation came of age in these post-war years when nationality, narrowly conceived and bound up with Christianity, had become dominant and when
Wissenschaft was the intellectual ideal. It reached maturity in a climate of
ideas very unlike that which greeted Mendelssohn when he came to Berlin
in 1743. How were the brightest and most sensitive young Jews of this
generation to grapple with the unremitting but changed dilemma of embracing the ideals of this new age while yet remaining loyal to Judaism?

The problems of the new Jewish generation—born in the last decade of
the eighteenth century—are best illustrated through the early life and
associations of one of its most significant representatives: Leopold Zunz.
In the course of some thirty years the young Zunz was exposed to the
Talmudic education of the traditional Jewish school, the pedagogic philosophy of the Maskilim, the purified ritual of the Reform movement, the ideal
of *Wissenschaft,* and the Hegelian philosophy. Out of the struggles of
his youth he finally emerged with a lifelong personal solution: *Wissenschaft des Judentums,* the science of Judaism. To present the intellectual
biography of the young Zunz is to discover reflected in the short span of
one man's youth the forces which shaped Jewish intellectual history in
Germany from the middle of the eighteenth century until well into the
nineteenth. It is to complete the transformation from a Jewish identity
expressed in the philosophical language of the eighteenth century into one
that draws upon the ideals of the nineteenth. And yet, as we shall see,
Zunz and his generation did no more than to replace the ephemeral and
personal solution of Mendelssohn with other solutions equally as fragile.

Zunz was born on August 10, 1794 in Detmold in the central German
principality of Lippe.[3] His traditionally Jewish family had been but
slightly touched by the rays of the Enlightenment. By the time the boy
was five years old he had already learned a Torah portion by heart and
begun to study Talmud. His father, a learned man who taught him Hebrew grammar, Pentateuch, and Judeo-German writing, died before Zunz

reached his eighth birthday. There was soon little choice for the widowed mother but to send her son to a free boarding school and so be relieved of the burden of his support. Thus, in 1803, Zunz entered the Samson Free School in Wolfenbüttel, a dismal *bet ha-midrash* of the most primitive kind.[4] It was then composed of two separate ramshackle buildings, in which walls, beds, and the bodies of students were often infested with vermin. The boys were woefully neglected: baths were unheard of; they washed only because Jewish law demanded it. At one point, Zunz later related, he literally had not a single pair of pants or socks in wearable condition. The institution offered its young pupils an education devoted almost exclusively to Talmud. Fifty years after Mendelssohn met Lessing, a bare four or five hours per week were devoted to secular studies, and the reading of German books was strictly forbidden. Pedagogy and discipline were primitive and crude; the school remained entirely untouched by the progressive influences of the Philanthropin and Pestalozzi. Yet, despite it all, a religious atmosphere prevailed and the students gained an enormous respect and reverence for the Jewish tradition.

One of Zunz's fellow students and close friends at the school was Isaac Marcus Jost, who later became the first Jew of modern times to write a comprehensive Jewish history. Jost relates that the young Zunz already manifested the keen, critical intellect which was to characterize him in later years. In spare hours he absorbed himself in mathematical puzzles; together with Jost, he studied Hebrew grammar and the *Josippon,* a Hebrew digest of Josephus which awakened in them at least a dim sense of history. Zunz's wit likewise appeared early; he wrote a Hebrew satire on the instructors which, regrettably, fell into their hands and was promptly burned. In these early years Zunz undoubtedly developed his ingrained hatred of the traditional Jewish school of which he later wrote: "The human being disappeared in the Jew."[5] But he also laid the foundation for his amazing knowledge of rabbinic literature.

Then, in the spring of 1807, under the new administration of Samuel Meyer Ehrenberg, the institution suddenly leaped out of the Middle Ages into the Haskalah; for Ehrenberg was a man of the stamp of Euchel, Wolfssohn, Fränkel, and that entire circle of Maskilim who sought to adapt the Jew to Western society and preserve Judaism simply as a religion. The school was renovated, the children properly clothed, and the curriculum broadened. Talmud was reduced to a few hours per week to make room for German literature, French, history, and geography. The institution became comparable to those established by the followers of Mendelssohn in Berlin, Breslau, Dessau, and Seesen. On August 22, 1807 Ehrenberg conducted at the school the first Jewish ceremony of confirmation ever to be held. (The thirteen-year-old confirmand was Leopold Zunz.) The ritual was replete with a public oral catechism culminating in the thirteen articles of Maimonides, a blessing by Ehrenberg, and an original Hebrew prayer by the confirmand. Three years later, when Israel Jacobson (who had installed Ehrenberg in his position) dedicated the Jacob's Temple in Seesen, Ehrenberg was present for the occasion, ever after preserving the memory of it as, in Zunz's words, "an oasis in the Jewish history of suffering." [6]

Ehrenberg's principal interest in life was his school. Like the other Maskilim he fervently believed that a proper education of Jewish youth was the greatest task incumbent upon his generation of Jewish leadership. The removal of the odious character traits of the peddler and money-lender—that constant concern with profit which society had dubbed "thinking and acting like a Jew"—seemed to him, an eminently practical man, the first consideration. He later wrote to Zunz: "In my school I feel I am in my proper place. I show my students the path Jews must tread if they want to appear better and more respected among the nations than heretofore." [7]

Ehrenberg's influence on the young Zunz was beneficial and significant. Like so many young men of genius Zunz was frequently morose, ungrateful, and phlegmatic. Ehrenberg tried to curb these tendencies in his prodigy with fatherly love and care, though, as Zunz's later life shows all too clearly, Ehrenberg was unable to subdue entirely the gruff and quarrelsome quality that became part of Zunz's permanent makeup. The pupil preserved a deep affection for his teacher that was expressed in a regular correspondence which lasted until Ehrenberg's death in 1853. But of greater importance for Zunz's intellectual development than the personal relationship with Ehrenberg was the weltanschauung his teacher represented. Ehrenberg opened up new horizons for Zunz, endowed him with respect for reason and a concern for the reform of Jewish life. He made Zunz receptive to the Reform movement as he would shortly encounter it in Berlin and implanted in his student the Haskalah dream of the Jew fully integrated into society, yet without conversion. It was to be a lasting influence on Zunz, one which would distinguish him from those young Jews who saw only negative implications in their Jewish birth. What Ehrenberg did not bequeath to Zunz was the ideal of *Wissenschaft,* to which the older man was never drawn. This stage of Zunz's development would come only in Berlin.

In April of 1809 Zunz completed his studies at the new Samson Free School and was admitted as the first Jewish student to the advanced department of the Wolfenbüttel high school. Concurrently he paid for his continued maintenance at the Samson School by serving as a member of its faculty. In 1811 he graduated from high school and, after a few further years of teaching and private studies in Hebrew literature, English, art, and music, determined to attend the new University of Berlin. In the fall of 1815 he was finally ready to leave Wolfenbüttel behind and travel to the Prussian capital where he would spend nearly all the succeeding years of his long life.

Berlin had undergone considerable change since the time of Mendelssohn. Once the focus of intellectual life during the Enlightenment, its cultural significance had dwindled after the death of Frederick the Great. Göttingen, Weimar, and Jena had become the centers of German classicism and romanticism, while Berlin retained significance only as a center of government, industry, and conviviality. It was not until the University of Berlin was established there in 1810 that the Prussian capital regained its role of intellectual leadership. However, the established Jewish community experienced little of this revival. The approximately three thousand Jews (two percent of the population) who lived in Berlin in 1815 went about their occupations as bankers, dealers in cotton, or pawnbrokers quite as they had before. The upper echelons continued the process of separation from the bulk of Jewry; they retained membership in the Jewish community, perhaps belonged to the Beer Temple, but they sent their children to non-Jewish schools and frequently had them baptized for the sake of their careers. Another portion of the community remained orthodox and opposed every effort at reform. A third segment, the very poor, often fell victim to the allurements of a new proselytizing society which was directed particularly at the uneducated. When Zunz arrived in 1815, the ebullient hopes that animated the Jewish community after the edict of emancipation in 1812 had already begun to settle, and in the years of political reaction that followed, apathy about Judaism and its future reached ever deeper into every corner of the community. They were a motley group as Zunz himself described them:

> Jews who are really Jews,... baptized Jews, enlightened (?) ones who devoutly spent all of Yom Kippur in Jacobson's temple, converts returned to Judaism, proselytes, Jews who are worse anti-Semites than born Christians, indifferentists ...a younger generation which doesn't know what it is, and some truly enlightened Jews—perhaps seven or eight.[8]

Arriving in Berlin, Zunz first visited his relative Ruben Samuel Gumpertz, a well-to-do elder of the Jewish community. Then, establishing himself as tutor in the home of the recently widowed Saisette Hertz,[9] he began a life that moved in two circles, each of which claimed a part of his time and personality. There was first the circle of the Jewish community and especially that branch of it engaged in reform. Prepared by Ehrenberg and highly sympathetic to the reformers' cause, Zunz entered into the internal world of Berlin Jewry, bringing to it his abilities as an educator and his talents as a preacher. At the same time he entered the university, was exposed to entirely new influences, and became associated with a circle of young Jewish friends whose approach to Jewishness differed radically from that of the ritual reformers. Although it would be too much to say that the young Zunz lived a double life in those early Berlin years, his spheres of activity were so different as to warrant taking up each of them separately.

Zunz had reached Berlin only two days before Yom Kippur. Since his relative Gumpertz was one of the leaders of the Reform movement—and undoubtedly also on account of his own desire—Zunz was present in Jacobson's home for services on the Day of Atonement. The experience made a deep impression upon him. Two days later he wrote a glowing report to his teacher Ehrenberg:

> Yesterday, or rather Saturday (the 14th), I spent in Jacobson's synagogue. People who for twenty years have had no close relationship with Jews spent the entire day there. Men who had already believed themselves above religious emotion poured out tears of devotion; the majority of the young people fasted. Of course we have three speakers here who would do honor to even the largest community. Mr. Auerbach expounds with philosophical clarity and inner genuineness; his voice is resonant and soft, his essence is purity. He even pronounces the Hebrew beautifully and is a good Hebrew poet. Kley is lively and audacious; his images arouse the imagination. When he said, "Now let us rise," everyone—although it

was five o'clock in the afternoon—jumped up as if by a stroke of magic. The latter I would compare to Ezekiel, the former to Jeremiah. The third, Günsburg, I
shall hear on the next holiday. Moreover the singing and the music were good;
Dr. Heinroth is bringing us the organ from Seesen.[10]

The "us" in the last sentence is significant. From the first, Zunz identified
himself with the strivings of the reform group, and though his enthusiasm
faltered from time to time, he continued to favor ritual reforms until the
rabbinical conferences of the 1840's.[11] He joined the ranks of Auerbach,
Kley, Salomon, and the others who carried on the reform program of
Friedländer and Jacobson. In almost every respect Zunz's educational and
religious philosophy was indistinguishable from theirs.

In September of 1817 Zunz wrote his first sermon, which he delivered
to a circle of several friends in Berlin. Entitled "On Religiosity," it closely
resembled the other sermons of the period. Like them it steered clear of
Jewish particularism: it summoned its listeners as human beings to a religiously oriented life. Apparently, Zunz was pleased with his effort, for he
thereafter seriously considered making the pulpit his career. When in
June of the following year the reform group in Hamburg was looking for
a preacher, Zunz expressed his interest in the position. To M. I. Bresselau,
one of its directors, he wrote:

> Not only am I generally inclined toward such [a position], but I am so especially
> toward one in Hamburg. There I find leadership by valiant and learned men
> with whom I should gladly work in preparing the way to the great goal we must
> set for ourselves. I would readily sacrifice for the sake of this work the peace and
> freedom which I enjoy as a student and take upon myself, together with the new
> burden, the attention of the world: that attention which always grows when its
> object advances upward, though it does not always make its object any happier.[12]

Despite the willingness Zunz here expressed to forsake the university
for the pulpit, a month later he had decided against competing for the
position, not on account of a loss of interest, but because he did not like
the specific circumstances and because he realized he would probably
not be chosen.[13] During the months following this unsuccessful attempt,
Zunz for the only time in his life seriously considered conversion. On
April 6, 1819 Jost wrote to Ehrenberg: "Baptism is very much on his mind,
although he struggles hard against the idea and does not like to consider
it. He stands too high above his coreligionists to be esteemed or supported
by them." [14] Like the erstwhile leaders of the Westphalian Consistory,
Zunz was dismayed by the reigning anarchy and felt the need for a central

authority to coordinate the process of reform. "So long as there is no authority to sanction the whole thing," he wrote to Ehrenberg, "nothing of consequence will happen. Everybody is his own reformer and makes himself silly. *Until the Talmud is overthrown nothing can be done.*" [15]

Yet at the very time that thoughts of abandoning Judaism were running through his mind, Zunz was putting down on paper a concerted plan for a thoroughgoing political and religious reform of the Jews. The work, entitled *Die Organisation der Israeliten in Deutschland* (*The Organization of the Israelites in Germany*), was commissioned by L. L. Hellwitz of Werl, who then published it in his own name. [16] The booklet is entirely typical of the views which had become characteristic of the Maskilim and religious reformers. It vehemently denounced the rabbis for lack of leadership and insisted that the state not consider them the genuine leaders of the Jewish community. It went on to speak of Judaism as one among the other "confessions" of Germany, and toward the end reiterated the very watchword of Mendelssohn's disciples: "The Israelite is no longer a member of an Israelite nation, rather only of an Israelite faith." [17] Its solution to the Jewish problem in Prussia was hardly novel. The booklet proposed two institutions: a great sanhedrin or Jewish concilium to lay down the guidelines for a religious and educational reformation, and a small sanhedrin or consistory, operating under the government ministry of religion, to carry on the day-to-day work of implementation. It was the old argument that the state must lend its authority and power of coordination to Jewish reform and that, given such reform, the Jew would then prove worthy of full political and social acceptance. There was even the old opposition to the use of the term "Jew" against which Friedländer had fought for so long:

> Since the name Jew is often misused as a derogatory epithet one should refrain from the use of this word in all public deliberations, documents, police lists, etc. Futhermore, the word Jew has never been the proper name of the nation; only a single tribe of the nation was called Judah, and from this arose, through an error of language, the name Jew. [18]

If these passages were all the work of Zunz it would mean that as late as 1819 his views were still entirely those of the older Maskilim. It appears, however, that after nearly four years in Berlin, Zunz's ideas had begun to diverge from those of Hellwitz, Friedländer, and Jacobson.

Shortly after the booklet appeared, Zunz wrote to Ehrenberg that he had reviewed his own work "à la [a missing word] in the *Gesellschafter*," a belletristic Berlin journal.[19] The review was signed only with "—e—." [20] It praised the *Organisation* as outstanding in comparison with the many other works on the subject. But not only did Zunz heap praise upon himself, he also subjected to criticism those few portions of the work which had apparently been forced upon him or added later by Hellwitz himself. Thus Zunz criticizes the booklet for its grandiose scheme of a concilium on the French model and, more importantly, for its rejection of the term "Jew." Indeed, it was the conscious return to the use of this designation rather than "Israelite" which was shortly to symbolize the separation of Zunz and his circle from the older generation. Noteworthy also, in the light of Zunz's scholarly interests, is his insistence in the review that henceforth no one meddle in Jewish affairs without consulting "competent and educated Jews."

But the influence of Ehrenberg and the Haskalah upon Zunz remained in evidence. About a year after the *Organisation* was published, Zunz applied for the position of Jewish teacher of religion in Königsberg. In this connection he outlined, in March of 1820, his principles of Jewish religious education.[21] Like Friedländer, Zunz did not regard extensive knowledge of Hebrew as necessary for every boy; learning the "language of the land," however, he considered essential for all. Instruction in religion was nearly useless, he felt, unless it was coordinated with a synagogue employing German prayers and a German sermon, or at least an improved Hebrew service. He favored confirmations,[22] though along with certain other of the Maskilim, he chose to regard the ceremony as an identification with the totality of Judaism rather than a confession of faith. The aim of Jewish education which he projected was the eradication of ignorance and egotism and the restoration of Jewish honor in the eyes of the nations.

However, Zunz was no more successful in obtaining this position than he had been in his application for the Hamburg preachership two years earlier. On April 4th, the elders of the Königsberg Jewish community, seeking information about Zunz's religious conduct, sent a letter to Meir ben Simcha Weyl, assistant rabbi of the Berlin community. Though Weyl's answer is not extant, in all likelihood it was negative since there is no further mention of Zunz's candidacy.[23] It is well known that until the forties Zunz did not adhere strictly to the ritual law, and it appears that he and Weyl were not on the best of terms.[24] The position was given instead to J. A. Francolm, subsequently the author of moralistic works of Jewish theology.

Failing to obtain a job in Königsberg, Zunz turned his attention to the Beer Temple in Berlin. Through the efforts of his relative Gumpertz, he was allowed to speak there on May 20, 1820. His sermon, on the subject of divine and human mercy, must have been well received since thereafter Zunz was allowed to preach at regular intervals; the proud young man even regarded the event as the beginning of a new age in Jewish history.[25] When the Hamburg temple that same year established a branch in Leipzig for the season of the fair, Zunz was engaged to deliver one of the two dedicatory sermons and to aid in conducting the worship. He made such an impression that a visitor offered him a job as preacher in London if he could give equally good sermons in English. In the flush of personal success—the recognition that he craved all his life and did not receive until near its end—Zunz wrote of the Leipzig services with ardent enthusiasm:

> The effect produced by the celebration, the likes of which has never been seen here before, is indescribable! It is to be compared to a storm which appears suddenly, at first moves about furiously in one spot like a whirlwind and then breaks out and sweeps everything away with it. Polish Jews, pious Jews, Christians, enlightened Jews, foreigners, etc.—nobody was dissatisfied, and with yesterday's and today's postal carriages the word goes out to all parts of Germany. The two dedicatory sermons are to be printed.[26]

Although he did not receive an official paid position at the Beer Temple until the late summer of 1821, Zunz's sermons were quite popular in the Berlin reform circle.[27] The reason was simple: in his sermons, as in his views on religious and educational reform, the young scholar shared the sentiments of his listeners. In almost every respect his views and his style are comparable to those of the other Jewish preachers of this generation. His homiletic talents were well developed, though his eloquence did not match that of his slightly older contemporary, Gotthold Salomon.[28]

In his sermons [29] Zunz addressed himself to the human being, not the Jew; what he preached was religion and morality, not specifically Judaism. In one of them, entitled "Self-Consciousness," he dwelt entirely upon universal moral considerations without regard for a possible specific self-consciousness pertaining to the Jew. Although his sermons—like the others of

the period—evidence some direct or indirect Kantian and romantic influence, they breathe the spirit of Mendelssohnian enlightenment.[30] Under
the aegis of reason all mankind is united: "That, my friends, is the power
of reason! By it we are men, by it we experience all that is glorious and
divine in this life and surmise the bliss of the future; reason it is which
rules the peoples and the world, which lends us dignity, esteem and
strength." [31] The philosophy of the sermons is the philosophy of the pre-
Kantian age: the conviction that God can be proven and the eudaemonism
which sees true happiness (*wahrhafte Glückseligkeit*) as the ultimate goal
of existence. Not unexpectedly, the purpose of the sermons is edification
(*Erbauung*).[32]

From the pulpit Zunz expressed little concern for the preservation of
Judaism. Even where we should certainly have expected it, in a sermon
against conversion entitled "Not to Leave One's Own," [33] he did not argue
that Judaism possessed intrinsic value but only that converts and indif-
ferentists were disloyal to their coreligionists: they withdrew themselves
from the struggle for religious and educational reform. As was the custom
among his colleagues, Zunz refrained from the use of rabbinic materials
—despite the fact that he had already achieved an extraordinary mastery
of the rabbinic literature and was actively engaged in its study. Nor was
his positive evaluation of the ceremonial law as a means to the end of
morality unusual in his day; it was an idea Saul Ascher had put forth
as early as 1792. In fact there is only one element, present in a few of the
Zunz sermons, that would lead us to suspect their author was animated in
part by an ideal different from that of his colleagues: the presence here
and there of the new value, *Wissenschaft*. "From the totality of the nation
or the fellowship (*Genossenschaft*) down to the communities, families
and individuals there is only one and always the same thing which is
worthy and lends dignity: it is the heavenly triad of religion, virtue and
science." [34] Yet Zunz, the preacher, never chose to make *Wissenschaft des
Judentums* (the science of Judaism) the topic of so much as a single sermon.

In view of the unexceptional character of Zunz's sermons and their
close coincidence with the weltanschauung of the circle in which they
were preached, the point of view they expressed cannot explain the brev-
ity of his tenure with the Beer Temple. On September 13, 1822, he re-
signed from the preachership a few weeks after a sermon he delivered

on the "Downfall of the Temple" had caused serious consideration of his dismissal. What Zunz said in this sermon (one of the few not preserved even in manuscript) was apparently nothing to which his listeners could in principle take exception. But he had made the fatal mistake of directing his religious and moral condemnations at individuals within the congregation instead of flattering influential members and voicing criticism only in vague and general terms. The leadership's apathy, inconsistency, and authoritarian control provoked his reproach. To his friend Isaac Noah Mannheimer, later preacher in Vienna, Zunz wrote:

> For two years now I have been preaching here, and not without success. Since September, 1821, I hardly gave a single sermon where I did not mix in some clear or dim allusions to the improvement of the temple, etc. Moreover, I personally made the people aware of malpractices, opposed the senseless liturgical measures they incompetently undertook, etc. I drew up statutes for them and together with Auerbach I suggested changes in the prayers; nothing helped. So, on the 17th of August, I gave a sermon on the Downfall of the Temple which did not spare the [Temple] Commission and which listed the lack of religiosity, the vanity, the arrogance, the pride in worldly possessions as the causes of the downfall.[35]

Though he still believed in reform, Zunz had broken with the Berlin circle because, like many a young idealist, he had been unable to bear the shortcomings of petty, average men.

The following spring Zunz issued in print a selection of the sermons he had given at the Beer Temple. Among those who awaited its publication was his good friend from a different circle, Heinrich Heine, a Jew whose romantic sensibilities had produced an attitude to Judaism far different from that of the older generation. The young poet hoped to find in this volume something more than the rationalistic Judaism of the Friedländer variety. In April of 1823 Heine wrote:

> I expect a great deal from his sermons, which are soon to be published; to be sure no edification and mild plasters for the soul; but something much better: an arousing of strength. It is precisely the last which is missing in Israel. A few chiropodists (Friedländer & Co.) have sought to heal the body of Judaism of its unfortunate *skin* disease by bloodletting, and as a result of their clumsiness and cobweb-like bandages of reason Israel will bleed to death.[36]

But in fact Zunz, the preacher, offered little more to his congregation than Friedländer's "bandages of reason." From the pulpit he provided nothing new, striking, or challenging. He differed from the Berlin circle only in his impatience with the progress of reform as he specifically envisioned it.[37] As reformer, educator, and preacher Zunz would merit little more attention than Isaac Auerbach, his Beer Temple colleague. If we would assess the significance of the young Zunz for the problem of Jewish identity we must turn to Zunz the scholar, the product of the Berlin University, and to that other circle in which he simultaneously moved: the *Verein für Cultur und Wissenschaft der Juden.*

Before the civil emancipation of the Napoleonic age few German Jews, except those studying medicine, had sought a university education. Mendelssohn wrote of his son Joseph: "He has no interest in medicine; and as a Jew he must become either a doctor, a businessman or a beggar." [38] But in the period of French domination and immediately thereafter new avenues seemed to lie open; young Jews flocked to the universities in the hope of gaining positions in government service or public instruction. To be sure, the life of the Jewish student who avowed his birth was not a pleasant one at a time when the concept of the German-Christian state was rapidly gaining dominance, especially in the universities. Some, like Heine when he was in Bonn and Göttingen,[39] preferred to move in Christian circles and insofar as possible to hide their Jewishness. Yet the younger generation was no longer satisfied to follow Mendelssohn's example of autodidaction, as most of the Maskilim had done. Self-study, they felt, produced a spotty type of education which rested more on cleverness than thorough knowledge and which lacked appreciation for proper form in language and behavior. At first the Jewish community leaders, themselves without a systematic education, could not understand why their young men wanted to attend a university. When Jost applied to the Westphalian Consistory for financial aid, he was turned down since there seemed to be no immediate practical value in his plan of studies.[40] But the next few years witnessed a shift in attitude. Israel Jacobson later supported Jost's studies, and Zunz was aided by gifts of books from his relative Gumpertz. The wealthy Jews came to realize that a proportion of Jewish university graduates could do much to break down the persisting stereotype of the Jew as peddler and moneylender. While the Jewish community leaders of Berlin refused to contribute financially to specifically Jewish scholarship, they generously donated funds to support Jewish students at the university.[41]

When Zunz entered the University of Berlin in 1815, it had already drawn to it some of the finest minds in Germany. In philosophy there was the brilliant young romanticist Karl Wilhelm Solger and, beginning in 1818, Hegel; in philology Friedrich August Wolf and August Boeckh; in law Friedrich Carl von Savigny; and in Bible Wilhelm de Wette. Its chancellor was the renowned theologian Schleiermacher. Zunz (who was later complimented for "most praiseworthy diligence" [42]) in his first semester registered for courses in logic (Solger), ancient history (Rühs), Plato's *Republic* (Boeckh), Greek antiquities (F. A. Wolf), and conical sections (Grüson). In succeeding terms he added a further course of lectures in mathematics, one in Arabic, one in Old Testament by de Wette, additional lectures by Boeckh and Wolf, and a course in Roman law by Savigny. Regarding his first semester Zunz recorded, "I leave Solger because he bores me and Rühs because he writes against the Jews. Boeckh instructs me, but F. A. Wolf attracts me." [43]

In judging the influences upon Zunz, these remarks should be taken seriously. He did not have a flair for philosophy; after the initial course by Solger he signed up for no further lectures with him, nor for any with Hegel. Rühs, who earlier in 1815 had published his article opposing Jewish integration, aroused Zunz in 1816 to compose a sarcastic reply—which, however, remained in manuscript.[44] The young Zunz, it appears, had little interest in speculative thought not bound by the strictures of mathematics and was repelled by an instructor whose attitude was inimical to the Jews.

There has been much dispute on the extent of Savigny's influence upon Zunz.[45] That Savigny was personally hostile to the Jews there can be no doubt. He was a member of the exclusivist *christlich-deutsche Tischgesellschaft,* and when Zunz's friend Eduard Gans sought a position on the Berlin faculty of law, he inspired a decision of that faculty to exclude Gans on the dubious grounds that a Jew could not teach canon law.[46] Savigny's anti-Jewish attitude was intimately linked to the viewpoint of the "Historical School" of law which he and K. F. Eichhorn founded in Germany. This school, which grew up in opposition to the French doctrine of natural rights as it was embodied in the Napoleonic Code, proposed the notion that in a healthy legal system—like that of classical Rome—the law exhibits a "gradual, wholly organic development." [47] In keeping with the Romantic movement as a whole (whose basic conceptions the Historical School applied to the field of law), Savigny was particularly interested in the Middle Ages; unlike the rationalists, he regarded this period as a creative epoch which was of particular concern for an understanding of the present.[48] It was perfectly in line with the approach of this school to apply to the contemporary Jew the precedent of his status in the Middle Ages. When the municipal Senate of Frankfurt am Main asked the Berlin law faculty to render an opinion on Jewish emancipation, the response, issued in 1818, pointed out that Jews in Germany historically had been foreigners and serfs of the Emperor and that legislation dating back to 1616 was still applicable.[49]

Zunz could hardly share Savigny's fondness for the Middle Ages; his own liberalism, his awareness of the extent of Jewish suffering in that period, and his hatred for the remnants of medievalism in Judaism prevented him from accepting Savigny's positive valuation. Zunz—and here we must remember his connections with reform—was not interested in preserving medieval institutions, but in overthrowing them. Although he shared Savigny's interest in the past, the young Zunz did not see it as a model for the present.

The greatest intellectual influence upon Zunz—as he himself indicated—came from the philologist Friedrich August Wolf, and to a lesser extent from Wolf's disciple, August Boeckh. In 1795 Wolf's *Prolegomena to Homer,* in which he proved that Homer's work was a composite of several authors, had launched the critical scholarship of the nineteenth century.[50] By 1811, Barthold Niebuhr, himself a pioneer of critical research, could report:

Philological studies in Germany during the last years have gained a momentum unknown to the most famous philologists and schools of earlier times. Strict interpretation and careful grammar are combined with inquiring research into the total scientific knowledge and opinions of the ancients as well as their history and institutions.

And Niebuhr thought the University of Berlin excelled all other universities of Germany in philological studies.[51]

Both Wolf and Boeckh conceived the discipline of philology in the broadest terms. It was not the study of antiquity only, or merely linguistics; it consisted of the critical examination of the language and literature of every people in every age: ancient, medieval, and modern. Boeckh defined it almost universally as the task of "recognizing and representing the entirety of available human knowledge." [52] It differed from history—as history was then defined—in that it was not principally concerned with political events. From these two giants of *Wissenschaft* Zunz learned philology and was inspired by its goals. Within a few years his love of the subject displaced an early inclination for mathematics, and philology became his principal interest. In fact the young Zunz is best understood, I believe, not as a philosopher or historian (though there are in his works some philosophical elements and indications of historical conceptualization) but as a *philologist*.[53]

Although by the time Zunz began his studies with him, Wolf was already a crabbed, disgruntled man whose lectures were no longer very popular,[54] his thoroughness and method still attracted the more talented and serious students. Politically he was—like Niebuhr and Boeckh—among those whom Zunz considered as not prejudiced against the Jews. The young Zunz came to regard this scholar, who espoused a sober empiricism that would have nothing to do with romanticizations,[55] as "one of the greatest men." He gradually came to see it as his life's task to create a Jewish philology utilizing the principles and methods of modern scholarship. He was not interested in the political history of the Jews, a centuries-long account of suffering which might have been that of any other people, but in their literary history, their creativity.[56] Much effort was being devoted to the Bible, but the Jewish creativity of the Middle Ages remained a virgin field, almost entirely unexplored by critical research. In this area he could make a basic, pioneering contribution.

Gathering together the results of his rabbinic studies, Zunz, in May of 1818, published a fifty-page pamphlet entitled *Etwas über die rabbinische Litteratur (On Rabbinic Literature)*.[57] Its inspiration was the ideal of *Wissenschaft* with which he was now imbued. In the preface he marked it as his principal concern and referred to it repeatedly throughout the work. The young scholar was disturbed that while science in general was making great advances, the science dealing with Jewish creativity found few partisans. He deplored its neglect: "How is it," he asks, "that our science alone is languishing?" Immediate effort must be devoted to it, lest a vast corpus of literature fall into oblivion. The present age—which Zunz regards as the close of the rabbinic period—provides a unique opportunity for gathering and ordering the material at a time when sources and requisite knowledge are still abundant.

> Just because we see the Jews in our day—only to consider the German ones—reaching for German language and German culture with greater seriousness and so—perhaps often without wanting it or suspecting it—carrying post-Biblical Hebrew literature to its grave, for that very reason science appears and demands an accounting from that which is closed.

Zunz proceeds to a topical survey of the medieval Hebrew literature, tossing out suggestions and questions, pointing to particular areas in special need of research, and trying to stimulate interest. Toward the end, he returns to the universal ideal of science espoused in the beginning. Ultimately the study of Jewish literature is to be seen as a contribution to the understanding of mankind: "Thus every historical datum, which diligence has discovered, acuteness deciphered, philosophy utilized and taste put in its proper place, becomes a contribution to the knowledge of man, which is the most worthy goal of all research."

While Zunz thus places Jewish studies under the aegis of *Wissenschaft,* he appears unwilling to let the scientific ideal exhaust his purposes. To be sure he dissociates himself from the approach of the Maskilim to this literature which was either to condemn it out of hand or search about in it for fragments that were presentable.[58] He states explicitly: "Here we are setting up the whole of Jewish literature in its fullest compass as an *object of research,* without worrying whether the total contents should be or can be also a *norm for our own judgments.*" Yet, while he rejects the spirit of the rabbinic literature as a guide for his own day and realizes that as a scientist he may not distort the genuine image even if it be unpleasant, Zunz is too much concerned with the present to be satisfied with a pure historicism. He notes that there is a practical reason as well for encouraging this study: his conviction that only a scientific approach to the Jewish past can result in a fair estimate of the nature of Judaism and of the Jew. Such an appraisal, Zunz confidently believes, would in turn produce intelligent efforts at political and religious reform. Scientific research will make it possible "to know and distinguish the old which is still of use, the antiquated which has become pernicious and the new which is desirable...."[59] Moreover, Zunz recognizes the value that an objective study would have for the literary and ethical gems it would yield. He would like to remove the prejudice with which the rabbinic literature—he prefers to call it neo-Hebraic or Jewish literature—is treated; even in the *Zohar*, the chief product of Jewish mysticism, he claims there is "many a kernel of gold."

Zunz also realizes that the configuration of the present is shaped by preceding centuries, but he does not speak of an evolution of the present out of the past or of any natural connection between the rabbinic age and the contemporary strivings for religious reform. Such terms as "development" (*Entwicklung*) and "organic" (*organisch*), though used by his teacher, Wolf, and later by Zunz himself, are notably absent here. For all of its concern with the present and future, this first document of *Wissenschaft des Judentums* already clearly displays the feature that was to characterize the early phase of the movement and differentiate it from previous Jewish learning: the assumption of a stand outside of and vis-à-vis the tradition instead of within it, approaching it with the discerning but cold eye of the scientist.[60]

On November 21, 1816, Zunz, the university student, had joined a group of young men motivated by the ideal of science to form a "Scientific Circle" (*Wissenschaftszirkel*) in which the members alternately gave lectures. It was a kind of general cultural organization, possibly modeled after similar Berlin discussion circles.[61] Although they were all Jewish, only one member, Joseph Hillmar, spoke to the group on a subject related to Judaism; even Zunz's three lectures, judging by their titles, dealt with matters of general interest.[62] These young Jews, who came together not particularly as Jews but as intellectuals, as yet felt no need for an organization with a specifically Jewish purpose. After an existence of somewhat less than a year the group broke up, its last meeting taking place on July 3, 1817.

But then two years later, in the wake of increased political reaction and the riots of 1819, seven young men, most of whom had been members of the Circle, held a meeting in the home of Joel Abraham List. Deeply concerned about the course of events, they undertook the ambitious task of trying to relate the new nineteenth-century ideals specifically to the problematic status of the Jew. The initiative came from a brilliant, personable and dynamic jurist, only twenty-one years of age: Eduard Gans.[63]

Unlike Zunz, Gans was born into a wealthy Berlin family and enjoyed all the comforts and social pleasures of Berlin Jewry's upper class. He received the finest secular education, and until his father died in 1813, was troubled by no financial cares. In 1816 he began his studies at the University of Berlin, later moved to Göttingen and in 1818 to Heidelberg where he came under the influence of the philosopher Hegel and the jurist Thibaut. As early as 1817, he clashed with a representative of political romanticism when Friedrich Rühs defamed his late father as a usurer. The nineteen-year-old Gans replied with a letter and article inserted at his own expense in the same newspaper that had printed Rühs's attack. He charged that the Berlin professor wanted only to connect usury with Jews.[64]

Hegel, Gans's mentor in Heidelberg, was very different from Rühs in his attitude toward the Jews. Although he attributed no great value to Judaism, he was an advocate of complete Jewish emancipation; his disciples at Heidelberg led the drive to admit Jews to the local branch of the *Burschenschaft*.[65] In his *Philosophy of Right* (1821), based on lectures given at Heidelberg, Hegel argued in favor of civil rights for the Jews, with a two-fold justification: prudence ("to exclude them is the silliest folly") and humanity ("they are, above all, *men*").[66] When Gans returned to Berlin from Heidelberg in the fall of 1819, he was philosophically an Hegelian, determined to apply Hegel's insights to his own chosen field of law. He also met again with his old Jewish friends from the *Wissenschaftszirkel* and spurred this young intellectual elite to consider what, as men of modern cultural outlook, being Jewish might still mean for them.

The seven who gathered that November of 1819 to form a new association, a *Verein,* were—aside from Gans and Zunz—Moses Moser, the close friend of Heine who later dubbed him "the soul of the *Verein*"; Isaac Marcus Jost, then already started on his *History of the Israelites;* Isaac Levin Auerbach, preacher at the Beer Temple; Joel List, a slightly older man who in 1821 broke with the *Verein* on account of a dispute with Gans; and Joseph Hillmar, who at first took over the job of president but later relinquished it to List and dropped out of the group.

The problem before these young men at that first meeting was the same one encountered by Mendelssohn and later by the Maskilim: what is it that makes one a Jew? But they were both too divorced from Jewish practice to answer with Mendelssohn "the ceremonial law" and too conscious of history to answer with the Maskilim "our religious confession."

They had to create for themselves a new justification for being Jewish that would be as much in keeping with the intellectual climate of the nineteenth century as Mendelssohn's was with the eighteenth. Spurning the alternative of conversion, they sought to forge an ideology of Judaism for the intellectual, whom birth, emotion, and rejection by society bound to the Jewish community.

Two of those present, List and Moser, read proposals of purpose to the group. List posed the question which must have been on all their minds in view of the disabilities associated with being a Jew and the chaos of a fragmented, uncertain Judaism: "Why a stubborn persistence in something which I do not respect and on account of which I suffer so much?" [67] Since the exile from Palestine the Jews had held together in the face of persecution like the inhabitants of a beleaguered fortress, placing their trust in the God of Israel. But the Enlightenment and increasing political emancipation changed that. New goals individualized and atomized a growing percentage of the Jewish community. Human aspirations took the place of Jewish ones; the bond of religion broke because Judaism commanded strict adherence to the ceremonial law. What was left? List's reply to this question is significant because it vividly sets the *Verein* apart from the Maskilim and reformers. From this maelstrom of conflicting identities there arises neither a purified religion nor a drive for political equality, but a primal consciousness that Judaism is an inseparable part of one's being. The romantic idea of individual existence through the group finds expression in List's formulation:

We thus have a clear idea of our existence, and indeed of our communal existence, for otherwise we would no longer be ourselves and therefore nothing at all. But now it is most characteristic of an idea that what is necessary within it is also possible and the possible also necessary. If we feel the inner necessity of our continued existence, then its inner possibility is undeniable. And, my friends, do we not ourselves constitute the most irrefutable proof of this truth? But what is true of us here must also be true of thousands of our fellow Jews. So we would have, then, a true idea of our inner unity; to spread it or make it outwardly possible shall be our striving and the ultimate goal of our *Verein*.

Not only is List's point of departure in Jewish self-consciousness rather than theology a radical change from the Haskalah, but so also is the content with which that consciousness is filled: the essence of Judaism is not religion, but something which List calls "nationality." Unlike the generations of Friedländer, Ascher, and Fränkel the *Verein* replied to the romanticists' insistence that the Jews were a people by the affirmation that they were one indeed. Their problem was to discover what it meant. Certainly it was not a nationa*lism* in the modern sense of the word: they considered themselves no less German patriots than the Maskilim. What they felt was a kind of *Volkstümlichkeit* which they did not want to hide. List put it this way:

> Still, my friends, we feel and recognize that that which is peculiar to our nation, our pure nationality, is not a mere product of time, not a passing phenomenon. ... As Jews our national worth must be more important to us than anything else, otherwise letting ourselves be called Jews isn't worth a straw.

But what made up the "felt" peoplehood which List—probably under the influence of Herder—wanted to preserve for the Jew? He has no answer and can only suggest that each member bring to the next meeting "a kind of sketch of our *Volkstümlichkeit.*"

Moser's speech [68] lacks the depth of List's. Its central concept is Jewish *culture,* which for Moser encompasses both religion and folkways. He considers it the purpose of the *Verein* to effect a harmony between this culture and the European. Such a reconciliation is to be distinguished from an abdication of Jewish culture, which in practice would mean conversion to Christianity. He chooses to see it as an advance toward the ideal of humanity, as that ideal is now conceived, not as a uniformity but as a harmony of cultures. The *Verein* must discover the cultural content of Judaism and to this end a thorough study of Bible and Talmud should be undertaken, sifting out the precious metal from the sand. On the basis of these discoveries, Moser hopes, an acceptable justification for the preservation of national unity (*Nationaleinheit*) can be erected. He thus looks to a program of scientific Jewish research to determine an essence of Judaism. Like List, he has no answers himself.

Succeeding meetings produced further plans and ideas, but it was not until 1821 that a name for the *Verein* was finally chosen and its statutes promulgated. Zunz's five suggestions for a name—only one of which would have marked the organization as Jewish—were rejected in favor of Gans's proposal: *Verein für Cultur und Wissenschaft der Juden* (Society for Culture and Science among/of the Jews).[69] In the course of this discussion the phrase *Wissenschaft des Judentums* occurred for the first time— also in a proposal by Gans, who earlier that year had taken over the presidency.[70] The purpose of the *Verein,* as finally stated in the first paragraphs of its statutes, was much more practical and less philosophical than the formulations of List and Moser or, as we shall see, the speeches of Gans. The combined work of Gans, Moser, and Zunz,[71] the statutes suggested that the more educated Jews had a responsibility to help overcome the incongruity between Jewish life as it then existed and the European world. To this end, scientific and educational efforts from above were to join with vocational redirection from beneath "gradually to vanquish every peculiarity that resisted the totality."[72] From the desire to formulate a philosophically acceptable Jewish *Volkstümlichkeit* in List's speech three years earlier the emphasis here had shifted to the means of overcoming Jewish peculiarities not consistent with the whole of European culture. The goals of the *Verein,* as formulated in the statutes, were no longer very different from those of the Maskilim.

The ideology of the *Verein* received its most eloquent and interesting expression in the three presidential reports rendered by its new president, Eduard Gans.[73] In nearly every paragraph they manifest the Hegelian philosophy which inspired many of the *Verein*'s members—though not Zunz. The *Verein,* as Gans conceives it, is a group of intellectuals spiritually and doctrinally alienated from the Jewish community; yet birth, relations, upbringing, friendships, and childhood memories tie them to their fellow Jews. Since they constitute the most advanced element in the community, they must accept the humanitarian obligation of bringing their lagging brethren up to their own point of cultural awareness. The problematic character of identification with the Jewish group could be eased by engaging in the noble endeavor of raising that group to a higher level and going about this task with scientific clarity. Gans was able to conclude his first report on a rousing, messianic note:

> Arise you who set science, the love of your own people, and benevolence above all else; arise, attach yourselves to this noble *Verein,* and see breaking forth in the strong fraternal union of such good men the messianic age, of which the prophets spoke, and which only the persistent corruption of the race has made a fable.[74]

Because Gans conceived the operation of history in accordance with Hegel's dialectical process, he was able to approach the question of Jewish status in Europe in a fresh way. While the Maskilim railed at the political reaction and decried it as a step backward from the Enlightenment, Gans could see it as part of history's necessary course. He could recognize the futility of the older generation's endeavor to prove their good qualities against their attackers. For Gans the romantic reaction and its Jew-hatred was in larger perspective simply a necessary response to the one-sidedness of the Enlightenment; in its turn it would produce the new form of a culturally integrated, but not monolithic Europe. Moreover, modern Jewish history had been undergoing its own inner dialectic. Haskalah provided orthodoxy with a reaction which went too far on the side of atomization, producing the need for a "return," a revival of fervor combined with increased depth:

> It is well enough known and not strange to the members gathered here or to any of those absent that about fifty years ago the light of better culture went out from Berlin to the German Jews; its partly beneficent results are still noticeable today. The bad mixture of a half oriental, half medieval life was dissolved; the dawn of a better education dispelled a completely alien culture; the previous assertion of a harsh total isolation gave way to inclination in a more universal direction. This break in the hitherto solid texture of Jewish life, which began especially with Mendelssohn and was then propagated by his disciples and followers, had the inevitable effect that those who left behind the solidity and intimacy of the community tried to stand only on their own. This constitutes the complete negation of the earlier condition and in fact is only of negative value. This standing on one's own—which, if one follows it further, makes up the character of that entire age, or the essence of the so-called *Aufklärung*—was just as necessary as it was beneficial. The subjective Spirit, freed of its fetters, had long to persist in the individual in his detachment and his negative condition in order to gain that strength which could move him to a voluntary return, not a forced one. This return is what matters. . . . The break with the intimacy (*Innigkeit*) of the old existence has indeed occurred, but the deeper return to this intimacy has not taken place. The enthusiasm for religion and the genuineness of the old relationships has vanished, but no new enthusiasm has broken forth, no new set of relationships has been built. We stuck fast in that negative *Aufklärung* which consisted of scorn and disdain for the traditional without taking pains to give that empty abstraction another content.[75]

The later Maskilim still spoke of "true *Aufklärung*"; Gans is clearly post-*Aufklärung*. His summons to "return," delivered in this last speech, is the call for a new synthesis.

The nature of Gans's proposed synthesis, however, remains most elusive. What is to be the content with which the "empty abstraction" of the Enlightenment can be filled? Instead of providing a clear answer, Gans chooses to dwell upon the past and future role of the Jews in relation to the larger scheme of European history. He sees Europe as a multiplicity whose unity lies only in the totality: it is a multi-limbed organism, each member possessing its own particular life, yet living only in the organic whole. Jewish history stands in stark contrast to this image of integration. It shows a people excluded by others and themselves exclusive, a history running parallel to world history but not a part of it. That course must now come to an end, not because it is the wish of the enlightened or because humanitarian principles demand it, but because the concept of Europe demands it, because history inexorably insists upon it, because it is the "impulse of the age." The Maskilim had argued for Jewish integration into *society;* Gans argues for a necessary Jewish re-integration into the course of *history*.

It was this process of re-integration which Gans described in the vague language of metaphor. He conceived it first as a total embodiment (*einverleiben*) of the Jews in Europe, then as a merging (*aufgehen*) of the Jewish world in the European—which, however, was not equivalent to extinction (*untergehen*). Gans could not wholly elude the point of view of his master Hegel that Judaism represents a single stage in the development of the human spirit but that the stage of independent existence is long past; that for it to persist beyond its day is an anachronism. Judaism's contribution is already contained in Europe. As Hegel put it, "The stages which the Spirit seems to have left behind it, it still possesses in the depths of its present." [76] The people must then rejoin its idea which long ago became part of the European fabric. For Gans this means a third way between total destruction of individuality and obvious distinctiveness. Echoing Hegel he says: "That is the consoling lesson of history well-understood: that everything passes away without disappearing and that everything persists when it has long been consigned to the past." His conclusion for Judaism is the often cited perplexing simile: "Therefore neither can the Jews perish nor can Judaism dissolve; but in the great movement of the whole it shall seem to have perished and yet live on as the current lives on in the ocean." [77]

It is incumbent upon the *Verein* to speed up this process of history. The members are to become what Hegel termed "world-historical men," [78] the clear-sighted ones who stand in advance of the masses because they recognize and will the course of events. To this end—the more rapid Europeanization of Jewry—the *Verein* was to be ultimately directed. Gans never did define what it was that made a Jew different or, in his terms, what made the Jewish limb of Europe different from any of the others. What he defined was the process of history as he thought it applied to the Jews of his day. In its ideology the *Verein* was no more and no less intent upon acculturation than the circles of the Maskilim and reformers—the process was simply ideologized in terms of history rather than eternal verities. The philosophy of the *Verein* gave no more basis for the preservation of the mute Jewish consciousness which all of its members felt than did the vapid rationalism of Friedländer. In the pronouncements of its president—and it would seem in its general orientation—the *Verein* lived very much in the shadow of Hegel, and in that shadow Jewish self-consciousness was destined to merge into the all-encompassing consciousness of the self as European.

The *Verein* engaged in various activities which included education and rehabilitation of the Jewish community as well as scientific pursuits. To the former category belongs the school which members of the *Verein* conducted for Jewish boys—many of them from Poland—who sought an education in Berlin but lacked the prerequisites for entry into public institutions; also certain unrealized projects for vocational training. To the latter belongs the Scientific Institute, formed from only a portion of the membership and dedicated to an objective treatment of Jewish subjects on the model of the earlier *Wissenschaftszirkel*. There was also an archives of modern Jewry, consisting of reports from members outside Berlin, and a small library of Judaica. The periodical of the *Verein,* the *Zeitschrift für die Wissenschaft des Judentums,* was intended both to be a scientific journal and to take into account the needs of the people.

For a time the *Verein* grew steadily. Its regular Berlin membership reached approximately fifteen and there were an additional twenty or so members in a branch of the organization in Hamburg.[79] It was the policy of the *Verein* to bestow membership upon outstanding Jewish leaders of the previous generation. Thus Friedländer, Bendavid, Jacobson, and Ehrenberg all were made regular or honorary members—as was Mordecai Manuel Noah in America. The *Verein* thought of itself as an elite group called upon to perform an historic task of which the humdrum Jewish community leadership was incapable. Such an attitude was bound to produce opposite effects on differing temperaments, a phenomenon we can observe most clearly in the examples of Marcus Jost and Heinrich Heine.

Isaac Marcus Jost, Zunz's schoolmate in Wolfenbüttel, had come to Berlin in 1814 to continue studies begun in Göttingen. In 1816 he became the principal of a modern Jewish school and later was one of the founding members of the *Verein*. Though a man of considerable intellectual ability, he lacked the genius of Zunz and the dynamism of Gans. In temperament he was a figure of the Enlightenment. He was a schoolmaster with a sober, practical outlook on life who eschewed wild notions and sought to avoid controversy wherever possible. In 1818 he began to write his multi-volumed *History of the Israelites,* which appeared from 1820 onward. The work was written in simple language in the hope that the unlettered Jew as well as the Christian statesman and scholar would read it. It was apologetic in character and possessed a definite rationalist bias. Unlike the *Verein,* Jost preferred to utilize the word *Israeliten* rather than *Juden,* offering a weak historical argument in justification.[80] He differed from the Maskilim only in finding history rather than debate the best tool of apologetics. In his introduction Jost says: "It is time to close the files on the value or lack of value of the Jews and Judaism and to begin an investigation of the phenomenon itself according to its origin and its development in order to apprehend its essence and, if it be found desirable, to change it." [81]

Jost did not regard the Jews as a "people" since they lacked the essential condition of a homeland. Estranged from religious practice, he saw the only purpose of Jewish leadership in occupational rehabilitation and humanization of the Jewish community. He frankly held no hope for the preservation of Judaism, and was not particularly concerned:

> If the Jews constituted a *people,* possessed land, put their weight into the scale of nations, in short made up a community through patriotism, a constitution and property, like the *Greeks* of today—it would be a different story. But under the circumstances, our efforts for the preservation of peculiarity are fruitless and perhaps they are harmful. Only this much may we wish: to lead human beings, debased through centuries filled with sufferings, back to humanity; to obtain a better mode of life for them and give their spirit a different direction, regardless of the result. That let us strive to achieve with all our might.[82]

The heady visions of the *Verein,* its willingness to clash with the established community leadership, and its ideal of pure *Wissenschaft* were completely out of keeping with Jost's temperament and philosophy.

In a discussion held by the *Verein* on its projected journal early in 1821, Jost argued against Zunz that grammatical studies of the Bible should not be included.[83] Pure philology, Jost apparently realized, would have little appeal to the average reader. Not long thereafter, on May 14, 1821, Jost left the *Verein*. Writing about the organization later to Ehrenberg, perhaps with some bitterness, he presented the *Verein* in a light in which it must have appeared to many Jews of the time:

> It is a product of the most wanton conceit and the most foolish arrogance: a few young men imagine themselves sufficiently eminent to change an entire nation, which they don't even know. The activities are similar to the foundation. The boastful, ridiculous statutes, the childish censoriousness of all that exists and the senseless journal bear witness to it. A good cause must be pursued with modesty, and young men who want to contribute to it should seek out a sober path, not regard themselves as so great at the very beginning that they *honor* the greatest men among their contemporaries by sending them *certificates of membership.*[84]

Yet this very audacity, the great expectations, the arrogant assertions of a new nineteenth-century Jewish intellectual elite—which repelled Jost—were precisely what attracted the very different Heinrich Heine.

On Gans's suggestion the *Verein* had accepted Heine as a member on August 4, 1822, and until he left Berlin the following May, he participated in its activities. He attended the meetings regularly, was in charge of a project to form a women's auxilliary (which however he did not carry out), and taught history three hours per week in the *Verein*'s school.[85] After he left Berlin he continued to be interested in the *Verein* and pressed his friend Moses Moser for information about it. Still in 1827, long after Heine had converted and the *Verein* been dissolved, he honored the rule that every member must send copies of his works to the *Verein*'s library. He sent his *Buch der Lieder* to Berlin inscribed: "To Dr. Zunz, librarian of the *Verein,* the author sends this book to be placed in the library in accordance with his obligation." [86]

Among the prominent members of the *Verein,* Heine was the only one who was truly a romantic. Like Rahel he reveled in the spiritual anguish which heightened the poignancy of sensation. Like her he appreciated the aloofness of the pariah and saw in it the essence of freedom.[87] Heine's first commitment was always to his own individuality not to any ideal construction, be it religious, philosophic or political. As he himself wrote to Moser: "Heine will and must always be Heine." [88] In Berlin he went about elegantly dressed, visited the finest cafes, and gained entry to the most sophisticated and influential circles; he was a frequent guest in the Varnhagen salon where he developed an admiration of Rahel bordering upon worship. He attended Hegel's lectures at the university, but unlike Gans and Moser did not become a disciple. Above all else Heine was an artist,[89] an aesthete who admitted that Lord Byron was the only man with whom he felt a relation of kinship.[90] From the vantage point of the artist the petty strivings of all masses become an object of scorn: "Oh how I despise the rabble of humanity," he wrote, "the circumcized along with those who are not." [91]

Heine had no love for the average Jews as he encountered them on the streets of Hamburg; they offended his sensibilities. Nor could the Reform movement appeal to him, since it was so much an imitation of the despised Christianity, lacked real spirit, and appeared an obvious remnant of out-dated Enlightenment thought. But the *Verein* attracted him, precisely because it was not mundane, not the old *Aufklärerei*. It consisted of a group of bright young men in contact with the intellectual currents of the age who felt they possessed a responsibility to their backward brethren. Such a group was noble, even heroic. As Heine said later, they possessed "a lofty, great, though unrealizable idea." [92] He found that he could identify with the type of Jew represented by many of the members of the *Verein,* and he gained a boundless respect for Zunz and Moser, a respect he retained long afterwards.

Because he was not a rationalist Heine could sense that Jewish identity was not a readily definable thing, that what made an individual decide to remain Jewish in spite of pressures to conversion could not be put in religious or philosophical terms. Simple emotions and traditions (eating *kugel*) knit the Jewish community together, not ideas. As a romanticist Heine looked to the Jewish past for the kind of spiritual greatness which Novalis tried to find in medieval Christendom. In his *Rabbi of Bacharach* the young Heine romanticized the Jewish Middle Ages, lending artistic form to a mode of life which in its contemporary expression repelled him for its pettiness.

After his opportunistic conversion in 1825, Heine frequently regretted the step, not because he loved Judaism or believed in its preservation, but because he felt he had betrayed himself. In leaving Judaism he had performed an ignoble act, an act of cowardice. Heine, who frequently fought duels to protect his honor, had besmirched it himself. He was ashamed to tell Moser about this compromise of his valued integrity and hoped that his friend would not condone it. Through the years Heine could not entirely rid himself of the notion that Zunz and Moser, in choosing to remain Jewish, had acted more nobly than he.

The examples of Jost, the *Aufklärungsmensch,* and Heine, the romantic, show the *Verein* as from two wings of a stage. Both of them had their essential being outside the organization, one in his work of apologetics and acculturation, the other in the depths of his poetic sensitivity. By the time Heine left Berlin in the spring of 1823, the *Verein* was already, in Gans's words, "in a state of complete dissolution." [93] It dragged on into February of 1824 before the meetings were finally suspended. With the exception of the school, its practical accomplishments in the four years of its existence were minor: mostly plans imperfectly carried out or barely conceived. Its single great achievement—to which we must now turn— was the conception and first realization of a *Wissenschaft des Judentums.* "The esoteric purpose of the *Verein,*" as Heine put it, "was none other than a reconciliation of historical Judaism with the modern science which, one supposed, in the course of time would gain world dominion." [94]

In two lectures given in the Scientific Institute of the *Verein,* Immanuel Wolf (afterwards Wohlwill) addressed himself to the problem of defining such a science of Judaism. Later his ideas were formulated into a program which opened the first issue of the *Verein's* journal.[95] Like Gans, Wolf was inspired by Hegel, and the program clearly shows the great philosopher's influence; but unlike the Gans speeches, the Wolf program reintroduces Zunz's ideal of *Wissenschaft* as the summit of values.

By "Judaism" Wolf means above all else a single dominant religious idea which constitutes its essence. He defines it as the idea of the unconditional unity of all being in eternity, which is symbolized by the Hebrew Tetragrammaton. The Jewish people became the bearers of this spiritual principle and communicated it to the world; though a particular people, they possessed a universal idea. In keeping with the Hegelian philosophy, Wolf saw this idea as itself struggling and developing within the nation that bore it. Jewish history thus became primarily a history of Judaism, namely of its basic principle; the empirical history of the Jewish people was reduced to secondary importance. In the Roman Empire this idea, which had developed to a certain point within a relatively isolated little nation, found a vast domain for further expansion. Through the dying Empire the universal idea, in the shape of Christianity, gained universal diffusion.

For Hegel Jewish history in a spiritual sense ended here—with the rise of Christianity. But Wolf will allow the development and transmission of the idea to the world to represent only one stage of Jewish history: the political Jewish state. That state collapsed, having fulfilled its mission, but Judaism did not. The Jewish people continued to preserve the idea in its midst and modify it to meet changing circumstances. Yet the isolation and unique mode of life of the Jews in the Middle Ages often hid the inner idea. Not until Spinoza was Judaism's fundamental idea of unity revealed again in all of its purity. Centuries ahead of his time, yet closer to the spirit of Judaism than the rabbis, Spinoza understood its idea for the first time *reinwissenschaftlich*,[96] in the manner of pure science.

Wolf argues that because Judaism has played such a significant role in the progress of the Spirit and because it is still acknowledged by millions of Jews, it is therefore highly deserving of a special science. The task of such a science would be to interpret the documents of Jewish history and literature and to seek out Judaism's still living principle. Wolf stresses that it must treat its object for its own sake and not for any ulterior purpose. Only as such can it be both worthy and beneficial:

> It begins with no preconceived notion and is not concerned with the end result. It does not try to set its object in either a favorable or an unfavorable light in relation to prevailing opinions; rather it shows its object the way it is. Science is sufficient unto itself, is itself an essential requirement of the human spirit. It therefore needs to serve no purpose outside its own. But it remains no less true that every science exercises the most significant influence, not only upon other sciences, but also upon life....[97]

The most important influence the science of Judaism might have upon life would be the determination of whether or not Jews were fit for citizenship. Separating the essential from the accidental in a scientific manner would lend impartiality to a heated issue, beclouded by passions and prejudice. But as in Zunz's essay on rabbinic literature, so here too emancipation is not the central concern, and even less so religious reform. What lies at the heart of early *Wissenschaft des Judentums,* as defined in this program, is the desire to bring Judaism under the aegis of science, to make it respectable by bringing it into the light of *Wissenschaft*. Wolf's highest value is not Judaism as it then exists (it long since allowed the world to share its idea) but the great ideal of science which unites all men. Here are Wolf's closing sentences:

> The scientific attitude is the characteristic attitude of our time. But since the formation of a science of Judaism is an *essential need* of the Jews themselves, it is clear that Jews especially are *called* to its cultivation, even though the field of sciences is the common ground of all men. The Jews must again prove themselves as vigorous fellow-workers in the common task of mankind; they must raise themselves and their principle to the standpoint of science, for that is the standpoint of *European life*. On this level, the relation of strangeness in which Jews and Judaism until now stood to the outside world must vanish. If there is ever to be a bond which will embrace all humanity, it will be *the bond of science, the bond of pure rationality, the bond of truth*.[98]

The *Zeitschrift*, which opened with such a program, was radically different from previous Jewish periodicals. It was dedicated to no wealthy benefactors, bore no copper engravings, and carried no column of news items. There were no edifying stories, parables, or poetry. It considered itself above catering to the wealthy and it had no interest in the minutiae of daily life. Zunz, the editor, wrote in preface to the third issue: "Science can be neither obsequious and elegant just to please those in high places nor can it lower itself with anxious concern to the petty needs of the day." [99] It was not intended to educate and acculturate as were *Ha-Measef* and *Sulamith,* but rather to gain respect for Judaism in an intellectual milieu where science was the reigning value. It was self-consciously post-Haskalah: not enlightenment but science was to bind together the Jewish community and tie it to intellectual Europe. Zunz wrote: "We now have enough of educational tools. Only through science can we obtain for Judaism the status and appreciation which it deserves and gradually arouse and unite all the better forces in Israel. The *Zeitschrift* will maintain itself strictly on this level...." [100]

The difficulty with so scientific a Jewish periodical was that it could find no readership. Ehrenberg tried to sell subscriptions to Jews in Brunswick, but with little success. There were few Jews who could understand these articles which contained untranslated quotations in Greek and Latin and were for the most part written in highly abstract language and infelicitous style. According to Ehrenberg, people told him quite frankly that it was too learned for them, and he was forced to agree.[101] Even

Heine, who himself for a time was planning to contribute, criticized the *Zeitschrift* for its lack of form and argued that since *he* was unable to understand some of the articles, certainly the average Jew would not comprehend them at all.[102] And, indeed, who should have read the *Zeitschrift?* The traditional Jew had no interest in a scientific approach to the Jewish literature, while the acculturated Jew might have appreciated science but did not care for the subject matter.

Of the sixteen articles, contained in three issues, only a few can claim our attention. Friedländer and Bendavid of the older generation both made contributions rather out of keeping with the tone of the periodical. The articles of Gans are concerned with the legal status of the Jew in Roman law, the history of the Jews in England, and the Jewish law of inheritance. Unlike Wolf, Gans conceives the history of the Jewish spirit as a totally passive process of adaptation and the absorption of foreign elements. The centuries left their impress on Judaism; Judaism did not reach out to them.[103]

Gans also contributed the only piece which was not pure scholarship.[104] On the basis of a talk given in the *Verein*'s Scientific Institute he discussed a recent edict of the Russian Czar Alexander I. This decree provided for the dissolution of Jewish community organizations, and was supposedly carried out upon complaint of the Jewish poor against community elders. In dealing with the subject, Gans refrained from praising or criticizing the decree. In accord with the Hegelian point of view expressed in his speeches, he regarded it as representing simply another step in the history of the idea of freedom. The demise of the twin aristocracy of the rabbis and the rich was to be welcomed only because the old autocratic rule had been out of keeping with the progress of the World Spirit; Gans could claim that he viewed the decree with favor because it was in accord with the course of history. In the Hegelian sense his review of the edict was scientific and so fitted properly into the *Zeitschrift*. But consigning wealthy *parnasim* to the past could hardly win favor for the *Verein*. From what Gans said about community control by the rich in Poland, the implicit analogy to German communities was all too obvious.

The articles in the *Zeitschrift* which proved of most lasting significance were the three contributed by Zunz. In all of them he expressed his interest in the inner life of Judaism rather than the external forces operative upon the community. In introducing his first article Zunz stressed that

Jewish history, unlike that of other peoples, was essentially a history of ideas, a history of Judaism more than a history of Jews. Yet the subject of the article, Hispanic place names occurring in Jewish literature, was one of wider importance and showed most clearly the contribution a study of Jewish texts might make to historical scholarship in general. Zunz entitled another article "Outline for a Future Statistics of the Jews," meaning by "statistics" something much broader than the modern definition of the term: namely, everything one can say about the manner of existence of a collectivity at a given moment in time. Zunz's attraction to the concept—which remains essentially sociological—indicates once again his preference for a static framework, such as the philological one, over a dynamic one. History becomes "the result of an infinite number of statistics." [105] The Jewish past is seen in terms of stages rather than as a connected development; there is no conception of progress or teleology. The emphasis is on particular ideas or modes of life at particular times, not on how one idea or mode evolves out of the other.

The lengthiest and most important article in the *Zeitschrift* was Zunz's biography of Rashi. The other Jewish periodicals had presented sketches of Maimonides, Menasseh ben Israel, Mendelssohn, and others but had neglected the great Jewish commentator of feudal Christian Europe. Rashi's sphere of activity had been too narrow for him to serve as guide and exemplar for the Maskilim. But not only does Zunz's subject differ from those chosen by *Ha-Measef* and *Sulamith,* his method differs as well. Their interest was edification, his science. Rashi must be seen as he actually was in the context of his time, as a talmudic Jew:

It is in terms of this talmudic Jewish life that Rashi must be understood.... Those who carve out figures of bygone times according to the model of their cultured friends in Berlin mock world history. They boast of Rashi that he was a tolerant man who understood Persian, Arabic, Latin, Greek and German; that he probed astronomy and medicine, was a master of Kabbalah and Hebrew grammar; that he took journeys and performed wonders. Yet they observe a foolish, haughty silence in regard to his commentaries and his real world.

In contrast I say of my hero that, dominated by the Talmud, he was not at all tolerant; he knew nothing of Persian, Arabic, Latin or Greek; his knowledge of German, astronomy, geography and medicine was negligible; he was a stranger to the Kabbalah and was not free of superstition. Even in the Hebrew language his understanding was more the result of feeling and practice than of a conscious knowledge of grammar.[106]

For Zunz the purpose of Jewish biography is not to praise a man for virtue and enlightenment or to condemn him by silence; science demands full and objective treatment. Here apologetics is subordinated to the scientific, impartial pursuit of truth. Or, rather, the scientific attitude is its own apologetic. For in treating Rashi as objectively as possible Zunz is contributing to that much desired reconciliation of Judaism with the scientific ideal. The apologetic element—far from disappearing—has simply moved from the results to the method.

While the Maskilim may have violated the canons of science by making the Jewish past more enlightened than it was, their relation to Jewish history was for that very reason somewhat more intimate. They found individuals within it with whom they could identify. But Zunz could not identify with Rashi. On the contrary, in writing about him he was rather following Gans's line of thinking,[107] that if one examined something in its historical context one could see how inappropriate it was in the present. In his first article Zunz did claim that an examination of Jewish history would yield the means to separate the permanent from the changeable and the divine from the human, but none of his articles make an effort in that direction. Not until his *Die Gottesdienstlichen Vorträge der Juden (The Sermons of the Jews)* a decade later does Zunz endeavor to draw conclusions from the past for the present.

Only one volume of the *Zeitschrift* appeared. By the time it was complete—in June of 1823—the life of the *Verein* was waning rapidly. Another eight months and it was dead. Its demise was due to three separate factors, each of which must be given its proper weight: the deteriorating status of the Jew in Germany, the lack of support by the Jewish community, and the *Verein's* own ideology.

The reaction against Jewish civic equality which had begun in 1815 grew in the years of the *Verein's* existence. In his letters to Ehrenberg, Zunz complained repeatedly of the *Risches,* the ill-feeling toward Jews, which he encountered in Berlin.[108] Two months before the first meeting of the *Verein*—on September 15, 1819—the Prussian government issued a decree prohibiting Christian children from attending Jewish schools; in June of 1822 Jews were excluded from the higher ranks of the army; and on March 11, 1823 the government declared that the Jewish religion was only "tolerated." But what hurt the young intellectuals of the *Verein* most was the decision made on August 18, 1822 and announced on December 4th of that year which explicitly denied public academic posts to Jews. The relevant provision of the emancipation edict of March 11, 1812 was rescinded "because of the incongruities involved in carrying it out." [109]

A month after the first meeting of the *Verein* Gans had made application to the Prussian Minister of Education, von Altenstein, for an academic appointment.[110] Despite the intervention of State Chancellor von Hardenberg on his behalf, his case had dragged on for two and a half years, finally resulting in the negative decision of August 18, 1822. In despair some members of the *Verein* for a while even toyed with the idea of emigration to America. An official letter was written to Mordecai Manuel Noah which expressed interest in "the means of transplanting a vast portion of European Jews to the United States, and how such emigration may be connected with the welfare of those who would prefer leaving their country to escape endless slavery and oppression." [111] But it is inconceivable that many members of the *Verein* were serious about emigration to America: they were too much Europeans to give up even a tormented life in a cultured environment for Noah's proposed Jewish colony on the Niagara River. Certainly for Zunz, who could not live without libraries—or Gans or Heine—the America of the 1820's must have seemed most unattractive. Yet to remain in Germany meant either to remain a Jew and accept exclusion from intellectual life and public positions or to convert to Christianity. The pressure was great. Gans and Heine chose conversion; Zunz, Moser, and Wolf chose to remain Jewish.

The despair which the German-Christian reaction brought upon the *Verein* was augmented by internal dissension and a lack of response by the Jewish community. Within the *Verein* dues went unpaid and the bulk of the membership seemed apathetic; [112] the branch in Hamburg, led by Kley and Salomon, asserted its independence of the group in Berlin.[113] Even more disheartening to the leaders of the *Verein* was the complete failure to communicate the group's purpose to the Jewish community. David Fränkel, himself an honorary member of the *Verein,* did not devote even a single announcement to it in his *Sulamith.* The *Bikure ha-'Itim* of Vienna printed the first three paragraphs of the statutes and excerpts from Gans's speeches; but it chose only those portions of the speeches that dealt with organization and activities, leaving out the philosophy.[114] The average Jew probably felt much as Jost did that this *Verein* was a group of arrogant, inexperienced young men whose projects for the most part were of little value. And so they refused the *Verein* their financial support. They thus impressed upon its members the notion that Judaism was indeed what it was held to be by gentile intellectuals: petty, mechanical, and spiritless, devoid of self-consciousness.[115] Gans complained that the Jewish community did not oppose the ideas of the *Verein* with a counter-idea, which would have produced a creative dialectic; the idea of the *Verein* was met and opposed by "the purely external and material, the humdrum idleness of daily life."[116] "I know of nothing spiritual in the Jewish community that would demand a noble fight," wrote Moser in 1824. To Moser Judaism seemed no more than a mummy which fell apart when exposed to the free atmosphere of modern culture.[117] In the course of four years the burning hope of creatively reconciling Judaism with Europe had turned to ashes.

But if civil disabilities and community apathy played a role in the demise of the *Verein,* so did its own ideology. Though its leaders were concerned with giving expression to their consciousness of themselves as Jews, they failed to develop a rationale for a continued Jewish identification. Their conception of the future did not provide any incentive for the Jew to remain a Jew. The goal was integration into Europe without specification as to how it was to differ from total absorption. Their primary concern was the Jew as human being, not as Jew; they wanted only to lift him to a higher level of self-understanding. Moser's remarks, written after the break-up of the *Verein,* must be given full weight: "What we truly wanted we want even now and could still want if we were all baptized."[118] The *Verein* had failed to find any significance in continued Jewish existence. Beginning with emotional attachments, loyalties to family, and personal honor, it provided no further reason to resist external pressures. When the pressures grew, nothing in the ideology of the *Verein* could withstand them.

Unlike the others, Leopold Zunz found a personal sanctuary in his first love, the *Wissenschaft des Judentums.* After disillusion both as preacher and as member of the *Verein,* he decided to make Jewish research the focus of his life. Here he found refuge from the tumult and confusion of a Jewish life uncertain of its course. In the summer of 1824 he wrote his famous letter to Wolf:

I have come to the point of nevermore believing in a reformation of the Jews; someone should throw a stone at that spectre and scare it away.... The Judaism which we wanted to rebuild is torn apart, the prey of barbarians, fools, money-changers, idiots and *Parnassim* [community leaders]. Many years will yet roll over this race and find it as it is today: torn asunder; out of desperation flowing over into Christianity; vacillating, without principles; some of them—pushed aside by Europe—vegetating on in the old dirt, looking dry-eyed for the donkey of the Messiah or something else with long ears; some of them riffling government papers and encyclopedias—now rich, now bankrupt; now oppressed, now tolerated. Their own science died among the German Jews and they have no understanding for the European, because, disloyal to themselves, they were estranged from ideas and became the slaves of mere self-interest.... Everything is a pap of praying, bank notes and *Rachmones* [charity], with *Aufklärung* and *Chilluk* [Talmudic dialectics]! After this hideous sketch of Judaism you need no explanation why the *Verein* died away together with its *Zeitschrift* and they are missed as little as temples, schools and civil happiness. The *Verein* did not die on account of its branch organizations—which could only have been termed the result of an administrative failure—rather in reality it never existed. Five to ten enthusiastic men got together, and like Moses dared to hope for the propagation of this spirit. That was an illusion. The only thing that emerges permanently from this *Mabul* [deluge] is the *Wissenschaft des Judentums,* for it lives even if for centuries no one raised a finger for it. I must confess that, next to submission to the judgment of God, occupation with this science is my support and consolation. Those storms and experiences shall have no influence upon me which could bring me into discord with myself. I have done what I considered to be my duty. Because I saw that I was preaching in the wilderness, I stopped preaching.... Nothing remains for the members but to work within their limited circles, remaining true to themselves and leaving the rest to God.[119]

Despairing of the Jewish present, Zunz took comfort in the ideal of science, applied to the Jewish past.

Over the course of half a century German Jewry had tried and failed to answer the troublesome query of Lavater: Why should a man of European culture remain a Jew? Mendelssohn's answer had been the obligation to observe a divinely ordained ceremonial law which God alone could abrogate. Friedländer, his disciple, forsook the law and turned deist. When romanticism won over the German spirit, the anemic rationalism with which modern Judaism had been identified became as despised as the ceremonial law. Sensitive spirits fled from its aridity into the arms of Schleiermacher or Schlegel. At the same time, within the community the Maskilim and reformers made a great effort to transform Judaism into a religious denomination with certain tenets of its own. And then, finally, the *Verein*: an attempt to do with *Wissenschaft* and philosophy of history what had earlier been attempted with enlightenment. But except for the orthodox Jew, in 1825 Lavater's question still stood unanswered.

Viable solutions were to come only later. Not until the next generation and thereafter was an attempt made to determine whether Judaism possessed unique character or content which could make its preservation imperative; only then did the Reform movement develop the idea of an ongoing Jewish mission. Not until the thirties was the Judaism of the present seen as a continuous development from the past and the study of Jewish tradition consciously utilized for the sake of the future. And not until much later did a few German Jews, who had themselves been a part of Europe, begin to think seriously of life as a national group outside of it.

The importance of our period lies not in its fragile answers but in its struggles with the question. From the time that Mendelssohn first openly confronted the problem of being both Jew and European until the disillusion of the young Zunz, the cultural environment changed radically but the existential problem of Jewish self-definition remained constant. Again and again a mute Jewish consciousness reached out for self-explanation, but ever fell short of an adequate justification.

Two centuries have now passed since Lavater's query and many variations have been added to the themes laid down then. But the problem today remains essentially the same—except that America has been substituted for Europe. The American Jew, desiring to be as much a part of American culture as Mendelssohn and his successors did of European, is engaged in the same quest for Jewish self-definition. At present it remains to be seen whether he will be able to draw significant content from the Jewish tradition to shape a uniquely Jewish identity. If not, Jewish consciousness will gradually dissipate and dissolve into the free American milieu, leaving only the religious heritage to live on—in Gans's image—"as the current lives on in the ocean."

ABBREVIATIONS

AZJ	*Allgemeine Zeitung des Judentums*
CCARY	*Central Conference of American Rabbis Yearbook*
Dubnow	Simon Dubnow, *Weltgeschichte des jüdischen Volkes*, VII–IX. Berlin, 1928–29.
Glatzer[1]	*Leopold and Adelheid Zunz: An Account in Letters, 1815–1885*, ed. Nahum N. Glatzer. London, 1958.
Glatzer[2]	*Leopold Zunz: Jude—Deutscher—Europäer*, ed. Nahum N. Glatzer. Tübingen, 1964.
Graetz	Heinrich Graetz, *Geschichte der Juden*, XI. 2nd ed.; Leipzig, 1900.
HJ	*Historia Judaica*
HUCA	*Hebrew Union College Annual*
JJGL	*Jahrbuch für Jüdische Geschichte und Literatur*
JQR	*Jewish Quarterly Review*
JSS	*Jewish Social Studies*
Jub	Moses Mendelssohn, *Gesammelte Schriften, Jubiläumsausgabe*, ed. I. Elbogen, J. Guttmann, and E. Mittwoch. Berlin, Breslau, 1929–38.
Kayserling[1]	M. Kayserling, "Briefe von und an Moses Mendelssohn." Pp. 485–569 in his *Moses Mendelssohn: Sein Leben und seine Werke*. Leipzig, 1862.
Kayserling[2]	M. Kayserling, *Moses Mendelssohn: Sein Leben und Wirken*. 2nd ed.; Leipzig, 1888.
Kayserling[3]	M. Kayserling, *Moses Mendelssohn: Ungedrucktes und Unbekanntes von ihm und über ihn*. Leipzig, 1883.
LBIB	*Leo Baeck Institute Bulletin*
LBIY	*Leo Baeck Institute Year Book*
MGWJ	*Monatsschrift für Geschichte und Wissenschaft des Judentums*
PAAJR	*Proceedings of the American Academy for Jewish Research*
REJ	*Revue des Études Juives*
Schriften	Moses Mendelssohn, *Gesammelte Schriften*, ed. G. B. Mendelssohn. Leipzig, 1843–45.
ZGJD	*Zeitschrift für die Geschichte der Juden in Deutschland*
ZWJ	*Zeitschrift für die Wissenschaft des Judentums*

NOTES

[Complete titles and publication data for all works, except those of only tangential significance, are given in the bibliography.]

CHAPTER 1

1. David Friedländer's proposed inscription for a planned Mendelssohn memorial, *MGWJ*, L (1906), 371.

2. Moritz Steinschneider, *Die hebräischen Uebersetzungen des Mittelalters und die Juden als Dolmetscher* (Berlin, 1893), pp. 461-62; article: "Hebraists, Christian" in *Jewish Encyclopedia*, VI, 300.

3. Jacob Katz, *Die Entstehung der Judenassimilation in Deutschland und deren Ideologie*, p. 22.

4. H. R. S. Van der Veen, *Jewish Characters in Eighteenth Century English Fiction and Drama* (Groningen, 1935), p. 40; Herbert Carrington, *Die Figur des Juden in der dramatischen Literatur des XVIII. Jahrhunderts*, p. 11.

5. Plays in which Jews appear as host desecrators were still produced in Germany as late as the beginning of the nineteenth century. See Charles Dejob, "Le Juif dans la Comédie au XVIIIᵉ Siecle," *REJ*, XXXIX (1899), 121.

6. Robert H. Murray, *Erasmus and Luther*, p. 365.

7. Andrew Dickson White, *Seven Great Statesmen in the Warfare of Humanity with Unreason*, p. 103; Jacob Meijer, "Hugo Grotius' *Remonstrantie*," *JSS*, XVII (1955), 104.

8. Heinrich Hoffmann, *Die Humanitätsidee in der Geschichte des Abendlandes*, p. 66.

9. Trans. Basil Kennett, p. 224.

10. *Die Religion in Geschichte und Gegenwart* (1927 edition), I, 637.

11. Locke's enlightened, though conservative views on religion are found in his "The Reasonableness of Christianity" (1695), *Works*, II, 471-541.

12. A similar idea is already expressed by Spinoza in his *Theologico-Political Treatise*, Chapter XIX.

13. "A Letter Concerning Toleration" (1689), *Works*, II, 253.

14. *Christianity not Mysterious*, p. xxvii. See also Max Wiener, "John Toland and Judaism," *HUCA*, XVI (1941), 215-42; Dubnow, VII, 520-23.

15. For the contrasting opinions of a number of English deists, see Samuel Ettinger, "Jews and Judaism as Seen by the English Deists of the 18th Century" [Hebrew], *Zion*, XXIX (1964), 182-207.

16. *Letters of Certain Jews to Monsieur de Voltaire*, pp. 62-63.

17. On the Marquis d'Argens see the excellent study by N. R. Bush, *The Marquis*

d'Argens and his Philosophical Correspondence; see also *Anekdoten von König Friedrich II. von Preussen,* I, 11 ff.

18. In the anonymous English translation, I, 265.

19. In 1737 the Marquis published his ideas under the title, *Philosophie du bon sens;* the work was promptly declared heretical by the Church in France.

20. C. F. Gellert, *Sämtliche Schriften,* V, p. 8.

21. Ibid., p. 143.

22. Van der Veen (*Jewish Characters...,* p. 46) suggests that Gellert's novel was a principal cause for the favorable portrayal of a Jew in Smollett's *Adventures of Count Fathom,* which appeared a year after the English translation of Gellert's work.

23. Michaelis recognized the similarity between Gellert and Lessing. In his review of *Die Juden* he wrote: "Man kann daher dieses Lustspiel nicht lesen, ohne dass einem die mit gleichem Endzweck gedichtete Erzählung von einem ehrlichen Juden, die in Hrn. Gellert's Schwedischer Gräfin stehet beyfallen muss."

24. Lessing's grandfather, however, was like himself an outspoken opponent of narrow prejudice. In 1670 he held a disputation entitled *de religionum tolerantia* in which he advocated no less than universal toleration (see K. G. Lessing, *Gotthold Ephraim Lessings Leben* [Berlin, 1793], pp. 3–4).

25. *Lessings sämtliche Schriften,* XVII, 18.

26. See Lessing's introduction to *Die Juden,* quoted in Erich Schmidt, *Lessing,* I, 144.

27. This represents a reversal of Gellert's *Schwedische Gräfin* where the count saves the life of the Jew who then shows his humble gratitude financially and through acts of friendship. In *Die Juden* Lessing's traveler saves the life of the baron and then cavalierly brushes aside the baron's efforts to reward him. He is not only moral and virtuous like the Polish Jew, but also virile and physically attractive. Gellert's Polish Jew is an ethical human being in the highest degree, but he remains in manner and dress recognizably a Jew. Lessing's traveler is in no way distinguishable from a Christian. Only the religious barrier remains.

28. Moritz Lazarus, "Moses Mendelssohn in seinem Verhältnis zu Juden und Judentum," *Deutsche Revue,* XI (1886), 217. Lessing probably began to write *Die Juden* when he was still living in Leipzig where Jews were admitted only for the fairs. See also Simon Bernfeld, *Dor tahpukhot,* I, 47.

29. Mendelssohn of course was not the first Jew to obtain a secular education. Aaron Gumperz and others—even some East-European Jews—had preceded him, but he was the first to make a name for himself in the intellectual community. For the earliest manifestations of Jewish enlightenment in Germany see J. Eschelbacher, "Die Anfänge allgemeiner Bildung unter den deutschen Juden vor Mendelssohn," *Festschrift zum siebzigsten Geburtstage Martin Philippsons,* 168–77; Isaac Eisenstein-Barzilay, "The Background of the Berlin Haskalah," *Essays on Jewish Life and Thought Presented in Honor of Salo Wittmayer Baron,* pp. 183–97; and especially the recent comprehensive study by Azriel Shohet, *Im hilufe tekufot.*

30. *Göttingische Anzeigen von Gelehrten Sachen*, I, No. 70 (1754), 621.
31. *Lessings sämtliche Schriften*, XVII, 40.
32. Fritz Bamberger, *Denkmal der Freundschaft*. These autograph inscriptions date from as early as 1762.
33. *Die Bestimmung des Menschen*, p. 56.
34. *Die vornehmsten Wahrheiten der natürlichen Religion* (4th ed.; Hamburg, 1772). Mendelssohn later utilized this work as one of the sources for the third dialogue of the *Phaedon* (*Jub*, III, 1, 155).
35. *Die vornehmsten Wahrheiten*, Preface.
36. Kayserling², p. 5.
37. Referring to *Jerusalem*, Ernst Cassirer says of Mendelssohn: "Er selbst durfte sich hier auf die grossen klassischen Vorbilder der jüdischen Religionsphilosophie mit recht berufen. Die 'Religion der Vernunft,' die er verkündet und verteidigt, war ihm nicht durch Wolff und durch den philosophischen Rationalismus nahegebracht worden,—sondern lange zuvor war sie schon dem zwölfjährigen Knaben im Studium des Maimonides aufgegangen" ("Die Idee der Religion bei Lessing und Mendelssohn," *Festgabe zum zehnjährigen Bestehen der Akademie für die Wissenschaft des Judentums*, p. 40). For the differences between Maimonides and Mendelssohn see Hans Joachim Schoeps, *Geschichte der jüdischen Religionsphilosophie in der Neuzeit*, I, 34–36.
38. By and large Berlin Jewry did not share Mendelssohn's love of philosophy. He was unable to gather sufficient subscriptions from the Berlin Jewish community to permit publication of a Hebrew philosophical work on the existence of God sent to him by its author, Herz Ullmann. See *Jub*, XVI, 203–4; Kayserling³, pp. 36–38.
39. *Jub*, XI, 346; see also *Schriften*, V, 171.
40. See, for example, the works of the "father of English deism," Herbert of Cherbury (1583–1648) and the excellent study of his thought by Harold R. Hutcheson, *Lord Herbert of Cherbury's De Religione Laici* (New Haven, 1944). Leibniz composed a prayer which could be invoked by "not only every Christian but also every Jew and every Mohammedan" (Jacob Auerbach, "Moses Mendelssohn und das Judenthum," *ZGJD*, I [1886], 7, note 1). Auerbach also points out certain parallels between the philosophy of Leibniz and Judaism.
41. Rudolf Unger, *Hamann und die Aufklärung*, p. 58.
42. Quoted in Beate Berwin, *Moses Mendelssohn im Urteil seiner Zeitgenossen*, p. 24. See also Karl Lungwitz, *Die Religionsphilosophie Johann August Eberhards*.
43. *Schriften*, VI, 414. Bernfeld (p. 64) claims on the basis of the record book of the Berlin Jewish community (*Jub*, XIV, 384) that Mendelssohn only *translated* this sermon (and the others). But such a view contradicts Mendelssohn's personal testimony in letters to Lessing (*Schriften*, V, 139 and 173) as well as the note of Nicolai (ibid., pp. 223–24).
44. *Jub*, XVI, 27, 42.
45. Lavater to Breitinger, quoted in ibid., VII, xii.
46. The letter from Eybeschütz is in ibid., XVI, 2–3; the Emden correspondence is in ibid., pp. 114, 130–32, 157–59, 161–63, 166–68, 178–83.

47. Although it has been usually ascribed to the year 1750, H. Borodianski has argued convincingly for the later date (ibid., XIV, iii–iv).

48. Isaac Euchel, *Toldot rabenu he-hakham Moshe ben Menahem,* p. 13; Ludwig Geiger, *Geschichte der Juden in Berlin* (Berlin, 1878), I, 86; Joseph Klausner, *Historia shel ha-sifrut ha-'ivrit ha-hadasha,* I, 51–55. Perhaps the rabbis noticed that the passages Mendelssohn chose were precisely in keeping with the prevailing optimism of the Leibnizian system and feared the pamphlets might be used to propagate secular philosophy. Borodianski, however, thinks the venture failed because of lack of response rather than suppression (*Jub,* XIV, iv–v). Both issues (each exceedingly rare) are reprinted in ibid., pp. 1–21, and in *Festschrift zum 50 jährigen Bestehen der Franz-Josef-Landesrabbinerschule in Budapest* (Budapest, 1927), pp. 62–76.

49. Kayserling², p. 215, note 2. Cf. *Schriften,* V, 221–23.

50. *Jub,* XVI, 142.

51. *Schriften,* IV, 1, 529. See also the reviews by Mendelssohn of the same work in ibid., IV, 2, 134–41, 292–99.

52. Ibid., VI, 436–43.

53. Friedrich Nicolai, *Ueber meine gelehrte Bildung,* pp. 43–44. It has been recently shown that Mendelssohn—and even David Friedländer—were closely acquainted with a strangely universalistic Jewish kabbalist who spent the years 1779–81 in Berlin (Jacob Katz, "Moses Mendelssohn und E. J. Hirschfeld," *LBIB,* VII [1964], 295–311).

54. *Schriften,* V, 509.

55. *Jub,* XVI, 131.

56. *Schriften,* IV, 2, 68. In his *Philosophische Gespräche* (ibid., I, 204) Mendelssohn has Philopon say: "Werden die Deutschen niemals ihren eigenen Wert erkennen? Wollen sie ewig ihr Gold für das Flittergold ihrer Nachbarn vertauschen?"

57. Berwin, *Mendelssohn im Urteil . . . ,* p. 87.

58. Arnold Bodek, "Moses Mendelssohn als deutscher Nationalschriftsteller," *Lessing-Mendelssohn Gedenkbuch,* pp. 154–55.

59. *Jub,* XI, 181.

60. "Preussische Kriegslieder, in den Feldzügen 1756 und 1757," *Sämtliche Schriften* (Karlsruhe, 1780), I, 273–318.

61. "Dichtung und Wahrheit," Seventh Book, *Goethes Werke* (Weimar, 1889), XXVII, 104.

62. Friedrich Hertz, "Wesen und Werden der Nation," *Jahrbuch für Soziologie* (Karlsruhe, 1927), first supplementary volume: *Nation und Nationalstaat,* p. 28.

63. For example by Lessing (*Jub,* XI, 38) and by Mendelssohn (*Schriften,* V, 494). Other references are given by Isaac Eisenstein-Barzilay, "Moses Mendelssohn," *JQR,* LII (1961), 172, note 82. See also Ismar Elbogen, "Die Bezeichnung 'Jüdische Nation,'" *MGWJ,* LXIII (1919), 200–8.

64. See Josef Feiner, *Gewissensfreiheit und Duldung in der Aufklärungszeit,* p. 11. Frederick's maxim for ruling was: "Räsoniert, soviel ihr wollt und worüber ihr wollt, aber gehorcht!"

65. When the cornerstone of the first synagogue in Berlin was laid in 1712, a prayer for the king and his family was placed in a copper box and buried in the ground (Geiger, *Geschichte der Juden...*, I, 23). The Peace of Dresden in 1745 was marked by special illumination of the synagogue and a Hebrew victory poem, which Aaron Gumperz translated into German (Kayserling[2], pp. 14–15).

66. M. Kayserling, *Der Dichter Ephraim Kuh.* The volume also contains an appendix on Issachar Falkensohn Behr.

67. *Schriften,* V, 70–71.

68. See Offenburg, p. 24.

69. *Schriften,* V, 139.

70. Quoted in Koppel S. Pinson, *Modern Germany,* p. 16. For Lessing's indifferent attitude to Prussia and her king see Franz Mehring, *Die Lessing-Legende.* An opposite view is taken by Max Kirschstein, *Lessing und Berlin.*

71. In a letter to Lessing of May–June, 1763, he refers to his Hubertusburg sermon as rather soporific, but also modestly calls his commentary to Maimonides' logic one of his "Kleinigkeiten" (*Schriften,* V, 173).

72. *Schriften,* IV, 1, 439–57.

73. Ibid., IV, 2, 227.

74. Ibid., pp. 284–92.

75. Ibid., V, 325, 368.

76. Ibid., p. 440.

77. For example, Michaelis. See Ludwig Geiger, "Briefe von, an und über Mendelssohn," *JJGL,* XX (1917), 95–96. Less emancipated Christians, however, were somewhat reluctant to befriend even the most enlightened Jew. Mendelssohn complains to his fiancée, Fromet Guggenheim, in a letter of January 26, 1762: "Es kann mich nichts so sehr verdriessen, als wenn mir ein Christ seine Bekanntschaft so teuer anrechnet, und sich im Herzen zu erniedrigen dünkt, wenn er mit einem Juden vertraut ist. So bald ich so was merke, so werde ich trotzig" (*Jub* XI, 287).

78. *Schriften,* V, 229–369.

79. *Jub,* XI, 57.

80. In 1762 a Swiss patriotic society wrote to Mendelssohn in flattering terms asking him to join their group (ibid., XI, 343–44). Fritz Arnheim, "Moses Mendelssohn und Luise Ulrike von Schweden," *ZGJD,* III (1889), 283–84.

81. C. G. Schütz, who had eaten dinner in Mendelssohn's home, in a letter of January 13, 1769, wrote: "Moses ist bei seiner Gelehrsamkeit und Scharfsinn zugleich der scherzhafteste Mann, der Mann von dem edelsten Charakter, und der angenehmste Gesellschafter" (Geiger, "Briefe...," p. 132).

82. Carl Becker, "The Dilemma of Diderot," *Everyman His Own Historian* (New York, 1935), pp. 268–69.

83. Unger, *Hamann...,* I, 46.

84. Gottfried Fittbogen, *Die Religion Lessings,* p. 67.

85. *Schriften,* V, 544 (italics here and throughout the volume are those of the author of the quotation).

86. Ibid., III, 477.
87. Ibid., p. 478; cf. ibid., IV, 2, 135.
88. Ibid., III, 479.
89. Ibid., p. 477.
90. Kayserling[2], p. 162; Berwin, *Mendelssohn im Urteil*..., p. 36. It was only after the tremendous success of the *Phaedon* that Mendelssohn was considered for membership in the Berlin academy (M. Kayserling, *Moses Mendelssohns philosophische und religiöse Grundsätze*, p. 8). A letter from the literary critic Heinrich Christian Boie to G. A. Burger, dated December 11, 1778, makes it clear that Mendelssohn was deemed one of the outstanding intellectual leaders of Germany. Boie considers him "unter den ersten unserer Nation" (Geiger, "Briefe...," p. 124).
91. *Jub*, VII, 10. Rawidowicz, in his introduction to the Lavater-Mendelssohn literature, fails to grasp the crucial significance of this statement. He paraphrases it in the *present* tense (ibid., p. xxii).

CHAPTER 2

1. *Jub*, VII, 10.
2. *Schriften*, V, 366.
3. *Jub*, XI, 264.
4. Even many years after the Lavater dispute Mendelssohn must have felt somewhat ill-at-ease when discussing religion with gentiles. His young Christian admirer Maurus Winkopp relates: "Sonderbar war, dass er sich auf einem Schabbas niemals über Religionssachen mit mir besprach. Fing ich etwa davon an, wie das an andern Tagen sehr oft geschah, so brach er zwar nicht ab, lenkte aber das Gespräch gleich auf andere Dinge" (*Schriften*, V, 573). Cf. Friedrich Wilhelm Schütz, *Leben und Meinungen Moses Mendelssohns*, p. 99: "Ueberhaupt sprach Mendelssohn sehr ungerne über dergleichen Gegenstände der Religion...."
5. *Jub*, VII, 7–8.
6. Ibid., p. 3.
7. Letter of Nicolai to Lessing in *Lessings sämtliche Schriften*, XIX, 363.
8. *Jub*, VII, 14.
9. In his reply to Mendelssohn, Lavater asserts his personal conviction that it is the duty of every Christian to proselytize for his faith. But he recognizes that many of his fellow Christians (like Lessing and Nicolai) do not accept this obligation (ibid., p. 34).
10. Ibid., p xiii.
11. Ibid., p. 13. Lavater's attitude was shared by typical members of the German clergy. See, for example, the comments of Otto Justus Basilius Hesse, *Schreiben des Herrn Moses Mendelssohn*, pp. 100–1. For a possible additional millennialist motive see B. Mevorah, "The Background of Lavater's Appeal to Mendelssohn" [Hebrew], *Zion*, XXX (1965), 158–70.

12. *Jub*, VII, 27–37.
13. Ibid., p. 36.
14. Mendelssohn speaks here of *"meiner geoffenbarten Religion"* (ibid., p. 43). Judaism for Mendelssohn includes both the universal truths of natural religion and its own particular law.
15. Ibid., p. 48.
16. Ibid., p. 307.
17. Ibid., pp. 317–18.
18. Ibid., pp. 63–64. Rawidowicz (ibid., p. xxxiv) incorrectly assumes that it is the beginning of a new tract against Lavater, written in early March of 1770. The fragment is far more likely a product of the period directly following Mendelssohn's reception of Lavater's dedication. It contains many of the same ideas which Mendelssohn then expressed in the *Open Letter* of December 12, 1769 and which he would have had no reason to repeat thereafter. For example: Lavater's betrayal of his promise to keep Mendelssohn's 1763 statements secret; hatred of religious dispute; Judaism as not proselytizing; and salvation outside Judaism. Mendelssohn does not exhaust the fragment in the *Open Letter,* but what he does not include are points that would either provoke bitter feeling or lengthen the dispute.
19. Ibid., p. clxiv, note 41.
20. Ibid., p. 337.
21. See Mendelssohn's comments on the "additions" (ibid., pp. 59–60); see also Nicolai's letter to Lavater of March 10, 1770 (ibid., pp. 340–42).
22. Ibid., XVI, 139.
23. *Recherches philosophiques sur les preuves du Christianisme* (rev. ed.; Geneva, 1770).
24. Although Lessing and Nicolai also believed the preface was predated, since the *Postscript* appeared only in April, Rawidowicz is correct in his contention that Bonnet could well have taken Mendelssohn's objections not from the *Postscript,* but from the letter which Mendelssohn sent to him on February 9th and which contained largely the same arguments, particularly in regard to the dependence of revelation upon miracles (*Jub,* VII, xcii). Moreover, Bonnet's private remarks on the controversy (ibid., pp. 372–74), as also his whole attitude toward Mendelssohn, give no reason to suspect such an artifice.
25. See his letter to Lavater of December 4, 1770 (ibid., pp. 354–55).
26. This is Rawidowicz's conclusion (*Jub,* VII, xlv) which, however, is not convincing. It supposes that Mendelssohn would purposely make a false impression on his own relative and that Elkan Herz, a wealthy merchant, should want Mendelssohn to be more zealous in his attack on Christianity, despite the consequences, than another group of Jews (who could they then be?) who were holding Mendelssohn back. (Or does Rawidowicz think there is no substance at all to Mendelssohn's claim that considerable numbers of his fellow Jews wanted to quiet the dispute as quickly as possible?) Moreover, Mendelssohn begins the crucial paragraph to Herz with the question: "You ask me why I

got involved in a dispute?" If Herz had wanted Mendelssohn to become *more* involved, he would not have questioned *any kind* of involvement. Mendelssohn was expressing to Herz no less than his genuine sentiments of the moment.

27. Isaac Eisenstein-Barzilay, "Moses Mendelssohn," *JQR*, LII (1961), 77. Kayserling ignores the paragraph entirely.

28. Lessings' letter to Mendelssohn of January 9, 1771 (*Schriften*, V, 189).

29. *Jub*, XVI, 148.

30. Ibid., VII, 300–305.

31. Ibid., pp. 67–107.

32. Ibid., p. 98.

33. Kayserling fails to translate "ha-kozvot" in his German transcription (Kayserling[1], p. 495).

34. *Jub*, XVI, 151.

35. The extreme element within Christian orthodoxy did not argue that Mendelssohn must be a bad Jew since he was enlightened, but said that, being a Jew, he could not be tolerant of Christianity; and it was therefore unChristian to accord him honor and respect. Johann Melchior Goeze, the pastor in Hamburg who became the arch-foe of Lessing, in 1771 published a sermon (*Eine Predigt von der Liebe gegen fremde Religions-Verwandte*) which contains an appendix regarding Mendelssohn. To my knowledge, it has never before been recognized as part of the Mendelssohn literature. The most significant passage (pp. 63–64) reads: "Der jüdische Gelehrte hat sich, so viel mir bekannt geworden, bisher noch nicht öffentlich als ein angreifender Feind und Lästerer unsers Erlösers, und seiner allerheiligsten Religion bewiesen. Indessen ist er bey aller seiner übrigen Geschicklichkeit ein Jude, und seine abgegebne [sic] Erklärungen zeigen genugsam, wie er im Herzen gegen Jesum und gegen seine Lehre gesinnet sey. Die übertriebenen Lobsprüche und Schmeicheleyen, mit welchen er von Christen, von Gelehrten, von Gottesgelehrten beehrt worden, sind daher unwidersprechlich der Ehre unsers Erlösers nachtheilig, und können mit den Gesinnungen, welche wahre Christen gegen denselben haben müssen, nimmermehr bestehen; sie machen die ganze ohnedem schon so stolze Nation der Juden noch stolzer, und sind eben so starke Hindernisse ihrer Bekehrung, als die offenbaren Aergernisse, die ihnen von unsrer Seite gegeben werden."

36. *Jub*, XVI, 150.

37. Ibid., VII, 340.

38. *Briefe Daniel Chodowieckis an die Gräfin Christiane von Solms-Laubach,* ed. Charlotte Steinbrucker (Strassburg, 1927), p. 43.

39. *Jub*, VII, 9, 10.

40. See his letter of July 1782 to Abraham Wolf in Dessau (*Schriften*, V, 600–4).

41. Ibid., p. 351.

42. Contained in Siegfried Silberstein, "Mendelssohn und Mecklenburg," *ZGJD*, I (1929), 284–86.

43. *Jub*, XVI, 157, 161–66.

44. *Schriften*, V, 669.

45. Hennings wrote to Mendelssohn: "Selbst in Berlin, wo die Juden wenigstens im äussern Anstriche der feinen Sitten gebildeter sind, als in den meisten andern Städten, und wo sie einen Mendelssohn unter sich haben, dessen Beispiel sie zu einer bessern Denkungsart führen könnte, giebt es wohl sehr wenige Juden, die sich nicht klüger dünken als Sie, weil Sie gemeinnützig denken, und iene die Kunst verstehen sich zu bereichern." A note in Hennings' hand adds: "Ich habe in Berlin mehr als einen *vernünftigen* Juden sagen hören, Mendelssohn ist ein Phantast" ("Briefe von, an und über Mendelssohn," *ZGJD*, I [1887], 122).

46. *Schriften*, V, 663.

47. Friedländer, *Moses Mendelssohn*, p. 35.

48. The cool tone of Mendelssohn's letter to Campe (*Schriften*, III, 419–22) is probably largely due to the fact that the Philanthropin was quite as much concerned with getting Jewish financial support as with showing its lack of prejudice. Mendelssohn's attitude to Jewish education and his practical efforts are exhaustively treated in Mordechai Eliav, *Ha-Hinukh ha-yehudi be-Germania*, pp. 25 ff., 71 et passim.

49. *Ha-Measef*, I (1784), 44.

50. *Lesebuch für jüdische Kinder* (Berlin, 1779).

51. *Jub*, XVI, 279; XIV, 243.

52. Kayserling[1], p. 522.

53. *Jub*, XIV, xcii.

54. *Schriften*, V, 605; Sabattia Joseph Wolff, *Maimoniana*, p. 87.

55. *Jub*, XIV, 242; XVI, 252.

56. See the comprehensive analysis of the translation and commentary by Perez Sandler, *Ha-Beur la-Torah shel Moshe Mendelssohn ve-si'ato* (Jerusalem, 1940).

57. *Schriften*, V, 516, 517.

58. *Jub*, XVI, 287; Kayserling[3], p. 48.

59. *Jub*, XIV, 211, 213, 218.

60. Sandler, p. 196; Eliav, p. 34.

61. Kayserling[2], p. 296; Graetz, p. 43.

62. Kayserling[1], pp. 521–22, 524.

63. Kayserling[2], pp. 296–300; "Briefe von, an und über Mendelssohn," p. 114.

64. *Jub*, XVI, 296.

65. *Schriften*, III, 201–2.

66. Ibid., V, 640, 680.

67. *Jub*, XVI, 236–37; *Schriften*, V, 544–45.

68. Ibid., pp. 492–94, 623–30; III, 366.

69. Simon Bernfeld, *Dor tahpukhot*, I, 102.

70. *Jub*, XVI, 278; *Schriften*, V, 671, 677. The high estimation of the Emperor which Mendelssohn expressed in a letter of May 7, 1782 to Joseph Galico (*Jub*, XVI, 281–82) was only temporary.

71. *Schriften*, V, 655.

72. See, for example, the review of the preface in *Der Teutsche Merkur*, XXXIX, 3 (1782), 180.

73. *Schriften*, V, 655.
74. *Das Forschen nach Licht und Recht in einem Schreiben an Herrn Moses Mendelssohn.*
75. Jacob Katz, "To Whom Was Mendelssohn Replying in *Jerusalem?*" [Hebrew], *Zion*, XXIX (1964), 112–32.
76. *Das Forschen...*, p. 40.
77. *Schriften*, V, 612; III, 306–7.
78. Simon Rawidowicz, "The Philosophy of *Jerusalem*" [Hebrew], *Sefer Bialik*, p. 131; *Aus Herders Nachlass*, II, 231.
79. Friedländer, *Moses Mendelssohn*, p. 35.
80. *Schriften*, III, 297.
81. Ibid., p. 307.
82. Rawidowicz, p. 133.
83. *Schriften*, III, 321.
84. A list of the writings directly provoked by *Jerusalem* is given by Rawidowicz, p. 136, note 1. See also Fritz Bamberger, "Die geistige Gestalt Moses Mendelssohns," *MGWJ*, LXXIII (1929), 81–82.
85. *Theologico-Political Treatise*, Chapter V.
86. See, for example, Johann David Michaelis, *Mosaisches Recht* (2nd ed.; Reutlingen, 1785), I, 2 ff.
87. *Schriften*, V, 669.
88. *Jub*, VII, 98.
89. *Schriften*, I, 36–37, 42; Kayserling², pp. 493–94; *Anekdoten von König Friedrich II. von Preussen*, III, 278–79; *Briefe Daniel Chodowieckis...*, p. 50.
90. Mendelssohn did not keep the law "only out of force of habit and uncertainty," as claimed by Immanuel Heinrich Ritter, *Geschichte der jüdischen Reformation*, Pt. I: *Mendelssohn und Lessing* (Berlin, 1858), p. 94.
91. *Schriften*, V, 521.
92. *Schriften*, V, 673, 680.
93. Friedländer, *Moses Mendelssohn*, p. 35.
94. Conversions also had become more common in the last years of Mendelssohn's life. In a letter to Elkan Herz of January 11, 1785 (*Jub*, XVI, 297) Mendelssohn is overjoyed that the Prussian courts upheld the will of Moses Chalfan, which excluded from the inheritance any of his children who would change their religion.
95. In his final letter to Sophie Becker of December 27, 1785 Mendelssohn wrote: "Allein im Grunde können wir uns, auch der Vernunft nach, die Gottheit nicht stark, nicht lebhaft genug als *gegenwärtig* vorstellen; und alle Versinnlichung reicht nicht hin, uns den Enthusiasmus mitzutheilen, welchen wir bei dieser Vorstellung haben sollten" (*Schriften*, V, 649).
96. Bamberger, "Die geistige Gestalt...," pp. 87–88.
97. René Wellek, *A History of Modern Criticism*, I, 148.
98. Kayserling², p. 174; cf. *Schriften*, V, 530–31.
99. Although the German word "Schwärmerei" is broader and less extreme than

the English term "fanaticism," the translation is more justifiable than any other, especially since Mendelssohn himself equated "Schwärmer" with "Fanatiker" (Kayserling[1], pp. 552–54).

100. Kayserling[3], p. 17.

101. *Schriften*, III, 13.

102. Ibid., II, 237; III, 414.

103. Ibid., V, 577.

104. Ibid., p. 373.

105. Ernst Cassirer, *The Philosophy of the Enlightenment*, p. 274. See especially Immanuel Kant, "Beantwortung der Frage: Was ist Aufklärung?" (1784), *Immanuel Kants kleinere Schriften zur Logik und Metaphysik*, pp. 109–19.

106. *Schriften*, V, 509.

107. Ibid., p. 706.

108. Ibid., pp. 614, 637.

109. Ibid., pp. 631–32.

110. Ibid., II, 237.

111. Friedrich Nicolai, *Ueber meine gelehrte Bildung*, pp. 40–41.

112. L. F. G. Goeckingk, *Friedrich Nicolais Leben und literarischer Nachlass* (Berlin, 1820), p. 19.

113. *Schriften*, V, 342.

114. Ibid., p. 368; Nicolai, pp. 40–41; Isaac Euchel, *Toldot rabenu he-hakham Moshe ben Menahem*, p. 123. Note also the immense erudition in Mendelssohn's Pentateuch introduction (*Jub*, XIV, 229 ff.).

115. *Schriften*, V, 587.

116. Ernst Simon, "Lessing und die jüdische Geschichte," *Jüdische Rundschau*, January 22, 1929, p. 1.

117. *Schriften*, V, 582.

118. Cassirer, *Philosophy of the Enlightenment*, pp. 190 ff.

119. The dynamic, evolving character of reason, as it is here conceived, represents the clearest refutation of the Spinozism with which Jacobi charged Lessing after his death.

120. *Schriften*, III, 317–18. Hazard is far from the truth when he suggests on the basis of a passage in the *Phaedon* (*Jub*, III, 1, 114) that Lessing derived his idea of a "progressive intellectual ascent" from Mendelssohn. In the *Phaedon* Mendelssohn refers only to the individual, not to mankind, just as he does here in the *Jerusalem* (Paul Hazard, *European Thought in the Eighteenth Century*, p. 429).

121. *Schriften*, V, 648–49.

CHAPTER 3

1. Kayserling[2], pp. 509 ff.

2. Salomon Maimon, *Lebensgeschichte*, II, 181.

3. Lazarus Bendavid, *Etwas zur Characteristick der Juden,* p. 45.

4. *Ha-Sharon* to *Ha-Carmel,* VII, 5 (1866), 36–38. This correspondence between Friedländer and Joseph Pesseles took place in 1783 and represented an attempt to work out a rapprochement between Mendelssohn and Dubno.

5. *Jub,* XIV, 268.

6. *Berlinische Monatsschrift,* VIII (1786), 528.

7. How long Friedländer served in this capacity is open to some dispute. In a letter to Zunz, written in 1825, Friedländer claimed he gave up the position in 1783 (*ZGJD,* V [1892], 263). On the basis of a document dated January 8, 1784, Moritz Stern extends his directorship of the school into 1784 (*ZGJD,* VI [1935], 121, 169). Immanuel Heinrich Ritter, in the only full-length biography of Fried-länder, claims that he held the position to the end of the century (*Geschichte der jüdischen Reformation,* Pt. II: *David Friedländer, sein Leben und sein Wirken,* p. 39). Apparently Friedländer gave up direct supervision of the school early in 1784—perhaps because of a disagreement in policy, as the letter to Zunz would indicate—but retained his position as director of the Hebrew publishing house until at least 1789, as indicated by the preface to Saul Berlin's *Mitspe Yoktel,* pseudonymously published by the Free School that year with a preface by Fried-länder and Isaac Daniel Itzig, who referred to themselves as leaders of the society responsible for the school.

8. In 1782 Friedländer translated into German Wessely's *Divre shalom ve-emet* which advocated the educational reforms proposed by Joseph II of Austria. The translation appeared in Berlin, Breslau, and Vienna but bore the name of neither author nor translator. A new edition was published in 1798.

9. *Berlinische Monatsschrift,* VII (1786), 406. Also quoted in Ritter, p. 53.

10. *Berlinische Monatsschrift,* VIII (1786), 523–50.

11. *Gebete der Juden auf das ganze Jahr.* See Ismar Elbogen, "David Friedländers Uebersetzung des Gebetbuchs," *ZGJD,* VI (1935), 130–33. The prayerbook trans-lation received a very favorable review in *Ha-Measef* of 1786 (pp. 138–41) despite the fact that one of the journal's editors, Isaac Euchel, himself issued a translation —though in German characters—the same year. Later, Friedländer's translation also appeared in German characters. Aside from the Prayerbook, Friedländer translated Ecclesiastes and portions of Isaiah and Job.

12. For Friedländer's personal life and economic activity see Ernst Friedlaender, *Das Handlungshaus Joachim Moses Friedlaender;* Hugo Rachel and Paul Wallich, *Berliner Grosskaufleute und Kapitalisten,* II, 378.

13. Josef Meisl, *Protokollbuch der jüdischen Gemeinde Berlin,* pp. 326, 342, 344, 358.

14. But class consciousness and personal interest must not be conceived as the only motives behind all of Friedländer's plans and projects. Raphael Mahler's treat-ment of Friedländer is so grossly distorted—and abusive—because he will see only this one side of Friedländer's make-up (*Divre yeme Yisrael,* II [Merhavia, 1954], 144 ff. and especially 342 ff.).

15. The article against Purim: *Berlinische Monatsschrift,* XV (1790), 377–81; Fried-länder's reply: ibid., pp. 563–77.

16. See, for example, Friedländer's *An die Verehrer, Freunde und Schüler Jerusalems Spaldings, Tellers, Herders und Löfflers* (Leipzig, 1823), p. 102.
17. Letter to Herz Homberg, September 22, 1783, in *Schriften*, V, 669.
18. E.g. Christian Wilhelm Dohm, *Ueber die bürgerliche Verbesserung der Juden*, I, 34–35; Grafen von Mirabeau, *Ueber Moses Mendelssohn*, pp. 135, 156, 203.
19. *Berlinische Monatsschrift*, XVIII (1791), 353.
20. *Sendschreiben an die deutsche* [sic] *Juden*. This brief work appeared without pagination as a special supplement to the fourth volume of *Ha-Measef*. It is directed against the *'Olat Tsibur* of Elazar Fleckeles in which this Prague rabbi condemned all translations of sacred texts into a modern language.
21. *Akten-Stücke die Reform der jüdischen Kolonieen in den Preussischen Staaten betreffend*, pp. 24–26. Friedländer's contempt for the rabbis is also responsible for his publishing, together with Isaac Daniel Itzig, Saul Berlin's aforementioned polemic against Rabbi Raphael Cohen and providing it with a preface disguising the identity of the author.
22. Eleven of Friedländer's letters to Eger were written in the German language with Hebrew characters and occasional Hebrew phrases; the remaining two are entirely in Hebrew. Six of the letters were published by Ludwig Geiger in German transliteration and translation in *ZGJD*, I (1887), 256–73. All thirteen extant were later published in their original language and characters by Josef Meisl as "Letters of David Friedländer" [Yiddish], in *Historishe Shriften*, II, 390–412. Meisl's dating is more accurate than Geiger's with one major exception. Meisl's letter no. 4 (= Geiger no. 1) should be dated September 20, 1789, not October 1, 1788. This is so because Meisl's no. 4 presupposes his no. 8; because a year interval in discussing the same topic—with other topics in between—is most unlikely; and because the here suggested dating yields a plausible interval of eleven days between the letters.
23. Meisl, p. 402.
24. Dohm, pp. 101–2.
25. Mirabeau, p. 203.
26. Reinhold Lewin, "Die Judengesetzgebung Friedrich Wilhelms II.," *MGWJ*, LVII (1913), 82 ff.
27. Ismar Freund, *Die Emanzipation der Juden in Preussen*, I, 34–35; idem, "David Friedländer und die politische Emanzipation der Juden in Preussen," *ZGJD*, VI (1935), 78.
28. *Akten-Stücke . . .*, p. 56.
29. As early as 1785 the *Berlinische Monatsschrift* (VI, 167–68) carried the anecdote of a soldier in Strasburg who by requesting Jewish burial had revealed his religion. It noted with satisfaction that Jews even volunteered for the army, something previously thought impossible. In the petition for naturalization of the Friedländer family, January 20, 1792 (*Akten-Stücke . . .*, pp. 48–51), the family promised to promote the well-being of the state "mit Gut und Blut," as had the Itzig family. A year later, March 3, 1793, Friedländer wrote to the Prussian state official von Schroetter that those Jews who would not serve in the army were

not entitled to the rights of citzenship. His frustration with orthodox Jewry is apparent: "Wollen die Juden wirklich nicht alle Pflichten eines Staatsbürgers übernehmen, so weise man die Unverschämten ab; sie können, sie dürfen nicht gehört werden." The letter is found in Ernst Friedlaender, *Das Handlungshaus...*, pp. 44–46.

30. *Akten-Stücke...*, p. 131.

31. Mahler (*Divre yeme Yisrael*, pp. 345 ff.) was the first to emphasize the class character of these documents, which had previously been regarded as rather noble efforts. But his interpretation exclusively in terms of capitalist self-interest, egotism and treason against the Jewish people is no closer to the truth. In fact there was self-interest, but also concern for the common Jew—at least for the one in Prussia.

32. Lewin, pp. 466–67.

33. *Gallerie der ausgezeichneten Israeliten aller Jahrhunderte*, p. 103; Geiger, *Geschichte der Juden...*, II, 162.

34. See Hannah Arendt-Stern, "Aufklärung und Judenfrage," *ZGJD*, IV (1932), 65–77.

35. *Akten-Stücke...*, p. 9 note.

36. In succeeding years Friedländer continued to urge the abolition of the term "Jew." But his preference for a substitute designation changed from "of Old Testament faith" to "Israelite." The latter was used by Christian theologians in reference to the ancient Hebrews and provided a fitting appellation for a non-Talmudic Jew. The letter to Teller retains the word "Jewish" while polemizing against it. Later writings all refer to "Israelites" and the "Israelite Religion" with the notable exception of Friedländer's article in Zunz's *Zeitschrift für die Wissenschaft des Judentums* where editorial policy apparently required the retention of both "Jews" and "Judaism." In the *Akten-Stücke* Friedländer uses both the terms "colony" and "nation." The former was regularly used of the French residents in Prussia; the latter must not be taken as indicative of any modern Jewish nationalism, but as a synonym for the former. See Ismar Elbogen, "Die Bezeichnung 'Jüdische Nation,'" *MGWJ*, LXIII (1919), 200–8. For a discussion of Friedländer's efforts at the turn of the century to eliminate the use of "Jew" in public documents, see Jacob Jacobson, "Zu David Friedländers Bemühungen um Abschaffung des Namens 'Jude,'" *AZJ*, LXXVI (1912), 379–80.

37. E.g. the reviewer of Friedländer's *Akten-Stücke* in the *Neue allgemeine deutsche Bibliothek*, III (1793), 155. See also *Tagebücher von K. A. Varnhagen von Ense*, XIII, 13–14; *Friedrich Schlegels Briefe an seinen Bruder August Wilhelm*, p. 52. It is noteworthy that Maimon is not mentioned in any of Friedländer's published writings or extant letters. Sabattia Wolff reports that Friedländer was at first a friend and benefactor of Maimon but later grew more indifferent to him (*Maimoniana*, p. 117).

38. Maimon, *Lebensgeschichte*, II, 180–83.

39. J. G. Fichte, "Beitrag zur Berichtigung der Urtheile des Publicums über die französische Revolution" [1793], *Sämtliche Werke* (Berlin, 1845), VI, 149–50.

40. "Letters of David Friedländer," p. 403.

41. In 1799 Friedländer wrote to Aaron Wolfssohn: "Ich halte die Nation, wie sie ist, bei allem Schein von Cultur, Geschmack und Gelehrsamkeit, en gros für unverbesserlich schlecht und alle Aufklärung durch 'Measphim' für unnütz. Alle unsere hebräisch geschriebenen Bücher liest Keiner...." In 1804 he wrote: "Mit der Sache des Judenthums ist es aus, völlig aus!" (Leopold Stein, *Die Schrift des Lebens*, II [Strassburg, 1877], pp. 444–45.) Not surprisingly, Friedländer's name does not appear on the subscribers' list of the 1809 *Ha-Measef*.

42. *Sendschreiben an Seine Hochwürden, Herrn Oberconsistorialrath und Probst Teller zu Berlin, von einigen Hausvätern jüdischer Religion.*

43. Friedländer had published rabbinic stories from Talmud and Midrash which supported his own philosophy in the *Berlinische Monatsschrift* (XVII [1791], 494–97; XVIII [1791], 117–19; XXV [1795], 385–87) and continued the "Proben rabbinischer Weisheit," begun by Mendelssohn, for J. J. Engel's *Der Philosoph für die Welt*. He knew rabbinic literature, at least superficially (*AZJ*, LXXVI, 163–65; Glatzer[2], p. 86), and had an appreciation of its moral aspects. But he objected strenuously to overvaluing the post-Biblical tradition and to regarding the Talmud as an exclusive guide for life.

44. *Sendschreiben...*, p. 28. Cf. Lessing, *Die Erziehung des Menschengeschlechts*, 1780, paragraph 16: "Ein Volk aber, das so roh, so ungeschickt zu abgezogenen Gedanken war, noch so völlig in seiner Kindheit war, was war es für einer *moralischen* Erziehung fähig? Keiner andern, als die dem Alter der Kindheit entspricht. Der Erziehung durch unmittelbare sinnliche Strafen und Belohnungen."

45. *Sendschreiben...*, p. 34.

46. Mendelssohn's influence is apparent at various points in the epistle. Friedländer even claims that Mendelssohn's principles are its basis (p. 11 note). Like Mendelssohn, he distinguishes between rational truths and historical truths, the former based upon personal conviction, the latter upon trust in the transmitted reports of witnesses. There are even striking parallels of language. Mendelssohn wrote to Lavater: "Ich darf sagen, dass ich meine Religion nicht erst seit gestern zu untersuchen angefangen" (*Jub*, VII, 8). Friedländer writes: "Wir haben die Betrachtung über Religion, Pflicht und Bestimmung nicht erst seit gestern angefangen" (p. 15).

47. Bendavid, *Etwas zur Characteristick...*, pp. 45, 64–65.

48. *Allgemeine Literatur-Zeitung* (1794), 343–44; *Intelligenzblatt der Allgemeinen Literatur-Zeitung* (1794), 301–2; and see Ellen Littmann, "David Friedländers Sendschreiben an Probst Teller und sein Echo," *ZGJD*, VI (1935), 103.

49. Immanuel Kant, *Der Streit der Fakultäten*, pp. 82–83. Dubnow (VIII, 268, note 1) thinks this work of Kant may well have influenced Friedländer's letter to Teller the following year.

50. See Nathan Rotenstreich, "Kant's Interpretation of Judaism" [Hebrew], *Tarbiz*, XXVII (1958), 388–405. In *Adrastea und das achtzehnte Jahrhundert*, Herder accepted Mendelssohn's interpretation of the law's validity as normative for

Judaism: "Nur der Gott ihrer Väter, der ihnen diese Gebote auflegte (meinen sie) kann sie ihnen entnehmen, und zwar nicht anders als durch einen so feierlichen Act, als die Gesetzgebung auf Sinai selbst war" (*Johann Herders sämtliche Werke*, X, 105).

51. Davidson is not mentioned by Graetz, Dubnow, or Mahler; nor is he listed in the *Encyclopaedia Judaica*. However Teller mentions him among the famous Jewish physicians of his day in his reply to the epistle (p. 16).

52. Wolf Davidson, *Ueber die bürgerliche Verbesserung der Juden*, pp. 114, 114 note, 117 note.

53. Other writings are discussed in Littmann, pp. 94 ff.

54. *Beantwortung des Sendschreibens einiger Hausväter jüdischer Religion.*

55. Benjamin Rippner ("David Friedländer and Probst Teller," in *Jubelschrift zum Siebzigsten Geburtstage des Prof. Dr. H. Graetz*, p. 169) thinks Teller decidedly rejected the epistle; Mahler (*Divre Yeme Yisrael ...*, p. 148) wrongly thinks he required a belief in secrets; Littmann (p. 104) maintains that "Bei Vermeidung jeder Schärfe im Ton ist seine Antwort in der Sache ablehnend." On the other hand, Dubnow (VIII, 204) considers Teller a proselytizer in the reply, which conflicts with Teller's own denial thereof (p. 27). Nor does it harmonize with Teller's support of the will of Moses Isaac Chalfan, excluding those of his children who converted from the inheritance (*ZGJD*, III [1889], 207).

56. *Beantwortung ...*, p. 40.

57. Friedländer himself later said that Teller "beehrte mein Schreiben mit einer, nicht durchaus genügenden Antwort." (*An die Verehrer ...*, p. 15.)

58. For the most complete listing of this literature (twenty-three pamphlets plus ten articles and reviews) and a discussion by categories: rationalists, dogmatists, and romantics, see Littmann, pp. 105 ff. Some of the writings are also discussed by Geiger, *ZGJD*, IV (1890), 57 ff.; and in the *Neue Allgemeine Bibliothek*, LVII (1801), 267–93.

59. Friedländer even sent a copy to Herder to get his reaction. The journalist Garlieb Merkel relates in his recollections: "Als im Jahre 1799 der berühmte David Friedländer zu Berlin Teller in einem gedruckten Sendschreiben öffentlich aufgefordert hatte, seine Meinung über den moralischen Wert der Judentaufe zu sagen, bat er mich, auch Herdern zu bewegen, dass er darüber etwas schreiben möge. Herder antwortete mir: Ich möchte Friedländer für das übersandte Exemplar des Sendschreibens danken und wenn ich eine höfliche Wendung dazu fände, hinzufügen, er wisse keine andere Antwort als den Zuruf Voltaires: Puisque vous êtes juif, soyez—le donc!" (*Thersites*, p. 59.) Further evidence that Friedländer's authorship was known or suspected: Aaron Wolfssohn, *Jeschurun*, pp. 115–16; "Letters of David Friedländer," no. 12. Moreover, if Schleiermacher's remark (cited below): "Wie tief verwundet muss besonders der treffliche Friedländer sein!" is intended to be ironic—which seems most likely—then the authorship must have been an open secret.

60. E.g. Hermann Daniel Hermes, *Ueber das Sendschreiben einiger Hausväter jüdischer Religion*, especially p. 37.

61. E.g. the anonymous *Treue Relation*, p. 19. Steinschneider (*Bodleian Catalogue*, II, col. 988) erroneously considers this pamphlet the work of a Jew. Also I cannot agree with the contention of both Steinschneider and Littmann (p. 111) that another of the pamphlets was by a Jewish author, the *Gespräch über das Send-schreiben*. This pamphlet seems rather the work of an enlightened Christian, although it indicates considerable familiarity with the Jewish community. The anonymous author finds Teller's conditions not unwarranted and looks forward to Jewish conversions. See especially pp. 30, 33, 35–36.

62. "Briefe bei Gelegenheit der politisch theologischen Aufgabe und des Send-schreibens jüdischer Hausväter," *Friedrich Schleiermacher's sämtliche Werke*; Pt. I: *Zur Theologie*, V, 1–39.

63. Ibid., p. 8.

64. "Letters of David Friedländer," no. 12; *Gespräch . . .* , p. 27.

65. "An die Hrn Verfasser des Sendschreibens an Hrn O. K. Rath Teller. Von Hrn Dr. Schönemann, jüdischer Nazion," *Neue Berlinische Monatsschrift*, IV (1800), 208–25. Of Schönemann I have been able to learn nothing further except that he contributed a translated excerpt from an allegorical Hebrew drama to the *Monatsschrift* the following year (V, 186–201), and that he lived in Driesen in the Neumark.

66. However, Lazarus Bendavid, not one of the family heads, undoubtedly had them in mind when he said in a speech of January 18, 1800: "Zu verargen ist es ihnen nicht, dass sie die besuchte und freudige Kirche, der verlassenen und traurigen Synagoge vorziehen und sich und ihre Kinder zu retten suchen. Aber gewonnen für das Ganze wird dadurch nichts, gar nichts. Es sind Splitter, die man von einem unbehülflichen Koloss scharf abschneidet; der Koloss, anstatt geschwächt zu werden, gewinnt vielmehr an Stärke, weil der Riss, den der Splitter andeutete, nun nicht weiter greift" (Bendavid, *Aufsätze verschiedenen Inhalts*, p. 132).

67. Yet Friedländer would never admit the reaction was justified. Recalling the *Sendschreiben* nearly twenty-five years later, he noted that of all the replies it produced, only the one of Teller himself and the review by Henke in the *Neue Allgemeine Deutsche Bibliothek* were worth reading (*An die Verehrer . . .* , pp. 15–16). The review by Henke (LVII, 267–93) is unusual precisely in that it completely excuses the turn away from the rest of Jewry. Henke was of the opinion that there was no hope of reforming Judaism in the immediate future and, since political rights were tied to reform, the family heads were without blame in trying to provide for their own.

68. Freund, "David Friedländer . . . ," pp. 82 ff.; idem, "Die rechtliche und politische Bedeutung der Emanzipation," *Gemeindeblatt der jüdischen Gemeinde zu Berlin*, March 8, 1912, pp. 28–29.

69. Freund, *Die Emanzipation . . .* , II, 332–35, 368–71.

70. *Gallerie der ausgezeichneten Israeliten . . .* , p. 105.

71. Reproduced in Freund, II, 455–59.

72. Rosa Dukas, *Die Motive der preussischen Judenemanzipation von 1812*, p. 64.

73. *Ueber die, durch die neue Organisation der Judenschaften in den Preussischen Staaten nothwendig gewordene Umbildung.*

74. E.g. *Licht und Wahrheit die Umbildung des Israelitischen Kultus betreffend.* Steinschneider (*Bodleian Catalogue*, II, col. 989) mistakenly attributes the pamphlet to Jeremiah Heinemann on the basis of a note indicating the forthcoming publication of a journal. The real author is Gotthold Salomon. See his *Selbst-Biographie* (Leipzig, 1863), p. 19.

75. E.g. L. B. Dohm, *Etwas zum Schutz des angegriffenen Gebrauches der ebräischen Sprache;* Abraham Muhr, *Jerubaal.*

76. Ludwig Geiger, "Nach dem Edikt vom 11. März 1812," *Gemeindeblatt der jüdischen Gemeinde zu Berlin,* August 9, 1912, p. 104. See also Mahler, *Divre Yeme Yisrael,* p. 364.

77. *Reden der Erbauung gebildeter Israeliten gewidmet* (1815); ibid., Erste Folge (1817); "Rede gehalten vor einer Gesellschaft gebildeter Israeliten," *Jedidja,* I, 1 (1817), 38–56; "Rede über Psalm 19," ibid., I, 2 (1817), 133–49.

78. Friedländer had been acquainted with Jacobson's reform efforts in Westphalia, but regarded them as too timid. On September 21, 1808 he wrote to Aaron Wolfssohn that Jacobson was temporizing, that he was trying not to offend and thus taking only half-measures (Joseph Cohn, "Einige Schriftstücke aus dem Nachlass Aron Wolfssohns," *MGWJ,* XLI [1897], 375–76). See also Glatzer[2], pp. 77–78.

79. Already in 1785 Friedländer had written "Briefe über die Moral des Handels" which breathe the same spirit. Here he had distinguished between petty trade, in which swindling and deceit are common, and large-scale trade, where a good reputation is of the essence, and honesty a prudential virtue. The "Briefe" first appeared in Zöllner's *Lehrbuch für alle Stände* and were then reprinted many years later in *Jedidja,* I, 1 (1817), 178–213.

80. *Reden* (1815), p. 76.

81. Isaac Marcus Jost, *Geschichte des Judentums und Seiner Sekten,* III, 333.

82. See note 16.

83. "Reformed," rather than "reform," is used advisedly of Friedländer. He did not have the conception of a progressive Judaism, continually reshaping itself, but only of an Israelite faith, which was as unchanging as the eternal truths of natural religion.

84. *Ueber die Verbesserung der Israeliten im Königreich Pohlen.* Friedländer's suggestions, however, apparently had little practical effect: see M. Wischnitzer, "Drei Briefe David Friedländers an den Erzbischof von Warschau, Franz Malczewski," *AZJ,* LXXII (1908), 353–54.

85. *Beitrag zur Geschichte der Verfolgung der Juden im 19ten Jahrhundert durch Schriftsteller.*

86. "Briefe über das Lesen der heiligen Schriften nebst einer Uebersetzung des sechsten und siebenten Capitels des Micha, als Beilage," *ZWJ,* I (1822–23), 68–94. While Friedländer here praised reading of the Hebrew Bible and stressed its aesthetic as well as its moral value, he saw no need to impose it upon the average pupil not destined for an academic career.

87. *J. J. Engels Schriften* (Berlin, 1801).
88. *Briefwechsel zwischen Goethe und Zelter,* passim.
89. *ZGJD,* V (1892), 263.
90. And indeed some still thought he was. When Gotthold Salomon in 1829 issued a biography of Mendelssohn with selections from his works, he dedicated it to Mendelssohn's son, Joseph, and to "des unsterblichen Meisters treustem Jünger Herrn David Friedländer."
91. In 1787 Friedländer had issued Mendelssohn's Hebrew extract from the *Phaedon, Sefer ha-nefesh* [*Book of the Soul*], and provided it with a Hebrew introduction. It was reissued in 1798 in Brünn with Friedländer's German translation of the introduction and Part I.
92. *Moses Mendelssohn,* p. 3.
93. *An die Verehrer . . . ,* p. 103.
94. Quoted in Ritter, *David Friedländer . . . ,* p. 25.
95. Ibid., p. 174.
96. Friedländer was pilloried by Graetz and his school, and to a lesser extent by Dubnow, for being an assimilationist, while recently he was indicted by Mahler for being a spokesman of the Jewish bourgeoisie. Jost, Ritter, and Ludwig Geiger, on the other hand, were insufficiently critical in their evaluations. The first unprejudiced—but fragmentary—studies on Friedländer appeared in an issue of the *ZGJD* (VI [1935]) devoted to Friedländer on the one-hundredth anniversary of his death.

CHAPTER 4

1. *Goethe-Jahrbuch,* XIV (1893), 51.
2. Ludwig Geiger, *Dichter und Frauen,* p. 129.
3. G. Schnapper-Arndt, "Jugendarbeiten Ludwig Börnes über jüdische Dinge," *ZGJD,* II (1888), 378.
4. Alfred von Martin, "Das Wesen der romantischen Religiosität," *Deutsche Vierteljahrsschrift für Literaturwissenschaft und Geistesgeschichte,* II (1924), 387.
5. See Ludwig Lesser, *Chronik der Gesellschaft der Freunde in Berlin.*
6. Georg Heinrici, "Briefe von Henriette Herz an August Twesten (1814–1827)," *Zeitschrift für Bücherfreunde,* N. S., V, Pt. 2 (1914), 344 note 5.
7. Sebastian Hensel, *Die Familie Mendelssohn 1729–1847,* I, 112–13.
8. Eric Werner, "New Light on the Family of Felix Mendelssohn," *HUCA,* XXVI (1955), 555–56.
9. Georg Wilhelm Friedrich Hegel, *Early Theological Writings,* p. 211 note 34; cf. Nathan Rotenstreich, "Hegel's Image of Judaism," *JSS,* XV (1953), 39.
10. *Schriften,* V, 667.
11. *Dorothea v. Schlegel geb. Mendelssohn und deren Söhne Johannes und Philipp Veit: Briefwechsel,* ed. J. M. Raich, I, [9].
12. Ibid., I, [2].

13. *Caroline und Dorothea Schlegel in Briefen,* ed. Ernst Wieneke, p. 14.
14. *Wilhelm und Caroline von Humboldt in ihren Briefen,* ed. Anna von Sydow, I, 176–79.
15. *Caroline: Briefe aus der Frühromantik,* ed. Georg Waitz, I, 564.
16. On September 18, 1790, which was the date of Yom Kippur in that year, Wilhelm von Humboldt wrote to Caroline, "Heute erst war ich bei Jetten [Henriette Herz] und Brendel.... Gestern hatten die Juden lange Nacht, wo sie nicht besuchbar sind...." (Sydow, I, 216.)
17. *Briefe von und an Friedrich und Dorothea Schlegel,* ed. Josef Körner, p. 20.
18. See Hugo Weizäcker, *Schleiermacher und das Eheproblem,* pp. 14, 22.
19. Letter to Gustav von Brinckmann, February 2, 1799, in *Henriette Herz: Ihr Leben und ihre Zeit,* ed. Hans Landsberg, p. 278.
20. Wieneke, p. 348.
21. *Athenaeum,* II, Pt. 1 (1799), 14.
22. *Florentin. Ein Roman,* ed. Friedrich Schlegel, I (Lübeck and Leipzig, 1801).
23. G. Brandes, *Die Hauptströmungen der Literatur des neunzehnten Jahrhunderts,* II, 80. *Florentin* was thought worthy of full republication in 1911 in volume seven of the seventeenth section of *Deutsche Literatur: Sammlung literarischer Kunst- und Kulturdenkmäler in Entwicklungsreihen,* pp. 89–244.
24. Raich, I, 224.
25. For example regarding Fichte, who was thinking of buying some of her Berlin furniture, she wrote, "... er wird doch seinen Juden Hass wenigstens damit sanctionieren, dass er sie mir christlich bezahlt" (letter to Schleiermacher, January 6, 1800, in "Briefe von Dorothea Schlegel an Friedrich Schleiermacher," *Mitteilungen aus dem Litteraturarchiv in Berlin,* N. S., VII, 26–27).
26. In her diary in Paris (Raich, I, 128).
27. *Mitteilungen ...,* p. 119. This portion is omitted in the earlier printing of the same letter in Raich, I, 109–13.
28. *Mitteilungen ...,* p. 124.
29. Raich, I, 163.
30. Ibid., p. 256.
31. In this respect too she differed from Prussian Jewry which, in the struggle for emancipation, was ever professing its patriotism. Dorothea, from an entirely different perspective, could consider her Jewish origin reason for *lack* of patriotism. On June 8, 1807 she wrote to Caroline Paulus, whose good friend she had become in Jena: "Um meines asiatischen Ursprungs willen wird man es mir wohl verzeihen, dass ich zu meinem angebornen Vaterlande keinen allzugrossen Trieb in mir spüre" (ibid., p. 225).
32. Ibid., p. 261.
33. *Briefe von Dorothea und Friedrich Schlegel an die Familie Paulus,* ed. Rudolf Unger, p. 67.
34. *Krisenjahre der Frühromantik: Briefe aus dem Schlegelkreis,* ed. Josef Körner, I, 485.
35. Raich, I, 155.

36. Ibid., p. 298.
37. The Jewish painter Moritz Oppenheim once told Philipp Veit the details of his grandfather's rejection of Lavater's importunities. In reply Veit sighed and muttered, "Wer weiss, was er jetzt dafür büssen muss!" (*Erinnerungen,* ed. Alfred Oppenheim [Frankfurt a.M., 1924], p. 90).
38. Raich, I, 437–38.
39. In her letter to Rahel of April 11, 1817 (ibid., II, 418).
40. This letter was first published by Ludwig Geiger in "Dorothea Veit-Schlegel," *Deutsche Rundschau,* CLX (1914), 133–34. But Geiger's interpretation of the letter as an act of extraordinary courage indicates a failure to understand Dorothea's religious orientation in this period of her life.
41. *Rahel,* II, 433.
42. There is some doubt as to whether Henriette or Recha was the youngest daughter. Despite the genealogy in Hensel (*Die Familie...,* II, 418), the first-hand report of Sophie Becker that Mendelssohn's middle daughter was "recht schön," which Henriette certainly was not, would seem to indicate Hensel's error on this point. Jacobson has recently given July 18, 1767 as the date of Recha's (Rechel's) birth, while Körner has determined that Henriette was only eleven years old at the death of her father in 1786. This would make Henriette considerably younger than Recha. See Sophie Becker, *Vor hundert Jahren: Elise von der Reckes Reisen durch Deutschland 1784–86* (Stuttgart, 1883), p. 192; Jacob Jacobson, "Von Mendelssohn zu Mendelssohn-Bartholdy," *LBIY,* V (1960), 252; Josef Körner, "Mendelssohns Töchter," *Preussische Jahrbücher,* CCXIV (1928), 176.
43. Waitz, *Caroline...,* I, 487.
44. Heinrici, "Briefe von Henriette Herz...," p. 342.
45. Letter to Theresia Unterkircher, March 4, 1832, quoted in Körner, *Briefe von und an Friedrich und Dorothea Schlegel,* p. 585.
46. K. A. Varnhagen von Ense, *Denkwürdigkeiten des eignen Lebens,* ed. Joachim Kühn (Berlin, 1922), II, 62.
47. Letter of Chamisso to Hitzig, February 18, 1810, quoted in *Krisenjahre,* III, 344.
48. Ibid., II, 167.
49. *Rahel,* III, 204. The name is here given only as "J." However, Hannah Arendt has discovered that the original text of the diary entry has "Jette Mendelssohn." This information is contained in a manuscript of corrections to *Rahel* on deposit at the Leo Baeck Institute in New York.
50. Hensel, I, 88.
51. *Henriette Herz. Ihr Leben und ihre Erinnerungen,* ed. J. Fürst, p. 28.
52. Johann Gottfried Schadow, *Kunst-Werke und Kunst-Ansichten,* pp. xix–xx.
53. Fürst, pp. 98–100.
54. See Rudolf Haym, *Die romantische Schule,* pp. 238–42.
55. 1797 letter of Böttiger to Schiller, quoted in Heinrich Heidenheimer, "Zur Geschichte und Beurteilung der Juden vom XV. bis XIX. Jahrhundert," *MGWJ,* LIII (1909), 268.

56. *Wilhelm von Humboldts Briefe an Karl Gustav von Brinkmann,* ed. Albert Leitzmann, p. 87.

57. In the *Allgemeine Literatur-Zeitung* of 1797 (no. 333, p. 167), there appeared a review of the anonymously published *Bambocciaden* by Bernhardi. A. W. Schlegel, the reviewer, quoted from it this little known lampoon on Henriette Herz which, though perhaps a bit unfair, does have a certain ring of truth: "Jene—Madam Moses ist eine Jüdin, und von ihr werden Sie wohl schon bemerkt haben, dass sie sich mit Mühe so viel Grazie erworben hat, dass sie dadurch ungemein misfällt. —Sie ist in dieser Gesellschaft die eigentliche *schöne Seele,* sie hat von Jugend auf viel Umgang mit guten Köpfen gehabt,—welche ihr eine runde Summe von allgemeinen durchgreifenden aesthetischen Ideen hinterliessen, die sie jetzt jedem neuen Bekannten groschenweise zuzählet. —Sie ist immer in irgend einen Goethischen Charakter masquirt—am liebsten zeigt sie sich als Prinzessin im Tasso, deswegen lernt sie auch jetzt Latein. Hat ihr Goethe den Charakter nicht recht auf den Leib gemacht, so schneidet sie ihn sich selbst nach der Mode. —Ihre begünstigten Liebhaber indessen behaupten, unter vier Augen wäre sie—Madam Moses."

58. *Wilhelm von Humboldts Tagebücher,* ed. Albert Leitzmann (Berlin, 1916–18), I, 69.

59. Kayserling[2], pp. 455–58.

60. Sydow, *Wilhelm und Caroline . . . ,* IV, 260.

61. Landsberg, *Henriette Herz . . . ,* p. 262.

62. Trans. John Oman (New York, 1958).

63. Ibid., p. 283. This passage appeared only in the first edition.

64. Ibid., pp. 238–41.

65. Landsberg, pp. 108–9.

66. Ibid., pp. 113, 129, 131, 139, 147.

67. Apparently Schleiermacher had without success tried to persuade her to convert earlier. On December 2, 1808 he wrote to his prospective bride, Henriette von Willich: "Ich möchte wol wissen, ob Jette ein Wort mit Dir sprechen wird über etwas, was von ihr verkannt, von ihrem zu uns gehören in Absich der Religion. Jetzt hält sie es leider noch aus; ob sie es aber noch aushalten wird, wenn sie Dich sieht das Abendmal aus meiner Hand empfangen, oder gar . . . wenn sie mich sieht unser erstes Kind taufen, das möchte ich doch bezweifeln" (*Friedrich Schleiermachers Briefwechsel mit seiner Braut,* ed. Heinrich Meisner, p. 261; see also p. 359).

68. Ludwig Robert, Rahel's brother, composed the following characteristic poem entitled "Hofräthin Jette Herz":

> Junonische Riesin
> Egyptische Marquisin
> Tugend verübend
> Treuer als liebend
> Entzückt mit Gewalt.
> Hundertfach herzlos,

> Edel und schmerzlos,
> Rüstig und kalt,
> Zu jung für so alt.

69. Sydow, III, 332.

70. *Briefwechsel zwischen Varnhagen und Rahel,* ed. Ludmilla Assing, II, 109.

71. *Briefwechsel des jungen Börne und der Henriette Herz,* ed. Ludwig Geiger (Oldenburg and Leipzig, 1905), p. 22. The seventeen-year-old Börne was overwhelmed by his beautiful "Pensionsmutter." But when he moved away to Halle his passion gradually disappeared, the letters became more detached and his famous irony and wit more apparent. Henriette tried to take the stance of a mother toward him, ever urging him to diligence in his studies. Undoubtedly his attachment to her flattered her vanity, but she was also genuinely concerned for his welfare. The later Börne, like the later Humboldt, turned away from Henriette when freedom replaced love as his highest value.

72. *Briefwechsel zwischen Rahel und David Veit,* ed. Ludmilla Assing, II, 55, 79-80.

73. For example the sisters Sara and Marianne Meyer, on whom see Ludwig Geiger's comments in *Goethe-Jahrbuch,* XIV (1893), 95–104.

74. Leitzmann, *Humboldts Briefe an Karl Gustav von Brinkmann,* p. 87.

75. *Rahel,* I, 237.

76. Hannah Arendt, *Rahel Varnhagen,* appendix: Aus unveröffentlichten Briefen und Tagebüchern in chronologischer Folge, p. 206. The passage reads: "Verkannt, gehasst, muss ich mich und mein Aeusseres immer erst legitimieren."

77. Arendt, appendix, pp. 201, 203, 207, 208.

78. Assing, *Briefwechsel zwischen Rahel . . . ,* II, 173.

79. *Rahel,* I, 311.

80. Ibid., II, 16.

81. Ibid., I, 586.

82. Assing, *Briefwechsel zwischen Rahel . . . ,* I, 76.

83. Letter of April 9, 1812 in *Rahel und Alexander von der Marwitz in ihren Briefen,* ed. Heinrich Meisner, pp. 234-35.

84. Arendt, appendix, p. 205.

85. *Rahel,* II, 367.

86. In a letter to Count Astolf de Custine of March 20, 1830, to be added to *Rahel,* III, 428, according to the Arendt manuscript of additions. The passage is as follows: ". . . et j'ai on la honte pour la première fois de ma vie, de m'ennuyer jusqu'aux larmes . . . mais pour manque d'images, de pensées, et d'idées! Pour la première fois je ne me trouvais pas exaltée, élevée, transportée dans une meilleure région par mes souffrances, j'étais devenue commune, au moins vide, creuse et ordinaire: et j'ai dû apprendre et j'ai appris: que ce que nous sommes n'est pas moins un don, que ce que nous avons. Enfin j'ai appris et j'ai souffert. . . ."

87. Carl Atzenbeck, *Pauline Wiesel,* pp. 217-18; see also pp. 185-86, 224.

88. "Ueber Rahels Religiosität," in *Ausgewählte Schriften von K. A. Varnhagen von Ense,* XIX, 281-82.

89. *Rahel*, II, 557.
90. *Angelus Silesius und Saint-Martin*, p. 104.
91. E.g. *Rahel*, II, 206: "O! ich fühle alles in meiner Noth. Gott schickt sie mir. *Ich küsse das Kreuz.* Er hat gewiss recht."
92. Ibid., I, 36–37, 227.
93. Ibid., II, 224; *Zur Judenfrage in Deutschland*, ed. Wilhelm Freund (Berlin, 1843), p. 181.
94. This was first noted by Gabriel Riesser in his "Jüdische Briefe: Zur Abwehr und Verständigung," *Gesammelte Schriften*, IV, 256–59.
95. "Ein Brief von Rahel," in *Zur Judenfrage in Deutschland*, pp. 181–82. Ludwig, whom Rahel considered her "Religionsbruder," wrote a poem at about the same time which shows that he too felt being a Jew was a pariah status indelibly imposed by society, but that religiously he could only be a Christian. This little known sonnet is to be found in Wilhelm Dorow, *Erlebtes aus den Jahren 1790–1827*, IV, 177–78:

> Wenn der ein Jud' ist, der im Mutterleibe
> Verdammt schon war zu niederm Sklavenstande,
> Der ohne Rechte lebt im Vaterlande,
> Dem Pöbel, der mit Koth wirft, eine Scheibe;
>
> Dem gar nichts hilft, was er auch thu' und treibe,
> Des Leidenkelch doch voll bleibt bis am Rande:
> Verachtungsvoll und schmachvoll und voll Schande?
> Dann bin ich Jud'—und weiss auch, dass ich's bleibe.
>
> Und wenn *der* Christ ist, der sich streng befleisset
> Sein Erdenkreuz in Demuth zu ertragen
> Und die zu lieben, die ihn tödtlich hassen;
>
> Glaubend, dass Alles, was sein Herz zerreisset,
> Der Herr, um ihn zu prüfen, zugelassen?
> Dann bin ich Christ! das darf ich redlich sagen.

96. *Rahel*, I, 43.
97. E.g. Hannah Arendt, who begins her biography with this quotation; also M. Kayserling in *Die jüdischen Frauen*, pp. 209–16.

CHAPTER 5

1. The esteem in which the Maskilim held Mendelssohn was boundless. They called him "the light of our generation" and said, "In his shadow we shall live among the nations." (*Ha-Measef*, I [1784], 20; II [1785], 43; III [1786], 66.) In verse they compared him to Newton:

> Koshet ve-dat tserura be-ofel mini dor dor
> 'Ade amar Elohim yehi Moshe! va-yehi or!
> [Truth and religion lay hid in night:
> God said, Let Moses be! and all was Light.] (Ibid., III [1786], 161.)

2. Ibid., I (1784), 6–10.

3. In "swearing by the flag of the Masoretes" (ibid., I [1784], first German supplement, p. 12) the Measfim showed themselves much more conservative than the Christian Bible scholars of the day. The only controversial issues which they raised were the permissibility of Bible translations into pure German and early burial of the dead, both issues on which they simply followed the lead of Mendelssohn. Early burial remained a matter for dispute well into the nineteenth century.

4. Ibid., VI (1790), 311.

5. *Ha-Measef,* VII (1794–97), 54 ff.

6. Ibid., fourth quarter; Raphael Mahler, *Divre yeme Yisrael,* II, 175.

7. "R' Henokh, oder vos tut me damit," *Arkhiv far der geshikhte fun yidishen te'ater un drame,* I (1930), 94–146. Similar in form and content is the play by Aaron Wolfssohn, *Leichtsinn und Frömmelei* [Hebrew characters], published in 1796. Euchel's play was still circulating in manuscript in Berlin Jewish circles in 1817, where the young Leopold Zunz amused his acquaintances by reading it aloud (Glatzer², p. 87).

8. *Ha-Measef,* VII (1794–97), German supplement to first quarter, 3–4.

9. *Jedidja,* IV, 1 (1822), 1.

10. *Sulamith, eine Zeitschrift zur Beförderung der Kultur und Humanität unter der jüdischen Nation,* ed. Fränkel and Wolf. Beginning with the third volume (1810), the title was changed to "unter den Israeliten."

11. Ibid., I, 1 (1806), 10.

12. Ibid., p. 164.

13. Ibid., II, 1 (1808), 217–32.

14. "Musterhaftes Betragen eines Rabbiners," ibid., I, 1 (1806), 183–84.

15. Judah Benzeev, *Yesode ha-dat,* first introduction.

16. *Erbauungen,* II, 22. These words are taken from the preface to the printed text of a sermon delivered by Eduard Kley, one of the editors, in May of 1814. Kayserling, in his *Bibliothek jüdischer Kanzelredner,* I, pp. 15–18, makes this preface part of the sermon, dates the sermon in May of 1813, and ascribes it to C. S. Günsburg. He is wrong on all three points. It is clearly not the sermon itself but a preface, written after the sermon was delivered (e.g., p. 21), which Kayserling has erroneously included in his *Bibliothek.* Furthermore, preface and sermon cannot be by Günsburg since the author claims to have been a tutor in Berlin for more than five years (p. 20). Günsburg did not come to Berlin until 1810 (*Bibliothek,* I, 15) and we have no knowledge of his having been a tutor. Of Kley it is known that he came to Berlin in 1809 and served as tutor in the home of Jacob Herz Beer, a job which he left only in 1815 (H. Jonas, *Lebensskizze des Herrn Doctor Eduard Kley,* pp. 6–8). The five years of tutoring also yields us a date of May, 1814—not 1813—for the sermon, a conclusion further substantiated by the fact that it appeared in the third quarterly installment of the *Erbauungen,* to be dated in 1814.

17. A bibliography of writings on and by Ascher is given in Ellen Littmann, "Saul Ascher," *LBIY,* V (1960), 107 note 3, 120–21.

18. J. G. Meusel, *Das gelehrte Teutschland*, pp. 52–53.

19. Quoted from the Prussian archives, Berlin-Dahlem, in Fritz Pinkuss, "Saul Ascher," rabbinical dissertation, *Hochschule für die Wissenschaft des Judentums* in Berlin. (Dr. Pinkuss, now in Brazil, was kind enough to lend me his manuscript.)

20. *Bemerkungen über die bürgerliche Verbesserung der Juden.*

21. See Hans Joachim Schoeps, *Geschichte der jüdischen Religionsphilosophie in der Neuzeit*, I, 42–43.

22. S. Ascher, *Eisenmenger der Zweite*.

23. *Leviathan . . .*, pp. 243–44.

24. Ibid., p. 227.

25. Ibid., pp. 171–72.

26. E.g. E. Kley, *Catechismus der mosaischen Religion*, iv; Herz Homberg, *Ben Yakir*, p. 83; *Erbauungen*, II, 8.

27. Littmann (p. 114) has tried to connect the *Leviathan* with Schleiermacher. But Schleiermacher was not yet living in Berlin in 1792 and he had as yet written no theological works!

28. *Leviathan . . .*, p. 14.

29. Max Wiener, "Saul Ascher and the Theory of Judaism as a Religion" [Yiddish], *Yivo Bleter*, XXIII (1944), 71.

30. *Leviathan . . .*, p. 160.

31. Ascher himself said later that his work was more acclaimed by Christians than Jews (*Die Germanomanie*, p. 58).

32. *Ha-Measef*, II (1785), 28–31. It seems, however, that this translation never did appear. Jagel's work, though earlier translated into Judeo-German, had not been utilized as a text for religious education (M. Eliav, *Ha-Hinukh . . .*, p. 260).

33. A number of them are listed in the bibliography. A detailed treatment of fifteen catechisms, which appeared from 1810 to 1868, is found in Jakob J. Petuchowski, "Manuals and Catechisms of the Jewish Religion in the Early Period of Emancipation," *Studies in Nineteenth-Century Jewish Intellectual History*, pp. 47–64.

34. E.g. J. M. Lilienfeld, *Patriotische Gedanken eines Israeliten*, p. 88.

35. Two favorite rabbinic quotations of the Maskilim were "dina de-malkhuta dina" ["the law of the land is law (for us)"] and "haside umot ha-'olam yesh la-hem helek le-'olam ha-ba" ["the pious of all nations have a share in the world to come"].

36. An example of the latter is the section entitled "Durch die Israeliten sollte der Glaube an einen einzigen und gerechten Gott, auch auf die andern Völker sich verbreiten," in Peter Beer, *Handbuch der mosaischen Religion*, II, 162–68.

37. Joseph Johlson, *Unterricht in der Mosaischen Religion*, p. 16.

38. Peter Beer, *Dat Yisrael*, I, xviii.

39. *Sulamith*, I, 2 (1807), 51 note.

40. Ibid., IV, 1 (1812), 246–54; *Jedidja*, II, 1 (1818), 207–16.

41. *Das wahre System der rein mosaischen Religion*, p. 6.

42. Peter Beer, *Geschichte, Lehren und Meinungen*, II, 416; Aaron Wolfssohn, *Jeschurun* (Breslau, 1804), p. 114.

43. *Predigten in dem neuen Israelitischen Tempel zu Hamburg*, II, 46.

44. Despite Isaac E. Barzilay, "National and Anti-National Trends in the Berlin Haskalah," *JSS*, XXI (1959), 165–92.

45. Gotthold Salomon, *Lebensgeschichte des Herrn Moses Philippsohn* (Dessau, 1814), p. 43 note. Cf. *Sulamith*, I, 2 (1807), 382; *Erbauungen*, II, 745; Benedikt Schottlaender, *Sendschreiben an meine Brüder*, pp. 16–18.

46. Jacob R. Marcus, "Israel Jacobson," *CCARY*, XXXVIII (1928), 386–498; Mahler, *Divre yeme Yisrael*, p. 151.

47. Salomon, *Lebensgeschichte . . .*, pp. 58–59.

48. Jacob R. Marcus, "The Love Letters of Bendet Schottlaender," *HUCA*, VII (1930), 542 note 10, 562 note 51.

49. It seems, however, that Christian teachers were no better paid (Felix Lazarus, "Das Königlich-Westphälische Konsistorium der Israeliten," *MGWJ*, LVIII [1914], 206 note 1).

50. Phoebus Philippson, *Biographische Skizzen*, II, 206.

51. M. Eliav, *Ha-Hinukh . . .*, p. 207.

52. David Fränkel, *Nachricht von der Jüdischen Haupt- und Frey-Schule in Dessau*, p. 60 note.

53. Schottlaender, p. 25.

54. *Sulamith*, II, 1 (1808), 70.

55. Ibid., I, 1 (1806), 215.

56. *Jedidja*, I, 1 (1817), 22–23.

57. As in the speech of Israel Jacobson at the dedication of his temple in Seesen: "Nur der gemeinschaftliche Fortschritt zum *Besseren*, zum letzten Ziele der *Vernunft* wird zwei verschieden denkende Partheien—wenn auch nicht zur Gemeinschaft, aber doch zum Näherseyn leiten; nur die Vernunft mit ihren ewigen Grundsätzen ist das Einzige, worin zuletzt die abweichendsten Partheien, die ungläubigsten Sekten, die weit entlegendsten Völker übereintreffen müssen" (*Sulamith*, III, 1 [1810], 309–10).

58. M. H. Bock, *Israelitischer Kinderfreund* (Berlin, 1811), xii; *Sulamith*, III, 2 (1811), 25.

59. Ibid., II, 1 (1808), 223–24.

60. *Führt uns die Religion auch nicht zurück?* (Altona, 1820), pp. 5–6. Cf. *Sulamith*, I, 2 (1807), 199–203, 249–57; V, 1 (1817), 32.

61. Ibid., III, 1 (1810), 336. Cf. ibid., I, 1 (1806), 314; III, 2 (1811), 371; V, 1 (1817), 163 note.

62. J. Wolf, *Sechs deutsche Reden, gehalten in der Synagoge zu Dessau* (Dessau, 1812–13), I, 55.

63. J. A. Dorner, *History of Protestant Theology*, trans. George Robson and Sophie Taylor, II (Edinburgh, 1871), 291.

64. Herz Homberg, *Rede bey Eröffnung der religiös-moralischen Vorlesungen für*

Israeliten in Prag (Prague, 1818), p. 5; Wolf, I, 103–19, II, 25–28; E. Kley, *Catechismus* ..., p. 1.

65. Wolfssohn, *Jeschurun*, pp. 118–21.

66. *Sulamith*, I, 2 (1807), 8–9.

67. Although Mendelssohn wrote sermons for patriotic occasions, the German sermon had not been a regular part of the Jewish service. It was not until 1805 that Joseph Wolf began giving German sermons in the Dessau synagogue on the first days of the festivals and on Kol Nidre eve (*AZJ*, LI [1887], 750). Wolf's sermon of October 1808, given on the occasion of Duke Franz's jubilee (*Sulamith*, II, 1 [1808], 276–85), is not, as commonly believed, the first extant German sermon to have been given by its author (Mendelssohn did not deliver the sermons he wrote). Earlier that same year a German sermon was delivered in the Cassel synagogue by Shalom Cohen, shortly to become the last editor of *Ha-Measef*. It was printed in *Sulamith*, II, 1 (1808), 15–30.

68. Ibid., II, 2 (1809), 296–305. See also the duties assigned to the congregational secretaries, pp. 305–12.

69. Ibid., III, 1 (1810), 15–17; cf. III, 1, 146–48, 294–97; V, 2 (1819), 399–401.

70. Given in ibid., III, 1 (1810), 366–80 and reprinted in 1842, without the threatening forty-third paragraph, in *Allgemeines Archiv des Judenthums*, I (1839), 328–39.

71. The Seesen Temple was not the first to possess an organ. Centuries earlier an organ had been installed in one of the old synagogues of Prague. In 1716 a new one was built for the same house of worship by a Jewish craftsman (Leopold Zunz, *Die Gottesdienstlichen Vorträge der Juden*, p. 476).

72. N. Friedland, *Zur Geschichte des Tempels der Jacobsonschule*, p. 5.

73. *Sulamith*, III, 1 (1810), 316–17.

74. E.g. by Fränkel in ibid., V, 2 (1819), 398–99 note, and by Heinemann in *Jedidja*, II, 2 (1819), 79–80. Also others continued to urge centrally controlled organization and reform: Johlson, *Unterricht* ..., p. xxi; J. Wolf and G. Salomon, *Der Charakter des Judenthums*, pp. 205–6.

75. Ironically, King Jerome of Westphalia had issued an order prohibiting such private services—which in Westphalia were held by the orthodox (*Sulamith*, III, 2 [1811] 211–13).

76. In November 1818 (Geiger, *Geschichte der Juden* ..., II, 221).

77. *Sulamith*, IV, 2 (1815), 66–70.

78. Israel Bettan, "Early Reform in Contemporaneous Responsa," *Hebrew Union College Jubilee Volume*, p. 434.

79. M. I. Bresselau, *Herev noḳemet neḳam berit*, pp. 5–6.

80. "Gründungs- und Vereinigungsurkunde des Neuen Israelitischen Tempelvereins in Hamburg," *Festschrift zum hundertjährigen Bestehen des Israelitischen Tempels in Hamburg 1818–1918*, p. 11.

81. *Ordnung der öffentlichen Andacht für die Sabbath und Festtage des ganzen Jahres.*

82. Ibid., pp. 106–7, 240–41.
83. Ibid., p. 62. See also p. 49 where in the Retse prayer " 'avoda" is translated as "den wahren Gottesdienst," and "ishe Yisrael" not as "Feueropfer" but simply as "Opfer."
84. Although the word "goel" is retained in the Hebrew text (p. 44), it is translated as "Erlösung."
85. *Ele divre ha-berit.*
86. Especially Bresselau, and Seckel Isaac Fränkel, *Schutzschrift des zu Hamburg erschienenen Israelitischen Gebetbuchs.*
87. Although his son, the famous fighter for Jewish equality in Germany, Gabriel Riesser, was later a director of the Hamburg Temple, Lazarus Riesser was not a member of the congregation—at least not in the beginning. His name is missing from the list of charter members given in Leimsdörfer, pp. 16–17.
88. Lazarus Jacob Riesser, *Send-Schreiben an meine Glaubens-Genossen in Hamburg.*
89. Gotthold Salomon, *Kurzgefasste Geschichte des neuen Israelitischen Tempels in Hamburg,* pp. 6–7.
90. *Ha-Measef* (II [1785], 17) spoke of "the justice of the peoples toward us, how daily their kindness toward us grows." Fränkel wrote in the *Sulamith* in 1808 (II, 1, 157) that it was a time "wo die Vernunft und Humanität die Oberhand gewonnen, wo die Regenten weise und milde herrschen, und im Menschen den Menschen ehren...."
91. Ibid., I, 2 (1807), 148–49.
92. Reinhold Steig, *Heinrich von Kleists Berliner Kämpfe,* pp. 21–23.
93. Ibid., p. 610.
94. *Achim von Arnims ausgewählte Werke,* II, 21–152.
95. Martin Philippson, "Der Anteil der jüdischen Freiwilligen an dem Befreiungskriege 1813 und 1814," *MGWJ,* L (1906), 1–21, 220–47.
96. *Zuruf an die Jünglinge,* pp. 5, 10.
97. A rare exception is presented by the Dessau pedagogue and Hebrew publisher, Moses Philippson. According to his son and biographer, he said as early as 1813: "Als *Israelit* muss ich bekennen, dass ich für die Gleichstellung meiner Glaubensgenossenschaft nach dem Sturze Napoleons wenig erwarte, man wird sie wieder in die alten Fesseln schlagen, die doch nur in einem kleinen Theile Deutschlands gebrochen oder gelüftet sind" (Philippson, *Biographische Skizzen,* I, 117).
98. Friedrich Rühs, *Ueber die Ansprüche der Juden an das deutsche Bürgerrecht;* J. F. Fries, *Ueber die Gefährdung des Wohlstandes und Charakters der Deutschen durch die Juden.* Rühs replied to his critics in *Die Rechte des Christenthums und des deutschen Volks.*
99. Sigmund Zimmern, *Versuch einer Würdigung der Angriffe des Herrn Professor Fries auf die Juden,* p. 4 note c. In his pamphlet Zimmern suggested that rabbinic authority would wither away by itself: "Engt uns nicht ein, und was ihr wollt, wird geschehen!" (p. 23). Five years later the stud. jur. of 1816 had received his doctorate and been baptized (Glatzer[2], p. 123).

100. M. Hess, *Freimüthige Prüfung der Schrift des Herrn Professor Rühs*, p. 90. See also *Sulamith*, V, 1 (1817), 3; Wolf and Salomon, *Der Charakter* . . . , p. 146.
101. Hess, p. 55.
102. *Sulamith*, IV, 2 (1815), 64.
103. David Fränkel, *Einige Worte an die Schüler der Franzschule in Dessau*, p. 16.
104. In a letter of January 1, 1819 to his teacher, S. M. Ehrenberg, Zunz noted having made Ascher's acquaintance and described him as "ein Mann von eigentümlichen Ansichten, Feind aller Schwärmerei, gegen die Deutschtümler: sein moralischer Charakter wird nicht geschätzt" (Glatzer[2], p. 96).
105. Saul Ascher, *Die Germanomanie*, p. 16.
106. Pinson, *Modern Germany*, p. 64.
107. Eleonore Sterling, *Er ist wie Du*, pp. 179–81, 189.
108. *Sulamith*, VI, 1 (1820), 34. *Jedidja* was completely silent.
109. Dubnow, IX, 39.
110. Eric Werner, "New Light on the Family of Felix Mendelssohn," *HUCA*, XXVI (1955), 558.

CHAPTER 6

1. Wilhelm von Humboldt, "Ueber die innere und äussere Organisation der höheren wissenschaftlichen Anstalten in Berlin," *Gedenkschrift der freien Universität Berlin*, pp. 193–202. On the change in intellectual "Modewörter" see Wilhelm Körte, *Leben und Studien Friedr. Aug. Wolfs*, II, 12.
2. Robert Reinhold Ergang, *Herder and the Foundations of German Nationalism* (New York, 1931), p. 248.
3. For biographical details of Zunz's early life the best single source is Zunz's own book of recollections and miscellaneous jottings, *Das Buch Zunz*, a portion of which, particularly covering the early years, was edited and published by Fritz Bamberger. David Kaufmann's article on Zunz in the *Allgemeine Deutsche Biographie* (reprinted in his *Gesammelte Schriften*, I, 333–51) draws heavily upon this source.
4. On the character of the school during the time Zunz was a student see: Philipp Ehrenberg, "Die Samson'sche Freischule zu Wolfenbüttel," *Literaturblatt des Orients*, V (1844), 65 ff.; Isaac Marcus Jost, "Vor einem halben Jahrhundert," in *Sippurim*, III (1854), 141–66; and Leopold Zunz, "Mein erster Unterricht in Wolfenbüttel," *JJGL*, XXX (1937), 131–38.
5. Glatzer[1], p. 24.
6. Leopold Zunz, *Samuel Meyer Ehrenberg*, pp. 27–28.
7. Glatzer[1], pp. 2, 28.
8. Ismar Elbogen, "Leopold Zunz zum Gedächtnis," *Fünfzigster Bericht der Lehranstalt für die Wissenschaft des Judentums in Berlin*, pp. 18–19; Glatzer[2], p. 77.
9. Not Henriettte Herz, as is incorrectly supposed by some scholars even today.

Glatzer notes that Saisette Hertz belonged to the Veitel Heine Ephraim family (Glatzer[2], p. 80). It appears that she was the recent widow of Heinrich Rudolf Hertz, a jeweler who had died in February of 1815 at the age of 38. See Jacob Jacobson, *Die Judenbürgerbücher der Stadt Berlin*, p. 73. Note also the entry in *Buch Zunz* (p. 24) under Sunday, May 13, 1821: "Sus. [Sais.?] Hertz stirbt."

10. Ludwig Geiger, "Zunz' Tätigkeit für die Reform (1817–1823)," *Liberales Judentum*, IX (1917), 114–15.

11. See for example the letter of Zunz, dated September 18, 1840, in which he proposes synagogal reforms for the Jewish community of London (ibid., pp. 119–20).

12. Siegmund Maybaum, "Aus dem Leben von Leopold Zunz," *Zwölfter Bericht über die Lehranstalt für die Wissenschaft des Judentums* (Berlin, 1894), p. 3.

13. Although he wrote to Bresselau that he was withdrawing in favor of his friend, the Hebrew and German poet L. M. Büschenthal (Maybaum, p. 4), he admitted to Ehrenberg that it was only an excuse (Geiger, p. 114).

14. Glatzer[1], p. 13; cf. p. 38.

15. Geiger, p. 114.

16. L. L. Hellwitz, *Die Organisation der Israeliten in Deutschland*. For many years historians, including Jost and Graetz, accepted Hellwitz as the author. But, as we now know from his self-compiled bibliography (*JJGL*, XXX [1937], 166) and his letters (Glatzer[2], pp. 99–100, 102, 109) Zunz was the author of the body of the work. Hellwitz wrote the preface (signed "Werl im März 1819") after Zunz completed his task and, as we know from the title page, paid the costs of publication from his own pocket. Although Zunz incorporated some of the opinions contained in documents written by others, given him for consideration in composing the work, he wrote to Ehrenberg that he was able to give the pamphlet a single spirit, put his own ideas into it, and that, if anyone was to be regarded as its author, he should be (Glatzer[2], p. 100). Wallach's contention that Zunz wrote a second work published in the name of Hellwitz and a third anonymous one dealing with Hellwitz is thus without foundation since Hellwitz was not a pseudonym for Zunz but a real individual. Moreover, it is inconceivable that Zunz, who meticulously listed all works he had written or in which he had had a share, should have excluded these two from his bibliography (Leopold Wallach, *Liberty and Letters*, pp. 53, 145–46).

17. *Die Organisation . . . ,* p. 62.

18. Ibid., pp. 35–36.

19. Glatzer[2], p. 99.

20. The significance of —e— remains a mystery, but perhaps this signature is what Ludwig Geiger (upon whose transcriptions Professor Glatzer in part based his second volume of Zunz correspondence) regarded as an ellipsis in the letter to Ehrenberg. As this brief review has not previously been available to scholars interested in Zunz, it is here reproduced in full from *Der Gesellschafter*, June 28, 1819, p. 420:

Literatur. "Die Organisation der Israeliten in Deutschland. Ein Versuch

von L. L. Hellwitz. Auf Kosten des Verfassers, zum Besten armer Hand-
werker." (Magdeburg 1819. In Commission bei Ferd. Rubach.)—Unter den
vielen über Juden erschienenen Schriften zeichnet sich die vorliegende durch
Klarheit der Sprache, durch Wärme und durch strenge Liebe zur Wahrheit
vortheilhaft aus. Daher verzeiht man dem Eifer für das bürgerliche Wohl und
die Erziehung der Juden manchen unausführbaren Vorschlag, wie den vom
Concilium; denn der grösste Theil der Juden wird sich schwerlich seinen
Talmud nehmen lassen. Aber zu wünschen ist die Beherzigung manches
zeitgemässen Wortes, das der Verfasser Juden und Christen sagt, und zu
hoffen: dass man nicht ferner in die jüdischen Angelegenheiten hinein
pfusche, ohne den Rath sachkundiger und unterrichteter Juden zu hören.
Wir nennen aber mit dem Verfasser die sogenannten Rabbiner dazu unfähig,
zumal solche, wie der zu Lemberg, der ganz kürzlich Mendelssohns Bibel-
übersetzung unterdrücken wollte. Was über die Erziehung (S. 40–48) gesagt
wird, fordert daher grosse Aufmerksamkeit. Des Verfassers Bann gegen das
Wort Jude (S. 36) theilen wir nicht; auch ist es durchaus kein Sprachfehler,
aus Jehuda entstanden. Desgleichen scheint uns das Verbot (S. 45) über die
Theilnahme an Religionstunden voreilig, da hierin bloss die Eltern bestimmen
können.—e—

21. Maybaum, pp. 5–6.
22. On August 12, 1817 he had written enthusiastically about a confirmation ceremony he attended, conducted by Auerbach in the Beer Temple (Geiger, p. 115).
23. H. Vogelstein, "Beiträge zur Geschichte des Unterrichtswesen in der jüdischen
Gemeinde zu Königsberg," *Sechsunddreissigster Bericht über den Religions-
Unterricht der Synagogengemeinde zu Königsberg i. Pr.* (Königsberg, 1903),
pp. 16–17.
24. Simon Bernfeld, *Toldot ha-reformatsyon ha-datit be-Yisrael*, p. 101. In *Buch
Zunz* (p. 21) Zunz mentions disparagingly "Simcha Weil & Consorten."
25. The entry in *Buch Zunz* (p. 23), after giving an outline of the sermon, reads:
"Seit Israel sind 8 Epochen jede zu 450 J., also in Allem 3600 J. verflossen,
bezeichnet durch Debora, Elischa, Nehemia, die Mischna, die Gemara, Saadia,
die Jahre 1370 u. 1820." The statement I think should be taken principally as
an expression of personal exhilaration and pride (see Maybaum, p. 7) rather
than as a consciousness of standing upon the threshold of a new age of world
history, as it is in Alexander Altmann, "Zur Frühgeschichte der jüdischen
Predigt in Deutschland," *LBIY*, VI (1961), 50. In the analysis of Zunz's sermons I have profited from Professor Altmann's recent thorough study, which
utilizes the sermons extant only in manuscript as well as the printed ones. However, I do not concur in all of his conclusions.
26. Geiger, "Zunz' Tätigkeit...," p. 116.
27. E.g. the reference in the letter from Ehrenberg of September 22, 1820: "Dass
Du am 2t Neujahrstag mit vielem Beifall gepredigt und denselben wirklich
verdient hast, habe ich durch Jost, dem es sonst nicht leicht einer recht macht,
erfahren" (Glatzer[1], p. 18).

28. See, for example, Gotthold Salomon, *Auswahl mehrerer Predigten.*

29. Sixteen of Zunz's sermons given in Berlin were published as *Predigten. Gehalten in der neuen israelitischen Synagoge zu Berlin.*

30. Altmann (pp. 21–42) places somewhat more emphasis upon Kantianism and romanticism.

31. *Predigten*, pp. 108–9.

32. See also Alexander Altmann, "The New Style of Preaching in Nineteenth-Century German Jewry," *Studies in Nineteenth-Century Jewish Intellectual History*, pp. 65–116.

33. *Predigten*, pp. 129–42.

34. Ibid., p. 106; cf. p. 141.

35. M. Brann and M. Rosenmann, "Der Briefwechsel zwischen Isak Noa Mannheimer und Leopold Zunz," *MGWJ*, LXI (1917), 97; Altmann, "Zur Frühgeschichte...," p. 6.

36. Ibid., p. 58 inset.

37. On June 25, 1822 Zunz reported to Ehrenberg: "Die hiesige deutsche Synagoge geht noch ihren alten schläfrigen Gang" (Geiger, p. 118).

38. *Schriften*, V, 722.

39. *Heinrich Heine Briefe*, IV, 106.

40. Jost, "Vor einem halben Jahrhundert," pp. 157–59.

41. Adolf Strodtmann, *Heines Leben und Werke*, I, 295.

42. *Zunz Archives*, File II.1. (according to the arrangement of photostats in the Leo Baeck Institute, New York).

43. *Buch Zunz*, p. 19.

44. *Zunz Archives*, File II. 43. Professor Glatzer, who has deciphered the manuscript, informed me that it differs little from the other Jewish replies.

45. The arguments in favor of a considerable influence by Savigny and the Historical School are advanced in Fritz Bamberger, "Zunz's Conception of History," *PAAJR*, XI (1941), 1–25. The influence has been minimized by Wallach (*Liberty and Letters*, p. 77) and by Nathan Rotenstreich in *Ha-Mahashava ha-yehudit be-'et ha-hadasha*, I, 38, note 6.

46. Joseph Lehmann, "H. Heine in Berlin, in den Jahren 1821–1823," *Magazin für die Literatur des Auslandes*, XXXVII (1868), 170. However, Savigny might have been expected to view Gans's candidacy with disfavor even if Gans were a Christian, since the young jurist was an avowed opponent of the Historical School.

47. Frederick Charles von Savigny, *Of the Vocation of our Age for Legislation and Jurisprudence*, p. 49.

48. Friedrich Carl von Savigny, *Geschichte des römischen Rechts im Mittelalter* (3rd ed.; Darmstadt, 1956), I, xv.

49. Graetz, pp. 318–19. Gotthard Deutsch once put it succinctly: "Das historische Recht bedeutete ja für die Juden ein verjährtes Unrecht" (*Westliche Blätter*, March 27, 1898, p. 12).

50. G. P. Gooch, *History and Historians in the Nineteenth Century*, pp. 28–29.

51. "Brief an den Chef der Sektion für Kultus und Unterricht im Ministerium des Innern Friedrich von Schuckmann vom 2.5. 1811." *Gedenkschrift der freien Universität Berlin,* p. 226.

52. August Boeckh, *Encyklopädie und Methodologie der philologischen Wissenschaften,* p. 16. For Wolf's conception see his "Darstellung der Altertums-Wissenschaft," *Museum der Altertums-Wissenschaft,* I (1807), 1–142.

53. Cf. I. Elbogen, "Neuorientierung unserer Wissenschaft," *MGWJ,* LXII (1918), 85.

54. Körte, *Leben und Studien Friedr. Aug. Wolfs...,* II, 72.

55. Ernst Troeltsch, "Der Historismus und seine Probleme," *Gesammelte Schriften* (Tübingen, 1922), III, 280.

56. *ZWJ,* pp. 114–16.

57. First published in Berlin by Maurer, it was reprinted in his *Gesammelte Schriften,* I, 1–31.

58. E.g. Jacob Weil, *Fragmente aus dem Talmud und den Rabbinen.*

59. Some Jewish leaders had earlier recognized the need for general scientific training as a prerequisite for the task of religious reform, but a scientific treatment of the Jewish literature was not proposed. The following excerpt is from an 1809 essay by H. J. Damier of Hamburg (*Sulamith,* II, 2, 418): "Wollen wir indessen die reinen göttlichen Lehren unter dem Schwall menschlicher Satzungen hervorsuchen, so müssen wir zuvörderst unsern Geist durch Wissenschaften aufzuklären suchen; denn nicht nur die Wissenschaften, welche auf Prinzipien der Vernunft, sondern selbst diejenigen, die auf wissenschaftlichen Datis beruhen, gewähren uns richtige Ansichten in der Religion."

60. Rotenstreich, I, 36–38.

61. Siegfried Ucko, "Geistesgeschichtliche Grundlagen der Wissenschaft des Judentums," *ZGJD,* V (1933–35), 3.

62. The titles were: "Anleitung zum Büchermachen," "Lob des Geldes," and "Von der Würde eines Konversationslexikons; eine Predigt ueber zwei Texte" (ibid.).

63. On Gans see the recently published first comprehensive biography, by Hanns G. Reissner, *Eduard Gans: Ein Leben im Vormärz.*

64. Ludwig Geiger, "Aus Eduard Gans' Frühzeit (1817)," *ZGJD,* V (1891), 91–99.

65. Shlomo Avineri, "A Note on Hegel's Views on Jewish Emancipation," *JSS,* XXV (1963), 145–51.

66. Georg Wilhelm Friedrich Hegel, *Philosophy of Right,* trans. T. M. Knox (Oxford, 1942), p. 169 note.

67. List's remarks are found in Ucko, pp. 9–11.

68. Ibid., pp. 13–16.

69. Gans made a point of the fact that "Wissenschaft der Juden" had a double meaning: Jews were to be both the scholars and the objects of their scholarship (ibid., p. 20).

70. Ibid., p. 19. Zunz, the young philologist, suggested, 1. Verein für Literaturfreunde, 2. Verein für Beförderung der Bildung unter den jüdischen Glaubensgenossen; 3. Academia; 4. Philagathia; 5. Symposion.

71. *JJGL*, XXX (1937), 166.
72. *Entwurf von Statuten*, p. 4.
73. They were reprinted with an introduction by Salman Rubaschoff (Shazar) under the title "Erstlinge der Entjüdung" in the periodical *Der jüdische Wille*, I (1918–19).
74. Ibid., p. 42.
75. Ibid., pp. 197–98.
76. Georg Wilhelm Friedrich Hegel, *Lectures on the Philosophy of History*, p. 82 (translation slightly modified). See also Nathan Rotenstreich, "Hegel's Image of Judaism," *JSS*, XV (1953), 33–52.
77. Rubaschoff, p. 113. Gans goes on to describe this future state with a quotation from Herder: "Es wird eine Zeit kommen, wo man in Europa nicht mehr fragen wird, wer Jude und wer Christ sei." This same passage formed part of the motto on the title page of Friedländer's *Akten-Stücke*, published in 1793.
78. Hegel, *Lectures . . .* , pp. 30–32.
79. For a complete listing see Reissner, pp. 172–89.
80. I. M. Jost, *Geschichte der Israeliten*, I, xii. See also Salo Baron, "I. M. Jost, the Historian," *PAAJR*, I (1928–30), 13 note 3. As late as 1832 Jost was opposed to the title, "Der Jude," which Gabriel Riesser chose for his journal (Glatzer[1], p. 64).
81. Jost, pp. viii–ix.
82. Glatzer[1], p. 35.
83. I. Elbogen, "Ein hundertjähriger Gedenktag unserer Wissenschaft," *MGWJ*, LXVI (1922), 90.
84. Letter of August 16, 1822 (Glatzer[1], p. 34).
85. *Heinrich Heine Gespräche*, pp. 29–31.
86. *Heinrich Heine Briefe*, I, 133, 174, 186, 192, 328.
87. Hannah Arendt, "The Jew as Pariah," *JSS*, VI (1944), 104.
88. *Heinrich Heine Briefe*, I, 134.
89. Hans Kohn, *Heinrich Heine*, p. 9.
90. *Heinrich Heine Briefe*, I, 175.
91. Ibid., p. 126.
92. "Ludwig Marcus: Denkworte," *Heinrich Heines Gesammelte Werke*, VIII, 250.
93. Rubaschoff, "Erstlinge der Entjüdung," p. 198.
94. "Ludwig Marcus: Denkworte," p. 253.
95. *ZWJ*, pp. 1–24. A translation of this piece, done by Lionel Kochan, appeared in *LBIY*, II (1957), 194–204. The translations given in the text are my own, though I have consulted the work of Mr. Kochan.
96. This term was also used by the Verein in reference to its own work (*Entwurf von Statuten*, p. 5).
97. *ZWJ*, p. 18.
98. Ibid., p. 24.
99. Ibid., third issue, p. iv.
100. *MGWJ*, LXVI (1922), 90.

101. Glatzer[1], p. 42; see also pp. 32, 37.
102. *Heinrich Heine Briefe*, I, 97. Copies of the first issue were sent to a number of gentile scholars and statesmen who viewed it with varying degrees of favor. Among them were Hardenberg, the French scholar Silvestre de Sacy, and the Berlin theologian and educator J. J. Bellermann.
103. *ZWJ*, pp. 420–21.
104. "Aus dem Archiv des Vereins," *ZWJ*, pp. 533–39. Though the comments are anonymous, Gans's authorship is certain, not only from the content but also because he spoke on this subject in the Wissenschaftliche Institut (Rubaschoff, p. 201).
105. *ZWJ*, p. 523. On Zunz's adaptation of the concept of Statistik from August Ludwig Schlözer see Luitpold Wallach, "Ueber Leopold Zunz als Historiker," *ZGJD*, V (1934), 247–52.
106. *ZWJ*, p. 285.
107. Ibid., p. 537.
108. Glatzer[2], pp. 77, 78, 81, 83, 103.
109. Ludwig von Rönne and Heinrich Simon, *Die früheren und gegenwärtigen Verhältnisse der Juden in den sämmtlichen Landestheilen des Preussischen Staates* (Breslau, 1843), p. 281.
110. Hanns G. Reissner, "Rebellious Dilemma," *LBIY*, II (1957), 181.
111. Samuel Oppenheim, "Mordecai M. Noah. A Letter to Him, Dated 1822, from Eduard Gans and Leopold Zunz, Relating to the Emigration of German Jews to America," *Publications of the American Jewish Historical Society*, XX (1911), 147–49.
112. Rubaschoff, pp. 201–3.
113. *Heinrich Heine Briefe*, I, 186.
114. *Bikure ha-'Itim*, IV (1823), 245–54.
115. E.g. Hegel, *Early Theological Writings*, p. 68.
116. Rubaschoff, pp. 196–97.
117. Strodtmann, *Heine's Leben* ..., I, 319, 326.
118. Ibid., p. 327.
119. Ibid., pp. 316–17.

BIBLIOGRAPHY

The following topical list is not an exhaustive bibliography for each of the subjects into which it is divided. The items it contains are those which proved of the greatest value for the specific question of Jewish identity. Under "Primary Sources" are included all contemporary writings as well as subsequent publications of primary material. All interpretive books and articles, including those based on unpublished documents, are listed under "Secondary Sources."

GENERAL WORKS

Arendt, Hannah. *The Origins of Totalitarianism.* 2nd ed. New York, 1958.

Arendt-Stern, Hannah. "Aufklärung und Judenfrage." *ZGJD,* IV (1932), 65–77.

Baron, Salo Wittmayer. *A Social and Religious History of the Jews,* II, III. New York, 1937.

Berlinische Monatsschrift, ed. F. Gedicke and J. E. Biester. 1783–1809.

Bernfeld, Simon. *Dor tahpukhot [A Perverse Generation].* 2 vols. Warsaw, 1914.

Dubnow, Simon. *Weltgeschichte des jüdischen Volkes,* VII–IX. Berlin, 1928–29.

Eliav Mordechai. *Ha-Hinukh ha-yehudi be-Germania be-yeme ha-Haskala veha-Imantsipatsia [Jewish Education in Germany in the Period of Enlightenment and Emancipation].* Jerusalem, 1960.

Eloesser, Arthur. *Vom Ghetto nach Europa: Das Judentum im geistigen Leben des 19. Jahrhunderts.* Berlin, 1936.

Geiger, Ludwig. *Berlin 1688–1840.* 2 vols. Berlin, 1895.

—— *Geschichte der Juden in Berlin.* 2 vols. Berlin, 1871.

Ginsburg, Sigmar. "Die zweite Generation der Juden nach Moses Mendelssohn." *LBIB,* I (1958), 62–72.

Graetz, Heinrich. *Geschichte der Juden,* XI. 2nd ed. Leipzig, 1900.

Jost, Isaac Marcus. *Geschichte des Judentums und seiner Sekten,* III. Leipzig, 1859.

Katz, Jacob. "Jewry and Judaism in the Nineteenth Century." *Cahiers d'Histoire Mondiale,* IV, 4 (1958), 881–900.

Klausner, Joseph. *Historia shel ha-sifrut ha-'ivrit, ha-hadasha [History of Modern Hebrew Literature],* I. 2nd ed. Jerusalem, 1952.

Lewkowitz, Albert. *Das Judentum und die geistigen Strömungen des 19. Jahrhunderts.* Breslau, 1935.

Mahler, Raphael. *Divre yeme Yisrael: dorot aharonim [History of the Jewish People in Modern Times],* II. Merhavya, 1954.

Offenburg, Benno. *Das Erwachen des deutschen Nationalbewusstseins in der preussischen Judenheit (Von Moses Mendelssohn bis zum Beginn der Reaktion)*. Hamburg, 1933.

Philippson, Martin. *Neueste Geschichte des jüdischen Volkes*, I. Leipzig, 1907.

Pinson, Koppel S. *Modern Germany: Its History and Civilization*. New York, 1954.

Rotenstreich, Nathan. *Ha-Mahashava ha-yehudit be-'et ha-hadasha* [*Jewish Thought in the Modern Age*], I. Tel Aviv, 1945.

Sachar, Howard M. *The Course of Modern Jewish History*. Cleveland and New York, 1958.

Schoeps, Hans Joachim. *Geschichte der jüdischen Religionsphilosophie in der Neuzeit*, I. Berlin, 1935.

Seligmann, Caesar. *Geschichte der jüdischen Reformbewegung von Mendelssohn bis zur Gegenwart*. Frankfurt a.M., 1922.

Stern, S. *Geschichte des Judentums*. Frankfurt a.M., 1857.

Stern-Täubler, Selma. "The Jew in the Transition from Ghetto to Emancipation." *HJ*, II (1940), 102–19.

—— "Die Judenfrage in der Ideologie der Aufklärung und Romantik." *Der Morgen*, XI (1935), 339–48.

Studies in Nineteenth-Century Jewish Intellectual History, ed. Alexander Altmann. Cambridge, Mass., 1964.

Weinryb, Dov. "Zionism Among German Jewry in the Haskalah" [Hebrew]. *Keneseth*, I (1936), 465–78.

Wiener, Max. *Jüdische Religion im Zeitalter der Emanzipation*. Berlin, 1933.

Zinberg, Israel. *Toldot sifrut Yisrael* [*History of Jewish Literature*], V, VI. Tel Aviv, 1959–60.

MOSES MENDELSSOHN

Primary Sources

Allgemeine Deutsche Bibliothek, XIII, 2 (1770), 370–96.

Anekdoten von König Friedrich II von Preussen, ed. Friedrich Nicolai. 6 vols. Berlin and Stettin, 1788–92.

Argens, Marquis d'. *The Jewish Spy*, trans. anon. 2nd ed., 5 vols. N.p., 1744.

Arnheim, Fritz. "Moses Mendelssohn and Luise Ulrike von Schweden." *ZGJD*, III (1889), 283–84.

Aus Herders Nachlass, ed. Heinrich Düntzer and F. G. von Herder, II. Frankfurt a.M., 1857.

Bamberger, Fritz. *Denkmal der Freundschaft: Stammbuchblätter und Widmungen von Moses Mendelssohn*. Berlin, 1929.

Beleuchtung des bekannten Antwort-Schreibens von Herrn Moses Mendelssohn zu

Berlin, an den Herrn Diaconus Lavater zu Zürich, aus Liebe zur Wahrheit verfasst und einem geehrten Publikum fürgelegt von einem Freund der Wahrheit. 2nd ed. Frankfurt and Leipzig, 1775.

Betrachtung über das Schreiben des Herrn Moses Mendels Sohn an den Diaconus Lavater zu Zürich. Leipzig, 1770.

"Briefe von, an und über Mendelssohn," ed. Ludwig Geiger and R. M. Werner. *ZGJD,* I (1887), 109–35.

"Briefe von, an und über Mendelssohn," ed. Ludwig Geiger. *JJGL,* XX (1917), 85–137.

Chubb, Thomas. *The True Gospel of Jesus Christ.* London, 1738.

Dohm, Christian Wilhelm. *Ueber die bürgerliche Verbesserung der Juden.* Berlin and Stettin, 1783.

Das Forschen nach Licht und Recht in einem Schreiben an Herrn Moses Mendelssohn auf Veranlassung seiner merkwürdigen Vorrede zu Manasseh Ben Israel. Berlin, 1782.

Friedländer, David. *Moses Mendelssohn: Fragmente von ihm und über ihn.* Berlin, 1819.

Gedanken über die Zumutung des Herrn Diaconus Lavater an Herrn Moses Mendelssohn ein Christ zu werden. Hamburg, 1770.

Geiger, Ludwig. "Mendelssohniana." *MGWJ,* IL (1905), 349–57.

Gellert, Christian F. *Leben der schwedischen Gräfinn von G**.* Vol. V of *Sämtliche Schriften.* Berne, 1775.

Goeze, Johann Melchior. *Eine Predigt von der Liebe gegen fremde Religions-Verwandte.* Hamburg, 1771.

Göttingische Anzeigen von Gelehrten Sachen, I (1754), 620–22.

Heinemann, J. *Moses Mendelssohn: Sammlung teils noch ungedruckter, teils zerstreuter Aufsätze und Briefe von ihm, an und über ihn.* Leipzig, 1831.

Herbert of Cherbury, Edward, Lord. *The Antient Religion of the Gentiles,* trans. William Lewis. London, 1705.

Hesse, Otto Justus Basilius. *Schreiben des Herrn Moses Mendelssohn in Berlin an den Herrn Diaconus Lavater zu Zürich, nebst Anmerkungen über dasselbe.* Halle, 1770.

Jerusalem, Johann Friedrich Wilhelm. *Betrachtungen über die Grundwahrheiten der Religion.* 2 vols. Brunswick, 1785.

Kant, Immanuel. "Beantwortung der Frage: Was ist Aufklärung?" Pp. 109–19 in *Kleinere Schriften zur Logik und Metaphysik.* Berlin, 1870.

Kayserling, M. "Briefe von und an Moses Mendelssohn." Pp. 485–569 in his *Moses Mendelssohn: Sein Leben und seine Werke.* Leipzig, 1862.

—— *Moses Mendelssohn: Ungedrucktes und Unbekanntes von ihm und über ihn.* Leipzig, 1883.

Kölbele, Johann Balthasar. *Schreiben an den Herrn Moses Mendelssohn über die Lavaterische und Kölbelische Angelegenheiten gegen Herrn Mendelssohn.* Frankfurt a.M., 1770.

—— *Zweytes Schreiben an Herrn Moses Mendelssohn insonderheit über den ehemaligen Mendelssohnischen Deismus, über das Kennzeichen einer Offenbarung, und kürzlich über die Glaubenswürdigkeit der Evangelischen Geschichte.* Frankfurt a.M., 1770.

Kurzes Sendschreiben an Herrn Moses Mendelssohn, seinen Entschluss zu ändern, von einem guten Freunde in Sachsen. N.p., 1771.

Lavater, Johann Caspar. *Rede bey der Taufe zweyer Berlinischen Israeliten so durch Veranlassung der Lavater und Mendelssohnischen Streitschriften zum wahren Christenthum übergetreten.* Frankfurt and Leipzig, 1771.

Lessing, Gotthold Ephraim. *Lessings sämtliche Schriften,* ed. K. Lachmann. 3rd ed. Leipzig, 1886–1919.

Locke, John. *Works.* 3 vols. London, 1714.

Mendelssohn, Moses. *Gesammelte Schriften,* ed. G. B. Mendelssohn. 7 vols. Leipzig, 1843–45.

—— *Gesammelte Schriften, Jubiläumsausgabe,* ed. I. Elbogen, J. Guttmann, and K. Mittwoch. 7 vols. (incomplete). Berlin, Breslau, 1929–38.

Montesquieu, Baron de. *The Spirit of the Laws,* trans. Thomas Nugent. 2 vols. New York, 1899.

Nicolai, Friedrich. *Über meine gelehrte Bildung.* Berlin and Stettin, 1799.

Pufendorf, Samuel. *Of the Law of Nature and Nations,* trans. Basil Kennett. 4th ed. London, 1729.

Reimarus, Herman Samuel. *Die vornehmsten Wahrheiten der natürlichen Religion.* 4th ed. Hamburg, 1772.

Spalding, Johann Joachim. *Die Bestimmung des Menschen.* 8th ed. Leipzig, 1764.

[Toland, John]. *Christianity not Mysterious.* London, 1696.

—— *Reasons for Naturalizing the Jews in Great Britain and Ireland on the Same Foot with all Other Nations.* London, 1714.

Verzeichnis der auserlesenen Büchersammlung des seligen Herrn Moses Mendelssohn. Berlin, 1926.

Vor Hundert Jahren: Elise von der Reckes Reisen durch Deutschland 1784-86. Nach dem Tagebuch ihrer Begleiterin Sophie Becker. Stuttgart, 1883.

Wolff, Christian. *Vernünftige Gedanken von dem gesellschaftlichen Leben der Menschen.* Halle, 1721.

Zöllner, Johann Friedrich. *Ueber Moses Mendelssohns Jerusalem.* Berlin, 1784.

Zum Siegesfeste: Dankpredigt und Danklieder von Moses Mendelssohn, ed. M. Kayserling. Berlin, 1866.

Secondary Sources

Auerbach, Jakob. "Moses Mendelssohn und das Judentum." *ZGJD,* I (1886), 1–44.

Badt-Strauss, Bertha. "Elise Reimarus und Moses Mendelssohn." *ZGJD,* IV (1932), 173–89.

Bamberger, Fritz. "Die geistige Gestalt Moses Mendelssohns." *MGWJ,* LXXIII (1929), 81–92.

—— "Mendelssohns Begriff vom Judentum." *Korrespondenzblatt des Vereins zur Gründung und Erhaltung einer Akademie für die Wissenschaft des Judentums,* X (1929), 4-19.

Barzilay, Isaac Eisenstein. "The Jew in the Literature of the Enlightenment." *JSS,* XVIII (1956), 243-61.

—— "Moses Mendelssohn." *JQR,* LII (1961), 69-93, 175-86.

Berwin, Beate. *Moses Mendelssohn im Urteil seiner Zeitgenossen.* Berlin, 1919.

Bush, Newell Richard. *The Marquis d'Argens and his Philosophical Correspondence.* Ann Arbor, 1953.

Carrington, Herbert. *Die Figur des Juden in der dramatischen Literatur des XVIII. Jahrhunderts.* Heidelberg, 1897.

Cassirer, Ernst. "Die Idee der Religion bei Lessing und Mendelssohn." Pp. 22-41 in *Festgabe zum zehnjährigen Bestehen der Akademie für die Wissenschaft des Judentums.* Berlin, 1929.

—— *The Philosophy of the Enlightenment,* trans. Fritz C. A. Koelln and James P. Pettegrove. Boston, 1955.

Dejob, Charles. "Le Juif dans la Comédie au XVIIIᵉ Siècle." *REJ,* XXIX (1899), 119-28.

Dilthey, Wilhelm. *Friedrich der Grosse und die deutsche Aufklärung.* Vol. III of *Gesammelte Schriften.* Leipzig and Berlin, 1927.

Eisenstein-Barzilay, Isaac. "The Background of the Berlin Haskalah." Pp. 183-97 in *Essays on Jewish Life and Thought Presented in Honor of Salo Wittmayer Baron.* New York, 1959.

Englander, Harry. "Mendelssohn as Translator and Exegete." *HUCA,* VI (1929), 327-48.

Eschelbacher, J. "Die Anfänge allgemeiner Bildung unter den deutschen Juden vor Mendelssohn." Pp. 168-77 in *Festschrift zum siebzigsten Geburtstage Martin Philippsons.* Leipzig, 1916.

Ettinger, Shmuel. "The Beginnings of the Change in the Attitude of European Society Towards the Jews." *Scripta Hierosolymitana,* VII (Jerusalem, 1961), 193-219.

—— "Jews and Judaism as Seen by the English Deists of the 18th Century" [Hebrew]. *Zion,* XXIX (1964), 182-207.

Euchel, Isaac. *Toldot rabenu he-hakham Moshe ben Menahem* [*Biography of Moses Mendelssohn*]. Berlin, 1788.

Feiner, Josef. *Gewissensfreiheit und Duldung in der Aufklärungszeit.* Leipzig, 1919.

Feuchtwanger, Ludwig. "Das Bild Mendelssohns bei seinen Gegnern bis zum Tode Hegels: Ein Beitrag zum Neuaufbau der geistigen Gestalt Mendelssohns." *ZGJD,* I (1929), 213-32.

Fittbogen, Gottfried. *Die Religion Lessings.* Leipzig, 1923.

Flajole, Edward S. "Lessing's Attitude in the Lavater-Mendelssohn Controversy." *PMLA,* LXXIII (1958), 201-14.

Gedenkbuch für Moses Mendelssohn, ed. Verband der Vereine für jüdische Geschichte und Literatur in Deutschland. Berlin, 1929.

Guttmann, Julius. "Mendelssohns Jerusalem und Spinozas Theologisch-Politisches Traktat." *Achtundvierzigster Bericht der Hochschule für die Wissenschaft des Judentums in Berlin*, pp. 33-67.

Guttmann, Michael. "Die Stellung Mendelssohns zur christlichen Umwelt." *MGWJ*, LXXIV (1930), 401-13.

Hazard, Paul. *European Thought in the Eighteenth Century from Montesquieu to Lessing*, trans. J. L. May. London, 1954.

Hoffmann, Heinrich. *Die Humanitätsidee in der Geschichte des Abendlandes*. Berne, 1951.

Holdheim, Samuel. *Moses Mendelssohn und die Denk- und Glaubensfreiheit im Judentume*. Berlin, 1859.

Horowitz, J. *Der Toleranzgedanke in der deutschen Literatur zur Zeit Moses Mendelssohns*. Stuttgart, 1914.

Jacob, Walter. "Moses Mendelssohn and the Jewish-Christian Dialogue." *CCAR Journal*, XIII (October 1965), 45-51.

Jacobs, Hans Haimar. *Friedrich der Grosse und die Idee des Vaterlandes* (Historische Studien no. 347). Berlin, 1939.

Kapp, Arno. "Elkan Herz, der Freund und Verwandte Moses Mendelssohns, der Vater der ersten Leipziger liberalen Judengemeinde." *ZGJD*, IV (1932), 198-202.

Katz, Jacob. *Die Entstehung der Judenassimilation in Deutschland und deren Ideologie*. Frankfurt a.M., 1935.

—— "Moses Mendelssohn und E. J. Hirschfeld." *LBIB*, VII (1964), 295-311.

—— "To Whom Was Mendelssohn Replying in *Jerusalem?*" [Hebrew]. *Zion*, XXIX (1964), 112-32.

—— *Tradition and Crisis: Jewish Society at the End of the Middle Ages*. New York, 1961.

Kayserling, M. *Der Dichter Ephraim Kuh: Ein Beitrag zur Geschichte der deutschen Literatur*. Berlin, 1864.

—— *Moses Mendelssohn: Sein Leben und Wirken*. 2nd ed. Leipzig, 1888.

—— *Moses Mendelssohns philosophische und religiöse Grundsätze mit Hinblick auf Lessing*. Leipzig, 1856.

Kirschstein, Max. *Lessing und Berlin*. Berlin, 1929.

Lazarus, Moritz. "Moses Mendelssohn in seinem Verhältnis zu Juden und Judentum." *Deutsche Revue*, XI (1886), 215-28.

Lessing-Mendelssohn Gedenkbuch. Leipzig, 1879.

Levy, Felix. "Moses Mendelssohn's Ideals of Religion and their Relation to Reform Judaism." *CCARY*, XXXIX (1929), 351-69.

Lewkowitz, Albert. "Mendelssohns Anschauung vom Wesen des Judentums." *MGWJ*, LXXIII (1929), 257-63.

Lovejoy, Arthur O. *Essays in the History of Ideas*. Baltimore, 1948.

Lungwitz, Karl. *Die Religionsphilosophie Johann August Eberhards*. Erlangen, 1910.

Mehring, Franz. *Die Lessing-Legende*. Stuttgart, 1893.

Meinecke, Friedrich. *Die Idee der Staatsräson in der neueren Geschichte*. Munich and Berlin, 1924.

—— *Weltbürgertum und Nationalstaat: Studien zur Genesis des deutschen Nationalstaates.* 2nd ed. Munich and Berlin, 1911.

Mevorah, B. "The Background of Lavater's Appeal to Mendelssohn" [Hebrew]. *Zion,* XXX (1965), 158–70.

Mirabeau, Honoré Comte de. *Ueber Moses Mendelssohn,* trans. anon. Berlin, 1787.

Moses Mendelssohn zur 200 jährigen Wiederkehr seines Geburtstages, ed. Encyclopaedia Judaica. Berlin, 1929.

Murray, Robert H. *Erasmus and Luther: Their Attitude to Toleration.* London, 1920.

Ozer, Charles L. "Jewish Education in the Transition from Ghetto to Emancipation." *HJ,* IX (1947), 75–94.

Patterson, David. "Moses Mendelssohn's Concept of Tolerance." Pp. 149–63 in *Between East and West: Essays dedicated to the Memory of Bela Horovitz.* London, 1958.

Philippson, Ludwig. "Die Stellung Moses Mendelssohns im und zum Judentume." *AZJ,* L (1886), 161 ff.

Rawidowicz, Simon. "Moses Mendelssohn" [Hebrew]. *Ha-Tekufa,* XXII (1929), 498–520.

—— "The Philosophy of *Jerusalem*" [Hebrew]. Pp. 99–140 in *Sefer Bialik,* ed. Jacob Fichmann. Tel Aviv, 1934.

—— "Mendelssohn's Translation of Psalms" [Hebrew]. Pp. 283–301 in *Sefer Klausner.* Tel Aviv, 1938.

Ritter, Immanuel Heinrich. *Geschichte der jüdischen Reformation.* Pt. I: *Mendelssohn und Lessing.* Berlin, 1858.

Rothman, Walter. "Mendelssohn's Character and Philosophy of Religion." *CCARY,* XXXIX (1929), 305–50.

Sandler, Perez. *Ha-Beur la-Torah shel Moshe Mendelssohn ve-si'ato* [*Mendelssohn's Edition of the Pentateuch*]. Jerusalem, 1940.

Schmidt, Erich. *Lessing: Geschichte seines Lebens und seiner Schriften.* 4th ed., 2 vols. Berlin, 1923.

Schütz, Friedrich Wilhelm. *Leben und Meinungen Moses Mendelssohns, nebst dem Geiste seiner Schriften in einem kurzen Abrisse dargestellet.* Hamburg, 1787.

Shohet, Azriel. "Beginnings of the Haskalah Among German Jewry" [Hebrew]. *Molad,* XXIII (1965), 328–34.

—— *Im hilufe tekufot: reshit ha-Haskala be-Yahadut Germania* [*Beginnings of the Haskalah Among German Jewry*]. Jerusalem, 1960.

Silberstein, Siegfried. "Mendelssohn und Mecklenburg." *ZGJD,* I (1929), 233–44, 275–90.

Simon, Ernst. "Lessing und die jüdische Geschichte." *Jüdische Rundschau,* January 22, 1929, p. 1.

Sommerfeld, Martin. "Aufklärung und Nationalgedanke." *Das literarische Echo,* August 15, 1915, pp. 1353–63.

Steinheim, Salomon Ludwig. *Moses Mendelssohn und seine Schule in ihrer Beziehung zur Aufgabe des neuen Jahrhunderts der alten Zeitrechnung.* Hamburg, 1840.

Stern-Täubler, Selma. "The Jews in the Economic Policy of Frederick the Great." *JSS*, XI (1949), 129-52.

Stockum, Th. C. van. *Lavater Contra Mendelssohn 1769-71. Verlicht Rationalisme en Christelijke Bekeringsijver.* Amsterdam, 1953.

Troeltsch, Ernst. "Die Aufklärung." Pp. 338-74 in *Gesammelte Schriften, IV.* Tübingen, 1925.

Unger, Rudolf. *Hamann und die Aufklärung.* 2nd ed. Halle, 1925.

Van der Veen, H. R. S. *Jewish Characters in Eighteenth Century English Fiction and Drama.* Groningen, 1935.

Wellek, René. *A History of Modern Criticism,* I. New Haven, 1955.

White, Andrew Dickson. *Seven Great Statesmen in the Warfare of Humanity with Unreason.* New York, 1912.

Wiener, Max. "John Toland and Judaism." *HUCA,* XVI (1941), 215-42.

Wolff, Alfred. *Der Toleranzgedanke in der deutschen Literatur zur Zeit Mendelssohns.* Berlin, 1915.

Wolff, Sabattia Joseph. *Maimoniana oder Rhapsodien zur Charakteristik Salomon Maimons.* Berlin, 1813.

Zarek, Otto. *Moses Mendelssohn: Ein jüdisches Schicksal in Deutschland.* Amsterdam, 1936.

Zscharnack, Leopold. *Lessing und Semler: Ein Beitrag zur Entstehungsgeschichte des Rationalismus und der kritischen Theologie.* Giessen, 1905.

Zunz, Leopold. *Rede gehalten bei der Feier von Moses Mendelssohns hundertjährigem Geburtstage.* Berlin, 1829.

DAVID FRIEDLÄNDER

Primary Sources

Allgemeine Literatur-Zeitung, April 3, 1794.

Bendavid, Lazarus. *Aufsätze verschiedenen Inhalts.* Berlin, 1800.

—— *Etwas zur Characteristick der Juden.* Leipzig, 1793.

Briefe Daniel Chodowieckis an die Gräfin Christine von Solms-Laubach, ed. Charlotte Steinbrucker. Strassburg, 1927.

Briefwechsel zwischen Goethe und Zelter, ed. Friedrich Wilhelm Riemer. 3 vols. Berlin, 1833-34.

Charlotte Sampson oder Geschichte eines jüdischen Hausvaters, der mit seiner Familie dem Glauben seiner Väter entsagte: Eine Geschichte der neuesten Zeit. Berlin, 1800.

Cohn, Joseph. "Einige Schriftstücke aus dem Nachlasse Aron Wolfssohns." *MGWJ,* XLI (1897), 369-76.

"Correspondence between Joseph Elias of Vilna and David Friedländer of Berlin regarding the Complaints of Solomon Dubno against Moses Mendelssohn" [Hebrew]. *Ha-Sharon* supplement to *Ha-Carmel,* VII, no. 5 (1866), 36-38.

Davidson, Wolf. *Ueber die bürgerliche Verbesserung der Juden.* Berlin, 1798.

Dohm, L. B. *Etwas zum Schutz des angegriffenen Gebrauches der ebräischen Sprache bei den Gebeten der Juden in den Königl. Preuss. Staaten.* Breslau, 1812.

Friedländer, David. *Akten-Stücke die Reform der jüdischen Kolonieen in den Preussischen Staaten betreffend.* Berlin, 1793.

—— *An die Verehrer, Freunde und Schüler Jerusalems, Spaldings, Tellers, Herders und Löfflers.* Leipzig, 1823.

—— *Beitrag zur Geschichte der Verfolgung der Juden im 19. Jahrhundert durch Schriftsteller.* Berlin, 1820.

—— "Briefe über das Lesen der heiligen Schriften nebst einer Uebersetzung des sechsten und siebenten Capitels des Micha, als Beilage." *ZWJ,* I (1822–23), 68–94.

—— "Briefe über die Moral des Handels, geschrieben im Jahr 1785." *Jedidja,* I, 1 (1817), 178–213.

—— *Für Liebhaber morgenländischer Dichtkunst.* Berlin, 1821.

—— Introduction to Moses Mendelssohn's *Phaedon* (1814). 7th ed. Berlin, 1856.

—— "Moses Mendelssohn." *Biographie Universelle* (1821), 274–82.

—— *Der Prediger. Aus dem Hebräischen nebst einer vorangeschickten Abhandlung: Ueber den besten Gebrauch der h. Schrift, in pädagogischer Rücksicht.* Berlin, 1788.

—— "Rede gehalten vor einer Gesellschaft gebildeter Israeliten." *Jedidja,* I, 1 (1817), 38–56.

—— "Rede über Psalm 19." *Jedidja,* I, 2 (1817), 133–49.

—— *Reden der Erbauung gebildeter Israeliten gewidmet.* 2 vols. Berlin, 1815–17.

—— *Sendschreiben an die deutsche* [sic] *Juden* [Hebrew characters]. Supplement to *Ha-Measef,* IV (1788).

—— *Sendschreiben an Seine Hochwürden, Herrn Oberconsistorialrath und Probst Teller zu Berlin von einigen Hausvätern jüdischer Religion.* 3rd ed. Berlin, 1799.

—— *Ueber die durch die neue Organisation der Judenschaften in den Preussischen Staaten notwendig gewordene Umbildung...Ein Wort zu seiner Zeit.* Berlin, 1812. New ed. by Moritz Stern as no. 6 of *Beiträge zur Geschichte der jüdischen Gemeinde zu Berlin.* Berlin, 1934.

—— *Ueber die Verbesserung der Israeliten im Königreich Pohlen: Ein von der Regierung daselbst im Jahr 1816 abgefordertes Gutachten.* Berlin, 1819.

—— trans. and notes, *Gebete der Juden auf das ganze Jahr* [Hebrew characters]. Berlin, 1786.

—— ed. and trans., *Sefer ha-nefesh le-he-hakham R' Moshe mi-Dessau* [Mendelssohn's Book of the Soul]. 2nd ed. Brünn, 1798.

Friedländer, David and Isaac Itzig. Preface to [Saul Berlin], *Mitspe Yoktel* [Watchtower of Yoktel]. Berlin, 1789.

Geiger, Ludwig. "Aus den Gemeindeakten." *Gemeindeblatt der jüdischen Gemeinde zu Berlin,* March 8, 1912, pp. 34–36.

—— "Ein Brief Moses Mendelssohns und sechs Briefe David Friedländers: B. Briefe David Friedländers (1789–1799)." *ZGJD,* I (1887), 256–73.

—— A Letter of David Friedländer to Leopold Zunz, in "Aus Zunz' Nachlass." *ZGJD,* V (1892), 263.

Bibliography

—— "Nach dem Edikt vom 11 März 1812," *Gemeindeblatt der jüdischen Gemeinde zu Berlin*, August 9, 1912, pp. 103–4.

—— "Ein talmudisches Gutachten David Friedlaenders." *AZJ*, LXXVI (1912), 163–65.

—— "Vor hundert Jahren: Mitteilungen aus der Geschichte der Juden Berlins." *ZGJD*, III (1889), 185–233.

—— "Zur Charakteristik David Friedländers (Ungedruckte Briefe 1816–1820)." *AZJ*, LVIII (1894), 220–23, 235–36, 246–48.

Gespräch über das Sendschreiben von einigen Hausvätern an den Probst Teller, zwischen einem christlichen Theologen und einem alten Juden. Berlin, 1799.

Herder, Johann Gottfried. *Sämtliche Werke: Zur Philosophie und Geschichte*, V, X. Tübingen, 1806–9.

Hermes, Hermann Daniel. *Ueber das Sendschreiben einiger Hausväter jüdischer Religion an den Herrn Oberconsistorialrath Teller und die von demselban darauf ertheilte Antwort.* Leipzig, 1799.

Jacobson, Jacob. "Aus David Friedländers Mussestunden." *ZGJD*, VI (1935), 134–40.

—— *Die Judenbürgerbücher der Stadt Berlin 1809–1851, mit Ergänzungen für die Jahre 1791–1809.* Berlin, 1962.

—— "Zu David Friedländers Bemühungen um Abschaffung des Namens, 'Jude.' " *AZJ*, LXXVI (1912), 379–80.

Kant, Immanuel. *Der Streit der Fakultäten* (1798), ed. Kurt Rossmann. Heidelberg, 1947.

"Letters of the Great Men of our Time" [Hebrew]. *Zion*, II (1842–43), 106–7.

Loewenberg, J. "Wilhelm und Alexander v. Humboldt im Verkehr mit ihren ältesten jüdischen Freunden." *Jahrbuch für Israeliten*, XII (1865–66), 41–72.

de Luc, J. A. *Lettre aux Auteurs Juifs d'un mémoire adressé à Mr Teller.* Berlin, 1799.

Maimon, Salomon. *Lebensgeschichte.* 2 vols. Berlin, 1792–93.

Meisl, Josef. "Letters of David Friedländer" [Yiddish]. *Historishe Shriften*, II (Vilna, 1937), 390–412.

—— *Protokollbuch der jüdischen Gemeinde Berlin, 1723–1854.* Jerusalem, 1962.

Muhr, Abraham. *Jerubaal oder über die religiöse Reform der Juden in preussischen Staaten.* Breslau, 1813.

Neue Allgemeine Bibliothek, LVII (1801), 267–93.

Nicolai, Friedrich. *Beschreibung der königlichen Residenzstädte Berlin und Potsdam*, I. 3rd ed. Berlin, 1786.

—— *Gedächtnisschrift auf Dr. Wilhelm Abraham Teller.* Berlin and Stettin, 1807.

Paalzow, Ludwig. *Die Juden, nebst einigen Bemerkungen über das Sendschreiben an Herrn Oberconsistorialrath und Probst Teller zu Berlin von einigen Hausvätern jüdischer Religion und die darauf erfolgte Tellersche Antwort.* Berlin, 1799.

Salomon, Gotthold. *Licht und Wahrheit die Umbildung des Israelitischen Kultus betreffend...Zur Beherzigung aller Israeliten, die noch Anhänglichkeit an der Religion ihrer Väter haben.* Leipzig, 1813.

Schleiermacher, Friedrich. "Briefe bei Gelegenheit der politisch-theologischen Aufgabe und des Sendschreibens jüdischer Hausväter, von einem Prediger ausserhalb Berlin." Pp. 1–39 in *Sämtliche Werke*. Pt. I: *Zur Theologie*, V. Berlin, 1846.

"Schreiben eines deutschen Juden, an den Präsidenten des Kongresses der vereinigten Staaten von Amerika." *Deutsches Museum*, VIII, 1 (1783), 558–66.

Stern, Moritz. "Gutachten und Briefe David Friedländers." *ZGJD*, VI (1935), 113–30.

Täubler, Eugen. "Zur Geschichte des Projekts einer Reform des Judenwesens unter Friedrich Wilhelm II." *Mitteilungen des Gesamtarchivs der deutschen Juden*, I (1909), 23–29.

Teller, Wilhelm Abraham. *Beantwortung des Sendschreibens einiger Hausväter jüdischer Religion an mich den Probst Teller*. 2nd ed. Berlin, 1799.

Thersites: Die Erinnerungen des deutsch-baltischen Journalisten Garlieb Merkel 1796–1817, ed. Maximilian Müller-Jabusch. Berlin, 1921.

Treue Relation des ersten Eindrucks den das neuerlich erschienene an den Probst Teller gerichtete Sendschreiben einiger Juden auf das Publikum machte: Ein Fingerzeig für die Juden. Berlin, 1799.

Ueber die physische und moralische Verfassung der heutigen Juden: Stimme eines Kosmopoliten. Germanien, 1791.

Wischnitzer, M. "Drei Briefe David Friedländers an den Erzbischof von Warschau, Franz Malczewski." *AZJ*, LXXII (1908), 353–54.

Wolf, Albert. "Ein Brief David Friedländers an Moses Moser." *MGWJ*, L (1906), 370–73.

"Ein Wörtchen über Juden ... Veranlasst durch die von Herrn Friedländer herausgegebenen Aktenstücke." *Neue allgemeine deutsche Bibliothek*, III (1793), 154–58.

Secondary Sources

Atlas, Samuel. "Solomon Maimon: The Man and His Thought." *HJ*, XIII (1951), 109–20.

Dilthey, Wilhelm. *Leben Schleiermachers*. Berlin, 1870.

Döring, Heinrich. "David Friedländer." *Allgemeine Encyclopädie der Wissenschaften und Künste*, Section One, LI, 268–70.

Dukas, Rosa. *Die Motive der preussischen Judenemanzipation von 1812 mit besonderer Berücksichtigung ihres Verhältnisses zu den Ideen der Judengesetzgebung der französischen Revolution*. Leipzig, 1915.

Elbogen, Ismar. "Die Bezeichnung 'Jüdische Nation.'" *MGWJ*, LXIII (1919), 200–8.

—— "David Friedländers Uebersetzung des Gebetbuchs." *ZGJD*, VI (1935), 130–33.

Fraenkel, Ernst. "David Friedländer und seine Zeit." *ZGJD*, VI (1935), 65–77.

Freund, Ismar. *Die Emanzipation der Juden in Preussen unter besonderer Berücksichtigung des Gesetzes vom 11. März 1812*. 2 vols. Berlin, 1912.

—— "David Friedländer und die politische Emanzipation der Juden in Preussen." *ZGJD*, VI (1935), 77–92.

Friedlaender, Ernst. *Das Handlungshaus Joachim Moses Friedlaender et Soehne zu Königsberg i. Pr.* Hamburg, 1913.

Geiger, Ludwig. "David Friedländer." *Algemeine Deutsche Biographie*, VII, 393–97.

Graupe, Heinz Moshe. "Kant und das Judentum." *Zeitschrift für Religions- und Geistesgeschichte*, XIII (1961), 308–33.

Guttmann, Jacob. "Lazarus Bendavid: Seine Stellung zum Judentum und seine literarische Wirksamkeit." *MGWJ*, LXI (1917), 26–50, 176–211.

Jacobs, Noah J. "Salomon Maimon's Relation to Judaism." *LBIY*, VIII (1963), 117–35.

Jacobson, Jacob. "Some Observations on the Jewish Citizens' Books of the City of Berlin." *LBIY*, I (1956), 317–30.

Kober, Adolf. "The French Revolution and the Jews in Germany." *JSS*, VII (1945), 291–322.

Lewin, Reinhold. "Die Judengesetzgebung Friedrich Wilhelms II." *MGWJ*, LVII (1913), 74–98, 211–34, 363–72, 461–81, 567–90.

Littmann, Ellen. "David Friedländers Sendschreiben an Probst Teller und sein Echo." *ZGJD*, VI (1935), 92–112.

Rachel, Hugo and Paul Wallich. *Berliner Grosskaufleute und Kapitalisten*, II. Berlin, 1938.

Rippner, Benjamin. "David Friedländer und Probst Teller." Pp. 162–71 in *Jubelschrift zum siebzigsten Geburtstage des Prof. Dr. H. Graetz*. Breslau, 1887.

Ritter, Immanuel Heinrich. *Geschichte der jüdischen Reformation*. Pt. II: *David Friedländer: Sein Leben und sein Wirken*. Berlin, 1861.

Rotenstreich, Nathan. "Kant's Interpretation of Judaism" [Hebrew]. *Tarbiz*, XXVII (1958), 388–405.

Samter, N. *Judentaufen im neunzehnten Jahrhundert*. Berlin, 1906.

Schmidt, H. D. "The Terms of Emancipation 1781–1812." *LBIY*, I (1956), 28–47.

Spazier, Richard Otto. "David Friedländer." Pp. 101–7 in *Gallerie der ausgezeichnetsten Israeliten aller Jahrhunderte, ihre Portraits und Biographien*. Stuttgart, 1834.

RATIONALISM AND ROMANTICISM

Primary Sources

Angelus Silesius und Saint-Martin: Auszüge und Bemerkungen von Rahel, ed. K. A. Varnhagen von Ense. 3rd ed. Berlin, 1849.

Athenaeum: Eine Zeitschrift, ed. August Wilhelm Schlegel and Friedrich Schlegel. 3 vols. Berlin, 1798–1800.

Aus dem Nachlass Varnhagens von Ense, ed. Ludmilla Assing. 2 vols. Leipzig, 1867.

Aus Schleiermachers Leben: In Briefen, ed. Ludwig Jonas and Wilhelm Dilthey. 4 vols. Berlin, 1858–63.

Behrend, Fritz. "Rahel Varnhagen an Schleiermacher." *Zeitschrift für Bücherfreunde,* N. S., IX, 1 (1917–18), 87–90.

"Ein Brief von Rahel." Pp. 180–84 in *Zur Judenfrage in Deutschland,* ed. Wilhelm Freund. Berlin, 1843.

Briefe von Dorothea Schlegel an Friedrich Schleiermacher. Vol. VII, N. S., of *Mitteilungen aus dem Literaturarchive in Berlin.* Berlin, 1913.

Briefe von Dorothea und Friedrich Schlegel an die Familie Paulus, ed. Rudolf Unger. Berlin, 1913.

Briefe von und an Friedrich und Dorothea Schlegel, ed. Josef Körner. Berlin, 1926.

Briefe von Wilhelm von Humboldt an eine Freundin, ed. Ludwig Geiger. 2 vols. Stuttgart, 1881.

Der Briefwechsel Friedrich und Dorothea Schlegels 1818–1820, ed. Heinrich Finke. Munich, 1923.

Briefwechsel des jungen Börne und der Henriette Herz, ed. Ludwig Geiger. Oldenburg and Leipzig, 1905.

Briefwechsel zwischen Rahel und David Veit, ed. Ludmilla Assing. 2 vols. Leipzig, 1861.

Briefwechsel zwischen Varnhagen und Rahel, ed. Ludmilla Assing. 6 vols. Leipzig, 1874–75.

Caroline: Briefe aus der Frühromantik, ed. Georg Waitz and Erich Schmidt. 2 vols. Leipzig, 1913.

Caroline und Dorothea Schlegel in Briefen, ed. Ernst Wieneke. Weimar, 1914.

Denina, Mr. l'Abbé. *La Prusse Littéraire sous Friedrich II.* 3 vols. Berlin, 1790.

Dorothea v. Schlegel geb. Mendelssohn und deren Söhne Johannes und Philipp Veit: Briefwechsel, ed. J. M. Raich. 2 vols. Mainz, 1881.

Dorow, Wilhelm. *Erlebtes aus den Jahren 1790–1827,* IV. Leipzig, 1845.

Friedrich Schlegels Briefe an seinen Bruder August Wilhelm, ed. Oskar F. Walzel. Berlin, 1890.

Friedrich Schleiermachers Briefwechsel mit seiner Braut, ed. Heinrich Meisner. Gotha, 1919.

Fürst, J., *Henriette Herz: Ihr Leben und ihre Erinnerungen.* 2nd ed. Berlin, 1858.

Geiger, Ludwig. "Einundzwanzig Briefe von Marianne von Eybenberg, acht von Sara von Grotthuss, zwanzig von Varnhagen von Ense an Goethe, zwei Briefe Goethes an Frau von Eybenberg." *Goethe-Jahrbuch,* XIV (1893), 27–142.

Heinrici, Georg. "Briefe von Henriette Herz an August Twesten (1814–1827)." *Zeitschrift für Bücherfreunde,* N. S., V, Pt. 2 (1914), 301–16, 337–47.

Hensel, Sebastian. *Die Familie Mendelssohn 1729–1847.* 18th ed., 2 vols. Leipzig, 1924.

Humboldt, Wilhelm von. "Ideen zu einem Versuch, die Gränzen der Wirksamkeit des Staats zu bestimmen." Pp. 1–188 in *Gesammelte Werke,* VII. Berlin, 1852.

Krisenjahre der Frühromantik: Briefe aus dem Schlegelkreis, ed. Josef Körner. 3 vols. Brünn, Bern, 1936–58.

Bibliography

Landsberg, Hans. *Henriette Herz: Ihr Leben und ihre Zeit.* Weimar, 1913.

Rahel und Alexander von der Marwitz in ihren Briefen, ed. Heinrich Meisner. Stuttgart, 1925.

Rahel: Ein Buch des Andenkens für ihre Freunde. 3 vols. Berlin, 1834.

Riesser, Gabriel. "Jüdische Briefe: Zur Abwehr und Verständigung. Pp. 175–296 in *Gesammelte Schriften,* IV. Frankfurt and Leipzig, 1868.

Schadow, Johann Gottfried. *Kunst-Werke und Kunst-Ansichten.* Berlin, 1849.

Schlegel, A. W. Review of *Bambocciaden. Allgemeine Literatur-Zeitung,* 1797, no. 333, p. 167.

[Schlegel, Dorothea]. *Florentin. Ein Roman,* ed. Friedrich Schlegel. Lübeck and Leipzig, 1801.

Schlegel, Friedrich. *Lucinde.* Berlin, 1799.

Schleiermacher, Friedrich. *Monologen,* ed. Friedrich Michael Schiele. 2nd ed. Leipzig, 1914.

—— *On Religion: Speeches to its Cultured Despisers,* trans. John Oman. New York, 1958.

—— *Vertraute Briefe über Friedrich Schlegels Lucinde.* Lübeck and Leipzig, 1800.

Schleiermacher als Mensch, sein Werden: Familien- und Freundesbriefe 1783 bis 1804, ed. Heinrich Meisner. Gotha, 1922.

Schleiermacher und seine Lieben, nach Originalbriefen der Henriette Herz. Magdeburg, 1910.

Schnapper-Arndt, G. "Jugendarbeiten Ludwig Börne's über jüdische Dinge." *ZGJD,* II (1888), 375–80; IV (1890), 201–74; V (1892), 194–222.

Schwenke, Paul. "Aus Wilhelm von Humboldt's Studienjahren." *Deutsche Rundschau,* LXVI (1891), 228–51.

Sulpiz Boisserée. 2 vols. Stuttgart, 1862.

Tagebücher von K. A. Varnhagen von Ense, ed. Ludmilla Assing. 15 vols. Leipzig, 1861–1905.

Varnhagen von Ense, K. A. *Ausgewählte Schriften,* XVIII, XIX. 3rd ed. Leipzig, 1875–76.

Werner, Eric. "New Light on the Family of Felix Mendelssohn." *HUCA,* XXVI (1953), 543–65.

Wilhelm und Caroline von Humboldt in ihren Briefen, ed. Anna von Sydow. 7 vols. Berlin, 1906–16.

Wilhelm von Humbolts Briefe an Karl Gustav von Brinkmann, ed. Albert Leitzmann. Leipzig, 1939.

Wilhelm von Humbolts Tagebücher, ed. Albert Leitzmann. 2 vols. Berlin, 1916–18.

Secondary Sources

Arendt, Hannah. *Rahel Varnhagen: The Life of a Jewess.* London, 1957; German ed.: Munich, 1959.

Atzenbeck, Carl. *Pauline Wiesel: Die Geliebte des Prinzen Louis Ferdinand von Preussen.* Leipzig, 1925.

Berdrow, Otto. *Rahel Varnhagen: Ein Lebens- und Zeitbild*. Stuttgart, 1900.

Brandes, G. *Die Hauptströmungen der Literatur des neunzehnten Jahrhunderts*, trans. Adolf Strodtmann. Vol. II: *Die romantische Schule in Deutschland*. 4th ed. Leipzig, 1894.

Deibel, Franz. *Dorothea Schlegel als Schriftstellerin im Zusammenhang mit der romantischen Schule*. Berlin, 1905.

Geiger, Ludwig. *Die deutsche Literatur und die Juden*. Berlin, 1910.

—— *Dichter und Frauen*. Berlin, 1896.

—— "Dorothea Veit-Schlegel." *Deutsche Rundschau*, CLX (1914), 119–34.

Graf, Emma. *Rahel Varnhagen und die Romantik*. Berlin, 1903.

Grau, Wilhelm. *Wilhelm von Humboldt und das Problem des Juden*. Hamburg, 1935.

Gundolf, Friedrich. "Schleiermachers Romantik." *Deutsche Vierteljahrsschrift für Literaturwissenschaft und Geistesgeschichte*, II (1924), 418–509.

Haym, Rudolf. *Die romantische Schule*. 2nd ed. Berlin, 1906.

—— *Wilhelm von Humboldt: Lebensbild und Charakteristik*. Berlin, 1856.

Hillebrand, M. "La Societé de Berlin de 1789 à 1815." *Revue des Deux Mondes*, LXXXVI (1870), 447–86.

Jacobson, Jacob. "Von Mendelssohn zu Mendelssohn-Bartholdy." *LBIY*, V (1960), 251–61.

Kayserling, M. *Die jüdischen Frauen in der Geschichte, Literatur und Kunst*. Leipzig, 1879.

Kohut, Adolph. *Moses Mendelssohn und seine Familie*. Dresden and Leipzig, 1886.

Körner, Josef. "Mendelssohns Töchter." *Preussische Jahrbücher*, CCXIV (1928), 167–82.

Liptzin, Solomon. *Germany's Stepchildren*. Philadelphia, 1944.

Mackowsky, Hans. *Johann Gottfried Schadow: Jugend und Aufstieg 1764 bis 1797*. Berlin, 1927.

Martin, Alfred v. "Das Wesen der romantischen Religiosität." *Deutsche Vierteljahrsschrift für Literaturwissenschaft und Geistesgeschichte*, II (1924), 367–417.

Mayer-Montfort, Elvira. "Dorothea Schlegel im Ideenkreis ihrer Zeit und in ihrer religiösen, philosophischen und ethischen Entwicklung." *Gelbe Hefte: Historische und politische Zeitschrift für das katholische Deutschland*, II, 1 (1925–26), 414–33, 489–517.

Meyer, Bertha. *Salon Sketches: Biographical Studies of Berlin Salons of the Emancipation*. New York, 1938.

Muncker, Franz. "Dorothea Friederike Schlegel." *Allgemeine Deutsche Biographie*, XXXI, 372–76.

Rinn, Heinrich. *Schleiermacher und seine romantischen Freunde*. Hamburg, 1890.

Scurla, Herbert. *Begegnungen mit Rahel: Der Salon der Rahel Levin*. E. Berlin, 1962.

Spiel, Hilde. *Fanny Arnstein oder Die Emanzipation*. Frankfurt a.M., 1962.

Stern, Selma. "Der Frauentypus der Romantik." *Der Morgen*, I (1925), 496–516.

Strich, Fritz. *Deutsche Klassik und Romantik*. 5th ed. Berne and Munich, 1962.

Susman, Margarete. *Frauen der Romantik*. 3rd ed. Cologne, 1960.

Teweles, Heinrich. *Goethe und die Juden.* Hamburg, 1925.

Weizäcker, Hugo. *Schleiermacher und das Eheproblem.* Tübingen, 1927.

Wiese, Benno von. *Friedrich Schlegel: Ein Beitrag zur Geschichte der romantischen Konversionen.* Berlin, 1927.

RELIGIOUS REFORM AND POLITICAL REACTION

Primary Sources

Almanach für die israelitische Jugend, ed. Jeremiah Heinemann. 3 vols. Berlin, 1819–21.

Arnim, Ludwig Achim von. "Halle." Pp. 21–152 in *Ausgewählte Werke,* ed. Max Morris, II. Leipzig, 1906.

Ascher, Saul. *Bemerkungen über die bürgerliche Verbesserung der Juden veranlasst bei der Frage: Soll der Jude Soldat werden?* N.p., 1788.

—— *Eisenmenger der Zweite, nebst einem vorangestezten Sendschreiben an den Herrn Professor Fichte in Jena.* Berlin, 1794.

—— *Die Germanomanie: Skizze zu einem Zeitgemälde.* Berlin, 1815.

—— *Leviathan oder Ueber Religion in Rücksicht des Judenthums.* Berlin, 1792.

Auerbach, Isaac Levin. *Sind die Israeliten verpflichtet ihre Gebete durchaus in der hebraischen Sprache zu verrichten? Aus den Quellen des Talmuds und der spätern Gesetzlehrer erörtert.* Berlin, 1818.

Beer, Peter. *Dat Yisrael oder Das Judenthum, das ist: Versuch einer Darstellung aller wesentlichen Glaubens- Sitten- und Ceremoniallehren heutiger Juden.* 2 vols. Prague, 1809–10.

—— *Geschichte, Lehren und Meinungen aller bestandenen und noch bestehenden religiösen Sekten der Juden und der Geheimlehre der Cabbalah.* 2 vols. Brünn, 1822–23.

—— *Handbuch der mosaischen Religion.* 3 vols. Prague and Vienna, 1818–21.

—— *Kelch des Heils.* Prague, 1802.

—— *Lebensgeschichte.* Prague, 1839.

—— *Sefer toldot Yisrael [History of Israel].* Prague, 1796.

Benzeev, Judah. *Yesode ha-dat [The Principles of Religion].* Vienna, 1811.

Bock, M. H. *Emunat Yisrael [The Faith of Israel] oder Katechismus der Israelitischen Religion.* Berlin, 1814.

—— *Israelitischer Kinderfreund oder Handbuch der gemeinnützigen wissenschaftlichen Kenntnisse.* Berlin, 1811.

Bresselau, M. I. *Herev noḳemet neḳam berit [A Sword Executing the Vengeance of the Covenant].* Dessau, 1819.

Buchholtz, Carl August. *Actenstükke die Verbesserung des bürgerlichen Zustandes der Israeliten betreffend.* Stuttgart and Tübingen, 1815.

—— *Ueber die Aufnahme der jüdischen Glaubensgenossen zum Bürgerrecht.* Lübeck, 1814.

Cohen, Shalom. *Katechismus der Mosaischen Religion: Zum ersten Unterricht für Israelitische Knaben und Mädchen.* Hamburg, 1812.

Die deutsche Synagoge, oder Ordnung des Gottesdienstes für die Sabbath- und Festtage des ganzen Jahres zum Gebrauche der Gemeinden, die sich der deutschen Gebete bedienen, ed. Eduard Kley and C. S. Günsburg. 2 vols. Berlin, 1817-18.

Diefenbach, J. G. *Jüdischer Professor der Theologie auf christlicher Universität.* 2 vols. Giessen, 1821.

Ele divre ha-berit [*These Are the Words of the Covenant*]. Altona, 1819.

Erbauungen, ed. E. Kley and C. S. Günsburg. 2 vols. Berlin, 1813-15.

Euchel, Isaac. "R' Henokh, oder vos tut me damit" ["Reb Henokh, or What do you do about it"]. *Arkhiv far der geshikhte fun yidishen te'ater un drame,* I (1930), 94-146.

Ewald, Johann Ludwig. *Einige Fragen und noch mehr unläugbare Wahrheiten, Juden- und Menschennatur, Juden- und Menschenbildung betreffend.* Karlsruhe, 1820.

—— *Ideen über die nötige Organisation der Israeliten in christlichen Staaten.* Karlsruhe and Baden, 1816.

Festschrift zum hundertjährigen Bestehen des Israelitischen Tempels in Hamburg, 1818-1918, ed. David Leimdörfer. Hamburg, 1918.

Fichte, Johann Gottlieb. "Beitrag zur Berichtigung der Urteile des Publicums über die französische Revolution" (1793). Pp. 40-288 in *Sämmtliche Werke,* VI. Berlin, 1845.

Frank, Christian. *Die Juden und das Judentum wie sie sind.* Cologne, 1816.

Fränkel, David. *Einige Worte an die Schüler der Franzschule in Dessau.* Dessau, 1817.

—— *Nachricht von der jüdischen Haupt- und Frey-Schule in Dessau.* Dessau, 1804.

Fränkel, Seckel Isaac. *Schutzschrift des zu Hamburg erschienenen israelitischen Gebetbuchs für die Mitglieder des Neuen-Tempelvereins nebst einer Beleuchtung des Rabbinismus.* Hamburg, 1819.

Fries, J. F. *Ueber die Gefährdung des Wohlstandes und Charakters der Deutschen durch die Juden.* Heidelberg, 1816.

Heinemann, Jeremiah. *Religiöse Gesänge für Israeliten insbesondere das weibliche Geschlecht und die Jugend.* Cassel, 1816.

—— *Todat emunat bet Yisrael 'al derekh she-ela u-teshuva* [*Confession of Faith of the House of Israel in Questions and Answers*]. Rödelheim, 1812.

Hess, Michael. *Freimütige Prüfung der Schrift des Herrn Professor Rühs, über die Ansprüche der Juden an das deutsche Bürgerrecht.* Frankfurt a.M., 1816.

Homberg, Herz. *Ben Yakir: Ueber Glaubenswahrheiten und Sittenlehren für die israelitische Jugend in Fragen und Antworten eingerichtet.* 2nd ed. Prague, 1826.

—— *Bne-Zion: Ein religiös-moralisches Lehrbuch für die Jugend israelitischer Nation.* Trieste, 1815.

—— *Rede bey Eröffnung der religiös-moralischen Vorlesungen für Israeliten in Prag.* Prague, 1818.

―――― *Imre shefer* [*Goodly Words*]. 2nd ed. Vienna, 1816.

Hundt-Radowski, Hartwig von. *Judenspiegel: Ein Schand- und Sittengemälde alter und neuer Zeit.* Reutlingen, 1821.

Hurwitz, Philipp Lazarus. *Ankündigung eines Unterrichts in der mosaischen Religion und in den dieselbe betreffenden Kenntnissen, in zweckmässigen Vorträgen und Unterhaltungen, für Israeliten.* Berlin, 1822.

Jacobson, Israel. *Untertänigste Vorstellung an Seine Hoheit den Fürst Primas.* Brunswick, 1808.

Jedidja, eine religiöse, moralische und pädagogische Zeitschrift, ed. J. Heinemann. 1817–31.

Johlson, Joseph. *Deutsches Gesangbuch für Israeliten: Zur Beförderung öffentlicher und häuslicher Andacht.* Frankfurt a.M., 1816.

―――― *Alume Yosef* [*The Sheaves of Joseph*]: *Unterricht in der Mosaischen Religion für die Israelitische Jugend beiderlei Geschlechts, nebst einem Anhange von den Ceremonialgesetzen und Gebräuchen.* 2nd ed. Frankfurt a.M., 1819.

Kayserling, M. *Bibliothek jüdischer Kanzelredner,* I. Berlin, 1870.

Kley, Eduard. *Catechismus der mosaischen Religion.* Berlin, 1814.

―――― *Predigten in dem neuen israelitischen Tempel zu Hamburg gehalten.* Hamburg, 1819.

Kley, Eduard and C. S. Günsburg. *Zuruf an die Jünglinge, welche den Fahnen des Vaterlandes folgen.* Berlin, 1813.

Lesser, Ludwig. *Chronik der Gesellschaft der Freunde in Berlin.* Berlin, 1842.

Lilienfeld, J. M. *Patriotische Gedanken eines Israeliten über jüdische Religion, Sitten und Erziehung.* Frankfurt a.M., 1812.

Marcus, Jacob R. "The Love Letters of Bendet Schottlaender." *HUCA,* VII (1930), 537–77.

Ha-Measef. 1784–90, 1794–97, 1809–11.

Neumann, Imm. Mor. *Vom Gebrauch der Bücher Moses in den jüdischen Schulen und Synagogen, mit Beziehung auf die projektirte Verbesserung des israelitischen Kultus.* Breslau, 1815.

Ordnung der öffentlichen Andacht für die Sabbat -und Festtage des ganzen Jahres, nach dem Gebrauche des Neuen-Tempel-Vereins in Hamburg, ed. S. I. Fränkel and M. I. Bresselau. Hamburg, 1819.

Paalzow, Christian Ludwig. *Helm und Schild: Gespräche über das Bürgerrecht der Juden.* Berlin, 1817.

Riesser, Lazarus Jacob. *Send-Schreiben an meine Glaubens-Genossen in Hamburg, oder eine Abhandlung über den Israelitischen Cultus.* Altona, 1819.

Rühs, Friedrich. *Die Rechte des Christentums und des deutschen Volks, verteidigt gegen die Ansprüche der Juden und ihrer Verfechter.* Berlin, 1816.

―――― *Ueber die Ansprüche der Juden an das deutsche Bürgerrecht.* Berlin, 1816.

Salomon, Gotthold. *Auswahl mehrerer Predigten zunächst für Israeliten.* Dessau, 1818.

―――― *Führt uns die Religion auch nicht zurück?* Altona, 1820.

—— *Predigt am Gedächtnisstage der Zerstörung Jerusalems.* Hamburg, 1822.

—— *Predigten gehalten beim israelitischen Gottesdienst in dem dazu gewidmeten Tempel zu Hamburg.* Dessau, 1819.

—— *Predigten in dem neuen Israelitischen Tempel zu Hamburg.* 3 vols. Hamburg, 1820–25.

—— *Selbst-Biographie.* Leipzig, 1863.

—— *Der wahrhaft Fromme stirbt nicht* (sermon in memory of Israel Jacobson). Altona, 1828.

Schottlaender, Benedikt. *Sendschreiben an meine Brüder die Israeliten in Westfalen die Errichtung eines Jüdischen Consistoriums betreffend.* Brunswick, 1808.

Sessa, K. B. A. *Unser Verkehr: Posse in einem Aufzuge.* 8th ed. Berlin, n.d.

Spiker, C. W. *Ueber die ehemalige und jetzige Lage der Juden in Deutschland.* Halle, 1809.

Sulamith, eine Zeitschrift zur Beförderung der Kultur und Humanität unter der jüdischen Nation. 1806–48.

"Ueber die Aufklärung der jüdischen Nation, zufolge der jüdischen Monatsschrift der Sammler." *Magazin für die biblisch-orientalische Literatur und gesammte Philologie,* I (1789), 193–208.

Ueber Juden-Reformation. Bavaria, 1819.

Das wahre System der rein mosaischen Religion: Ernstliche Schritte zur Beförderung der Wahrheit in Religions- und Glaubenssachen unter den Israeliten. Germany, 1815.

Weil, Jacob. *Bemerkungen zu den Schriften der Herren Professoren Rühs und Fries über die Juden und deren Ansprüche auf das deutsche Bürgerrecht.* Frankfurt a.M., 1816.

—— *Fragmente aus dem Talmud und den Rabbinern: Versuch eines Beitrags zu den Actenstücken für die Beurteilung dieser Werke.* 2 vols. Frankfurt a.M., 1809–11.

Wolf, Joseph. *Sechs deutsche Reden, gehalten in der Synagoge zu Dessau, nebst einer hebräischen Uebersetzung derselben.* 2 vols. Dessau, 1812–13.

Wolf, Joseph and Gotthold Salomon. *Der Charakter des Judentums nebst einer Beleuchtung der unlängst gegen die Juden von Prof. Rühs und Fries erschienen Schriften.* Leipzig, 1817.

Wolfssohn, Aaron. *Jeschurun, oder unparteyische Beleuchtung der dem Judentume neuerdings gemachten Vorwürfe.* Breslau, 1804.

Zimmern, Sigmund. *Versuch einer Würdigung der Angriffe des Herrn Professor Fries auf die Juden.* Heidelberg, 1816.

Secondary Sources

Barzilay, Isaac E. "The Italian and Berlin Haskalah (Parallels and Differences)." *PAAJR,* XXIX (1960–61), 17–54.

—— "National and Anti-National Trends in the Berlin Haskalah." *JSS,* XXI (1959), 165–92.

Bernfeld, Simon. *Toldot ha-reformatsyon ha-datit be-Yisrael* [*History of Jewish Religious Reform*]. Cracow, 1900.

Bettan, Israel. "Early Reform in Contemporaneous Responsa." Pp. 425–43 in *Hebrew Union College Jubilee Volume*. Cincinnati, 1925.

Dorner, J. A. *History of Protestant Theology*, trans. George Robson and Sophia Taylor, II. Edinburgh, 1871.

Eichstadt, Volkmar. *Bibliographie zur Geschichte der Judenfrage*. Hamburg, 1938.

Eisenstein-Barzilay, Isaac. "The ideology of the Berlin Haskalah." *PAAJR*, XXV (1956), 1–37.

——— "The Treatment of the Jewish Religion in the Literature of the Berlin Haskalah." *PAAJR*, XXIV (1955), 39–68.

Freudenthal, Max. "Ein Geschlecht von Erziehern." *ZGJD*, VI (1935), 141–68.

Friedland, N. *Zur Geschichte des Tempels der Jacobsonschule*. Seesen, 1910.

Hess, Michael. *Die Bürger- und Realschule der israelitischen Gemeinde zu Frankfurt a.M. von ihrer Entstehung im Jahre 1804 bis zu meinem Abtreten von derselben im Juli 1855*. Frankfurt a.M., 1857.

Jonas, H. *Lebensskizze des Herrn Doctor Eduard Kley, zunächst in seiner Wirksamkeit als Schulmann*. Hamburg, 1859.

Lazarus, Felix. "Das Königlich-Westphalische Konsistorium der Israeliten." *MGWJ*, LVIII (1914), 81–96, 178–208, 326–58, 454–79, 542–61.

Littmann, Ellen. "Saul Ascher: First Theorist of Progressive Judaism." *LBIY*, V (1960), 107–21.

Marcus, Jacob R. "Israel Jacobson." *CCARY*, XXXVIII (1928), 386–498.

Meusel, Johann Georg. *Das Gelehrte Teutschland im Neunzehnten Jahrhundert*. 5th ed. Lemgo, 1820.

Philippson, Martin. "Der Anteil der jüdischen Freiwilligen an dem Befreiungskriege 1813 und 1814." *MGWJ*, L (1906), 1–21, 220–47.

Philippson, Phoebus. *Biographische Skizzen*. 2 vols. Leipzig, 1864–66.

Philipson, David. *The Reform Movement in Judaism*. Rev. ed. New York, 1931.

Pinkuss, Fritz. "Saul Ascher, ein Theoretiker der Judenemanzipation aus der Generation nach Moses Mendelssohn." *ZGJD*, VI (1935), 28–32.

——— "Saul Ascher: Ein unbekannter Theoretiker des Judentums und der Juden-Emancipation" (unpublished rabbinical thesis, Hochschule für die Wissenschaft des Judentums). Berlin, 1931.

Salomon, Gotthold. *Kurzgefasste Geschichte des neuen Israelitischen Tempels in Hamburg während der ersten 25 Jahre seines Bestehens*. Hamburg, 1844.

——— *Lebensgeschichte des Herrn Moses Philippsohn, Lehrers an der israelitischen Haupt- und Freischule zu Dessau*. Dessau, 1814.

Schnee, Heinrich. *Die Hoffinanz und der moderne Staat*. 4 vols. Berlin, 1953–63.

Seaman, E. William. "An Analysis of the Social, Economic and Political Program Expressed in *Ha-Measef*" (unpublished rabbinical thesis, Hebrew Union College). Cincinnati, 1954.

Simon, Ernst. "Pedagogical Philanthropinism and Jewish Education" [Hebrew]. Pp. 149–87 in *Mordecai Kaplan Jubilee Volume*. New York, 1953.

Steig, Reinhold. *Heinrich von Kleists Berliner Kämpfe.* Berlin and Stuttgart, 1901.

Sterling, Eleonore. "Anti-Jewish Riots in Germany in 1819: A Displacement of Social Protest." *HJ*, XII (1950), 105-42.

—— *Er ist wie Du: Aus der Frühgeschichte des Antisemitismus in Deutschland (1815-1850).* Munich, 1956.

—— "Jewish Reaction to Jew-Hatred in the First Half of the Nineteenth Century." *LBIY*, III (1958), 103-21.

Stern, Siegfried. "Die Zeitschrift 'Sulamith.'" *ZGJD*, VII (1937), 193-226.

Stern, Sigismund. "Dr. Michael Hess: Ein Lebensbild." *Diesterweg's Pädagogisches Jahrbuch*, 1862, 1-38.

Stern-Täubler, Selma. "Der Literarische Kampf um die Emanzipation in den Jahren 1816-1820 und seine ideologischen und soziologischen Voraussetzungen." Pt. II, pp. 171-96 in *Hebrew Union College 75th Anniversary Publication.* Cincinnati, 1950-51.

Treitschke, Heinrich von. *Deutsche Geschichte im neunzehnten Jahrhundert*, II. 7th ed. Leipzig, 1912.

Weinryb, Bernard D. "Aaron Wolfsohn's Dramatic Writings in their Historical Setting." *JQR*, XLVIII (1957-58), 35-50.

Wiener, Max. "An Early Theory of Liberal Judaism." *Liberal Judaism*, December 1949, pp. 22-26.

—— "Moses Mendelssohn und die religiösen Gestaltungen des Judentums im 19. Jahrhundert." *ZGJD*, I (1929), 201-12.

—— "Saul Ascher and the Theory of Judaism as a Religion" [Yiddish]. *Yivo Bleter*, XXIII (1947), 55-79.

LEOPOLD ZUNZ AND THE SCIENTIFIC IDEAL

Primary Sources

Boeckh, August. *Encyklopädie und Methodologie der philologischen Wissenschaften*, ed. Ernest Bratuscheck. Leipzig, 1877.

Brann, Marcus and M. Rosenmann. "Der Briefwechsel zwischen Isak Noa Mannheimer und Leopold Zunz." *MGWJ*, LXI (1917), 89-116, 293-318.

Das Buch Zunz, künftigen ehrlichen Leuten gewidmet, ed. Fritz Bamberger. Berlin, 1931.

Ehrenberg, Philipp. "Die Samson'sche Freischule zu Wolfenbüttel." *Literaturblatt des Orients*, V (1844), 65 ff.

Entwurf von Statuten des Vereins für Cultur und Wissenschaft der Juden. Berlin, 1822.

Fichte, Johann Gottlieb. *Reden an die deutsche Nation.* Berlin, 1808.

Geiger, Ludwig. "Aus Eduard Gans' Frühzeit (1817)." *ZGJD*, V (1891), 91-99.

—— "Aus L. Zunz' Nachlass." *ZGJD*, V (1891), 223-68.

—— "Zunz im Verkehr mit Behörden und Hochgestellten." *MGWJ*, LX (1916), 245–62, 321–47.

—— "Zunz' Tätigkeit für die Reform (1817–1823) mit einem Anhang (1840)." *Liberales Judentum*, IX (1917), 113–20.

Hegel, Georg Wilhelm Friedrich. *Early Theological Writings*, trans. T. M. Knox. Chicago, 1948.

—— *Lectures on the Philosophy of History*, trans. J. Sibree. London, 1890.

Heine, Heinrich. *Gesammelte Werke*, ed. Gustav Karpeles. 9 vols. Berlin, 1893.

Heinrich Heine Briefe, ed. Friedrich Hirth, I, IV. Mainz, 1950–51.

Heinrich Heine Gespräche, ed. Hugo Bieber. Berlin, 1926.

Hellwitz, L. L. *Die Organisation der Israeliten in Deutschland*. Magdeburg, 1819.

Humboldt, Wilhelm von. "Ueber die Aufgabe des Geschichtsschreibers." Pp. 1–25 in *Gesammelte Werke*, I. Berlin, 1841.

Italiener, Bruno. "Briefe von Leopold Zunz an Immanuel Wohlwill." Pp. 46–60 in *Festschrift zum hundertzwanzigjährigen Bestehen des israelitischen Tempels in Hamburg 1817–1937*, ed. Bruno Italiener. Hamburg, 1937.

Jost, Isaac Marcus. *Geschichte der Israeliten*. 10 vols. Berlin, 1820–47.

—— "Vor einem halben Jahrhundert: Skizzen aus meiner frühesten Jugend." *Sippurim*, III (1854), 141–66.

Leopold and Adelheid Zunz: An Account in Letters, 1815–1885, ed. Nahum N. Glatzer. London, 1958.

Leopold Zunz: Jude—Deutscher—Europäer, ed. Nahum N. Glatzer. Tübingen, 1964.

Lips, Alexander. *Ueber die künftige Stellung der Juden in den deutschen Bundesstaaten*. Erlangen, 1819.

Maybaum, Siegmund. "Aus dem Leben von Leopold Zunz." *Zwölfter Bericht über die Lehranstalt für die Wissenschaft des Judenthums in Berlin*, 1894, 1–63.

Reissner, Hanns G. "Heinrich Heine an Eduard Gans: 'Quand Meme....'" *Zeitschrift für Religions- und Geistesgeschichte*, X (1958), 44–50.

Rubaschoff (Shazar), Salman. "Erstlinge der Entjudung: Drei Reden von Eduard Gans im Kulturverein." *Der Jüdische Wille*, I (1918), 30–42, 108–21, 193–203.

Savigny, Frederick Charles von. *Of the Vocation of our Age for Legislation and Jurisprudence*, trans. Abraham Hayward. London, 1831.

Wolf, Friedrich August. "Darstellung der Altertums-Wissenschaft." *Museum der Altertums-Wissenschaft*, I (1807), 1–142.

Zeitschrift für die Wissenschaft des Judentums, ed. Leopold Zunz. Berlin, 1822–23.

Zunz, Leopold. *Etwas über die rabbinische Litteratur, nebst Nachrichten über ein altes bis jetzt ungedrucktes hebräisches Werk*. Berlin, 1818.

—— *Gesammelte Schriften*. 3 vols. Berlin, 1875–76.

—— *Die Gottesdienstlichen Vorträge der Juden, historisch entwickelt*. Berlin, 1832.

—— "Mein erster Unterricht in Wolfenbüttel." *JJGL*, XXX (1937), 131–38.

—— "Meine Schriften." *JJGL*, XXX (1937), 140–72; XXXI (1938), 245–47.

—— *Predigten, gehalten in der neuen Israelitischen Synagoge zu Berlin*. Berlin, 1823.

───── *Samuel Meyer Ehrenberg, Inspektor der Samonschen Freischule zu Wolfenbüttel, ein Denkmal für Angehörige und Freunde.* Brunswick, 1854.

Secondary Sources

Altmann, Alexander. "Zur Frühgeschichte der jüdischen Predigt in Deutschland: Leopold Zunz als Prediger." *LBIY*, VI (1961), 3–59.

Arendt, Hannah. "The Jew as Pariah: A Hidden Tradition." *JSS*, VI (1944), 99–122.

Aster, Ernst von. "Aufklärung, Romantik und Gegenwart." *Der Morgen*, V (1929), 73–85.

Auerbach, Jakob. "Dr. I. M. Jost: Eine Biographische Skizze." *Volkskalender und Jahrbuch für Israeliten*, 1861, 129–64.

Avineri, Shlomo. "A Note on Hegel's Views on Jewish Emancipation." *JSS*, XXV (1963), 145–51.

Bamberger, Fritz. "Wissenschaft vom Judentum." *Der Morgen*, XII (1936), 5–9.

───── "Zunz's Conception of History: A Study of the Philosophic Elements in Early Science of Judaism." *PAAJR*, XI (1941), 1–25.

Baron, Salo. "I. M. Jost, the Historian." *PAAJR*, I (1928–30), 7–32.

Bieber, Hugo. "Leopold Zunz and the Society for Culture and Science Among the Jews" [Yiddish]. *Yivo Bleter*, XXV (1945), 298–303.

Cohon, Samuel S. "Zunz and Reform Judaism." *HUCA*, XXXI (1960), 251–76.

Deutsch, Gotthard. "Eduard Gans." *Westliche Blätter (Sonntagsblatt des Cincinnatier Volksblatt)*, March 27, 1898, p. 12.

Elbogen, Ismar. "Ein hundertjähriger Gedenktag unserer Wissenschaft." *MGWJ*, LXVI (1922), 89–97.

───── "Leopold Zunz zum Gedächtnis." *Fünfzigster Bericht der Lehranstalt für die Wissenschaft des Judentums in Berlin*, 1936, 14–32.

───── "Neuorientierung unserer Wissenschaft." *MGWJ*, LXII (1918), 81–96.

Friedlander, Albert H. "The Verein für Kultur und Wissenschaft der Juden: A Study in the History of Culture" (unpublished rabbinical thesis, Hebrew Union College). Cincinnati, 1952.

Gedenkschrift der freien Universität Berlin, ed. Wilhelm Weischedel. Berlin, 1960.

Glatzer, Nahum N. "Zunz's Concept of Jewish History" [Hebrew]. *Zion*, XXVI (1961), 208–14.

Gooch, G. P. *History and Historians in the Nineteenth Century*. London, 1913.

Guddat, W. "Heinrich Heine und der 'Verein für Kultur und Wissenschaft der Juden' in Berlin 1822 und 1823." Pp. 72–78 in *Festschrift zum 70. Geburtstage von Moritz Schaefer*. Berlin, 1927.

Jost, Isaac Marcus. "Actenmässige Darstellung des kurzen Daseins einer jüdischen Schul-Commission in der Berliner Gemeinde 1826." *AZJ*, XXIII (1859), 159 ff.

Kaufmann, David. "Leopold Zunz." Pp. 333–51 in *Gesammelte Schriften*, ed. M. Brann, I. Frankfurt a.M., 1908.

Kisch, Guido. "Zur Zunz-Biographie." Pp. 369–76 in *Festgabe für Adolf Leschnitzer*. Heidelberg, 1961.

Kohn, Hans. *Heinrich Heine: The Man and the Myth*. Leo Baeck Memorial Lecture 2. New York, 1959.

Körte, Wilhelm. *Leben und Studien Friedr. Aug. Wolfs des Philologen*. 2 vols. Essen, 1833.

Lehmann, Joseph. "H. Heine in Berlin, in den Jahren 1821–1823." *Magazin für die Literatur des Auslandes*, XXXVII (1868), 169–71.

Meinecke, Friedrich. *Die Entstehung des Historismus*. Vol. III of *Werke*. Munich, 1959.

Rabbinowitz, Saul P. *Yom Tov Lipman Zunz: hayav zemano u-sefarav [Leopold Zunz: His Life, Times and Works]*. Warsaw, 1896.

Reissner, Hanns G. "Der Berliner 'Wissenschaftzirkel' (1816–17)." *LBIB*, VI (1963), 101–12.

—— *Eduard Gans: Ein Leben im Vormärz*. Tübingen, 1965.

—— "Felix Mendelssohn-Bartholdy und Eduard Gans." *LBIY*, IV (1959), 92–110.

—— "Rebellious Dilemma: The Case Histories of Eduard Gans and some of his Partisans." *LBIY*, II (1957), 179–93.

Rotenstreich, Nathan. "Hegel's Image of Judaism." *JSS*, XV (1953), 33–52.

Steinschneider, Moritz. *Die Schriften des Dr. L. Zunz*. Berlin, 1857.

Strodtmann, Adolf. *H. Heines Leben und Werke*. 3rd ed. 2 vols. Hamburg, 1884.

Ucko, Siegfried. "Geistegeschichtliche Grundlagen der Wissenschaft des Judentums (Motive des Kulturvereins vom Jahre 1819)." *ZGJD*, V (1935), 1–34.

Wallach, Luitpold. *Leopold Zunz und die Grundlegung der Wissenschaft des Judentums: Ueber den Begriff einer jüdischen Wissenschaft*. Frankfurt a.M., 1938.

—— *Liberty and Letters: The Thoughts of Leopold Zunz*. London, 1959.

—— "Ueber Leopold Zunz als Historiker: Eine Skizze." *ZGJD*, V (1934), 247–52.

Weil, Gotthold. "Das Zunz-Archiv." *LBIB*, II (1959), 148–61.

Wiener, Max. "The Ideology of the Founders of Jewish Scientific Research." *Yivo Annual of Social Science*, V (1950), 184–96.

Zirndorf, Heinrich. *Isaak Markus Jost und seine Freunde*. Cincinnati, 1886.

SELECTED SUPPLEMENTARY BIBLIOGRAPHY

The following studies are among those which have been published since the first appearance of this volume in 1967.

Altmann, Alexander. *Moses Mendelssohn: A Biographical Study*. University, Alabama, 1973.

—— "The Philosophical Roots of Moses Mendelssohn's Plea for Emancipation." *JSS*, XXXVI (1974), 191–202.

Ettinger, Shmuel. "The Modern Period." Pp. 727–853 in *A History of the Jewish People*, ed. H.H. Ben-Sasson. Cambridge, Mass., 1976.

Fischer, Horst. *Judentum, Staat und Heer in Preussen im frühen 19. Jahrhundert*. Tübingen, 1968.

Friedlander, Albert. "The Wohlwill-Moser Correspondence." *LBIY*, XI (1966), 261–99.

Friedländer, David. *Igeret le-hod ma'alato ha-adon Teler [Open Letter to the Honorable Mr. Teller]*, Hebrew introduction by Richard Cohen. Jerusalem, 1975.

Glatzer, Nahum N. "On an Unpublished Letter of Isaak Markus Jost." *LBIY*, XXII (1977), 129–37.

Graupe, Heinz Mosche. *Die Entstehung des modernen Judentums*. Hamburg, 1969.

Das Judentum in der deutschen Umwelt, 1800–1850, eds. Hans Liebeschütz, and Arnold Paucker. Tübingen, 1977.

Kahn, Lothar. "Ludwig Robert: Rahel's Brother." *LBIY*, XVIII (1973), 185–99.

Katz, Jacob. *Emancipation and Assimilation: Studies in Modern Jewish History*. Westmead, 1972.

–––––– *Out of the Ghetto: The Social Background of Jewish Emancipation, 1770–1870*. Cambridge, Mass., 1973.

Pelli, Moshe. *Moshe Mendelssohn: be-khavle masoret [Moses Mendelssohn: Bonds of Tradition]*. Tel-Aviv, 1972.

Petuchowski, Jakob J. *Prayerbook Reform in Europe*. New York, 1968.

Richarz, Monika. *Jüdisches Leben in Deutschland: Selbstzeugnisse zur Sozialgeschichte, 1780–1871*. Stuttgart, 1976.

Sambursky, Miriam. "Ludwig Robert's Lebensgang." *LBIB*, XV (1976), 1–22.

Samet, M.S. "Mendelssohn, Weisel, and the Rabbis of their Time." [Hebrew]. *Studies in the History of the Jewish People and the Land of Israel*, I (1970), 233–57.

Schorsch, Ismar. "From Wolfenbüttel to Wissenschaft—The Divergent Paths of Isaak Markus Jost and Leopold Zunz." *LBIY*, XXII (1977), 109–28.

Schweid, Eliezer. *Toldot ha-hagut ha-yehudit be-et ha-hadasha [A History of Jewish Thought in Modern Times]*. Jerusalem, 1977.

Stern-Taeubler, Selma. "The First Generation of Emancipated Jews." *LBIY*, XV (1970), 3–40.

Toury, Jacob. *Der Eintritt der Juden ins deutsche Bürgertum: Eine Dokumentation*. Tel-Aviv, 1972.

Zondek, Theodor. "Dr. Med. David Veit (1771–1814)." *LBIB*, XV (1976), 49–77.

Index

Index

Index